Frances Nevins

Mid 20th Century Carmelite
friend, scholar, wife, nun and mystic

A Spiritual Biography

Joan Ward Mullaney

Printed and bound in the United States of America.

Book design by Greta Valuski, Berkshire Print Shop, Pittsfield, Massachusetts.

Cover design by Sister RuthAnn Fox, R.S.M., Sisters of Mercy of the Americas, Dallas, Pennsylvania.

Mullaney, Joan Ward
Frances Nevins: mid 20th century Carmelite, friend, scholar, wife, nun and mystic: a spiritual biography/Joan Ward Mullaney. - 3rd ed.
330 p.: Ill., plates; 24cm.
Includes bibliographical references and index.

ISBN 978-0-9824406-1-2

1. Nevins, Frances. 2. Carmelite Nuns - United States-Biography. I. Title.
BX4705.N495 M85 2013   255.9710092 - dc23
2013903642

To order additional copies of this book, contact:

Monastery Greetings
   Phone: 800-472-0425
   Fax : 216-249-3387
   or order online at: www.MonasteryGreetings.com

Title page: front gate with Carmelite shield. Monastery, Discalced Carmelites, 428 Duane Avenue, Schenectady, NY 12304

Dedication

For Sr. RuthAnn Fox, R.S.M.
an extraordinary Sister of Mercy.

and

For Cardinal Avery Dulles, S.J.
short term colleague
and
long time friend,
he rests in peace.

Sister Christine Marie of the Holy Spirit, O.C.D.
Solemn Profession and Veiling
October 8 and 9, 1965

Foreword

Today is the day to write this foreword. My day began with Mass in Saint Michael Cathedral Church in Springfield, Massachusetts, where Frances Nevins/Sister Christine of the Holy Spirit was baptized, July 1, 1931. I felt her there.

Perhaps always but at some times more than others, time and space enter us and make us who we are born to be. Today feels that way to me. At a key moment in tracking the story of Frances Nevins from her baptism to her death in the Schenectady Carmelite cloister where she would spend most of her adult life, Joan Mullaney makes this observation for her friend Frances, "For me, I have to be here to be. It's who I am."

On May 2, 1951 as outstanding senior at Connecticut College for Women, Frances Nevins delivered the Chapel Talk. At the time, one can deduce from her story, she was unaware of being a baptized Catholic. She opens with this advice: "It seems to me that to anyone who turns to Christianity with a desire to find out what it's about, the first thing it has to say is found in the Gospel of Matthew:

> Ask, and it shall be given you;
> seek, and ye shall find;
> Knock, and it shall be opened unto you:
> For everyone that asketh receiveth;
> and he that seeketh findeth;
> and to him that knocketh it shall be opened.
>
> (Matthew VII 7-8)

What she was asking then or at any given moment of her life as infant, child, adolescent, scholar, wife, or nun, one can profitably wonder. Joan Mullaney's spiritual biography of her friend who finds home in her Carmelite community helps a reader wonder meaningfully about this woman who asks, receives, and finds the mystery of God. Her half century of a quiet life leads her where we will all go, to Death. Death arrives at the hermitage like the one who stops for Emily Dickinson in her poem "Because I could not stop for Death". It comes like the dart that pierces the Cloud of Unknowing.

A few months before dying, Frances Nevins wrote: "Lord, the only heaven I want is an everlasting abundance of the life we have together here. It is impossible to desire a heaven that is wholly different from anything we know...My highest experiences are heaven with my eyes shut."

Reading these words, I recall feeling myself at sea and at home in baptismal waters at this morning's Mass. Writing this foreword, I recognize that Frances Nevins' life has become a keyhole through which I caught a glimpse of one woman opening her self utterly to God. Might others move through these pages toward their truest selves in Christ? Thomas Merton says that "For me to be a saint means to be myself." Is this quest not worth the wondering?

Jane F. Morrissey, ssj, Ph.D.
Former President, Congregation
of the Sisters of St. Joseph
of Springfield

Contents

Part II: The Call To Carmel

The Frances Nevins papers will be deposited
in the archives of
Connecticut College,
New London, Connecticut

Schenectady Carmel main building
viewed from the enclosure

Author's Preface

"Although her health was poor, the coming of the Angel of Death was swift and unexpected. On the morning of December 5th, Sister Christine did not answer the signal for rising. It was discovered that her bed had not been touched and a light was burning in an outdoor hermitage. To our shock and dismay, we found her on the floor of the hermitage, comatose and icy cold. The initial diagnosis was hypothermia (her body temperature was 80°), but by 8:00 P.M. a hemorrhage in the brain was discovered and immediate surgery was performed to release pressure. However, Sister Christine never regained consciousness and Our Lord came for her on Tuesday, December 16 at 9:30 P.M. She had just passed the twentieth anniversary of her entrance into Carmel.

The funeral was on Friday, December 19 and after the Liturgy, Sister Christine was laid to rest in the Monastery Crypt." [1]

Frances Nevins is an important and interesting person. One way to judge her life's story is by examining the facts about her extraordinary experiences of God as a woman, and as a nun.

Since her death on December 16, 1980, I have worked steadily on the congenial task of discovering, understanding, and documenting her remarkable journey. This documentation is contained in formal, official papers as well as her close-to-the-heart retreat notes and journal entries. She also had a gift for friendship. Letters to friends chronicle her tender concern for both their sorrows and their joys.

When Frances died, Sister Mary of St. John of the Cross, O.C.D., Prioress of the Schenectady Carmel, offered me the journals and retreat notes that Frances had written beginning early in her life in Carmel and extending to a very few hours before her death. As Frances' friend for nearly a quarter century, I accepted these precious pages with gratitude. The writings span 20 years of sea change in her own life, monastic life, and society. She writes about prayer and experiences we all face – death, love, disappointments, loneliness, contradictions, sickness, and change itself. She writes as the well-educated woman she is - at home with scripture, ideas, references, the clear sentence with a subject and a predicate, and the ease of the classic scholar using Greek, Latin, or the occasional French word better to make the case.

But, most of all, she writes about her extraordinary relationship with God, describing it with clarity, care, and unmistakable knowledge. Through prayer-filled words, her faith, love, and trust are evident. Her writings also show that, despite her omnipresent poor health, suffering did not become central; love was central. Trust in God, she affirmed over and over, will take care of everything.

Frances Nevins also brought with her to Carmel a vocation within a vocation – namely, to pray for priests and the priesthood. For her, the monastic life was a deeply focused life, and her focus on the holiness of priests was part of her Marian ideal and raison d'être. An important aspect of this special focus was Frances' respect for spiritual direction and the spiritual director. Father Henry Tansey, a Mill Hill Missionary, was her guide and confessor at the time of her death. There is evidence that Sr. Christine and Fr. Tansey contributed significantly and joyfully to one another's already mature life in goodness.

Father Tansey was much loved in the Albany diocese. Less than six weeks after Frances' death, Bishop Hubbard would again preside at a funeral liturgy, this time for Father Tansey. Perhaps only a few among the 1400 friends in the Albany Cathedral that morning would know how Father Tansey had both rejoiced and sorrowed when his friend in Carmel went home to God with the last words in her journal – Amen, Alleluia – still fresh on the page. Perhaps further study of these two lives will discover that, like Teresa and John, Francis and Clare, and Jane de Chantal and Francis de Sales, there are special relationships unique to their time, place, and spiritual gifts that God creates to do a certain work that cannot be done by one or the other separately.

As regards Frances' qualities and whether they "fit" with those the Church seeks among those to be honored, only time will tell. I do think the Saints stay close to the broken-hearted. They also live a love story with lots of ups and downs; they hang on and more. In her journal, Frances says she knows the suffering of the heart – fear, anguish, desolation of spirit. "They all have an echo in my own life and prepared me a little to stand beside you". She knew what it was like to inherit great wealth. She also knew what it was like to be brought up by nannies, to be a lonely child of divorce, to give up a husband she loved, to feel alone in Carmel. I think there are many who come to a Carmel monastery looking for help with just those kinds of anguish.

When preparing to enter Carmel, Frances Nevins courageously asked that visiting and writing privileges be granted to me, as a kind of next-of-kin modification. Father Albert, Carmelite Definitor General, and Mother Magdalene, D.C. agreed that I could visit for two hours twice a year and receive and send four letters.

For twenty years we spoke comfortably and laughed merrily through a serious metal grate in the small speak room reserved for visitors. In the early days, another Sister sat near Frances and out of my eye range. She kept busy with handiwork and, other than an occasional chuckle, was invisible. I knew, however, that when the black curtain began gently to move, the visit was definitely coming to an end.

As friends, the visiting privilege was important. We had already shared important transitions in our lives. Her life of scholarship took a new direction; her marriage ended; Catholicism and Catholic life became her life. And in a parallel universe, I began my academic/professional climb beginning at Boston College, followed by Harvard, Smith College, and Catholic University in Washington, D.C.

The visiting privilege was also important to Frances and her mother because I was a link between them. When Mrs. Tenney felt up to the one visit she did make, her chauffeur brought her to the monastery and I brought her back home to Connecticut when she felt ready to travel.

After twenty years, and despite regular visits and letters, I was not prepared for the unusual circumstances of Sister Christine's final illness and death. Nor was I prepared by friendship and scholarship to understand her rare gifts. Rather, I have come to understand her life through her journals and retreat notes. And she was not guarded in describing her struggles with illness, loneliness, poverty or opposition.

Her writings are the sum and substance of this book. They appear exactly as she wrote them, with no alteration whatsoever. I selected journal entries and retreat notes primarily from the last eighteen months of Sr. Christine's life.

The arbitrary limitation of time brings with it certain difficulties. Coherence inevitably requires inclusion of events and journal entries prior to the focus period. The reader is encouraged, therefore, to make use of the chronology. Another effect of the time choice is to focus on her at the top of the ladder, or, as she says, "standing on the tiptoes of my faith". Even with these caveats, there is sufficient evidence that Sr. Christine was given remarkable gifts that are given to few.

This book was written for friends of Sr. Christine, both within Carmel and out. When we look at her life and writings from one direction, she does not answer any major questions of the 21st century for us, but from another direction, she answers all of them.

Joan Ward Mullaney

2011

NOTES

1. The Circular Letter (Carmelite Monastery, Schenectady, NY, 1981). Obituary notice about Sister Christine Marie of the Holy Spirit, O.C.D. 1930-1980 sent to other Carmelite Monasteries.

Acknowledgments

First and foremost, grateful acknowledgment is made to Frances Nevins whose remarkable life and writings made this book possible and necessary.

Right Reverend Howard J. Hubbard, D. D. Bishop of Albany, offered the right mix of encouragement and good questions. He understood the specialness of Discalced Carmelite life in a way that proved the best possible guidance in understanding Sr. Christine and her place in that life.

Mother Mary John of the Cross,. O.C.D. was Prioress of the Schenectady Carmel at the time of Sr. Christine's death. She gave me the journals and retreat notes written by Sr. Christine during the entire 20 years of her Carmelite life. I treasure our continued correspondence. I also appreciate the generous assistance of Sr. Therese, O.C.D. and Sr. Paul, O.C.D. whose letters written as Novices and updated by Sr. Therese in 2008 are special to the purposes of this book.

Sr. Clare Joseph, O.C.D. (Theresa Lagoy) was a member of the Schenectady Carmelite community between 1960 and 1975. Visits and correspondence with Theresa have been invaluable in developing and testing my understanding of Sr. Christine's day-to-day Carmelite life. She is full to the brim with integrity and generosity. Sr. Mary of Jesus and St. Joseph, O. Carm., also a contemporary of Sr. Christine's, shared many details about her friend's early years in Carmel. Sr. Mary founded and is now Prioress of a new hermitage foundation. Gone to God is Sr. Alberta, O.C.D. extern sister at Schenectady Carmel, who made everyone's life easier, especially mine, during the days of Sr. Christine's final illness.

Sisters of the Good Shepherd were forthcoming and generous, anticipating correctly just what materials would be needed to understand Frances Nevins' entrance and departure from their Order. Sr. Mary Michael Kennedy, R.G.S., Frances' Mistress of Novices and Sr. Agnes Ertel, R.G.S., and I had many conversations about Frances' months with Sisters of the Good Shepherd.

Sisters of the Congregation of Our Lady of the Retreat of the Cenacle extended many courtesies and provided information that explained retreat experiences available to Frances Nevins in the 1950s.

I am grateful to members of the following religious communities who patiently answered my questions and offered many insights:

Order of Discalced Carmelite Friars
Order of Friars Minor Conventual
Boston College Jesuit Community
Mill Hill Missionaries (England and United States)

Fr. Paul Fohlin O.C.D., Boston MA, and Brother Martin Murphy O.C.D., Hubertus, WI accomplished the difficult and vital task of photo procurement.

A special measure of gratitude is offered to four reviewers who made their comments and criticisms with clarity, rigor, tact and promptness. These excellent people are: Joan D. Tallman, music educator and specialized librarian; Fr. William F. Eckert, parish priest and author of *The Prayer of the Priest*; Patricia Black Cashmore, wise Boston College colleague; and Cecilia Meighan, Sister of Mercy, lawyer, educator, and founder of the Institute of Law and Religious Life.

To my editor, Jane Morrissey, S.S.J., I am indebted for her sensitive and graceful editing. I learned quickly that she is wonderfully gifted. Formerly President of the Congregation of the Sisters of St. Joseph of Springfield, MA, she is a founder of innovative programs, Gray House and Homework House, in Holyoke, MA.

I owe a special debt to Linda Coll who was with me at the biblical beginning. Her intelligence, steadiness, integrity, computer wizardry and downright goodness made all the difference.

I admit the gestation for this book was long. Over time, the following people provided specialized knowledge important to this project: Joann Wolski Conn (theology and spirituality); Jean Bostley, S.S.J. (Exec. Dir. Catholic Library Association); Nola Brunner, C.S.J. (Vicar for Religious and Archivist, Diocese of Albany, NY) Eleanor Dooley, S.S.J. (Latin translations); Robert F. Drinan, S.J. (civil and canon law); David Farrell, C.S.C. (religious life and social vision); RuthAnn Fox, R.S.M. (photographics); Cecelia Harvey, (Nuns of New Skete); Kateri Maureen Koverman, S.C. (friend in all weather); Mildred Lemmerman, (Schenectady Carmel staff); Monsignor Frederick McManus, (canon law); Teresa Moran, S.S.J. (prayer and good works); Tom Newman, (my window to the Orthodox Church); Fr. Robert O'Grady, (Boston Archdiocese Communications Office); Peggy O'Neil, S.S.J. (Director of Pastoral Ministry, supplier of books and bestower of blessings); Dimitri Plionis, Ph.D. (Greek language, ancient and modern); Elizabeth Moore Plionis (excellent colleague); Patricia Stanley Ruel (perceptive observer of monastic life); William W. Sheldon, C.M. (Rector, Vincentian Seminary, Philadelphia: religious life in the 20th century); Eugene Tansey, brother of Fr. Henry Tansey, (hospitality and memories at his home, Stonepark, Keadue, Roscommon, Ireland).

Archivists were an invaluable resource in 'learning about learning'. The Masters School, Dobbs Ferry, NY; Connecticut College, New London, CT; Radcliffe/Harvard; and Boston College staff patiently answered letters, phone calls and in-person interviews without fuss. Connecticut College hosted a gathering of faculty and friends who knew, admired and remembered Frances Nevins. In ways that counted, classmates who had kept letters for twenty years shared them with me. I am indebted in so many ways to Mona Gustafson Affinito, Ph.D; Mary Helen "Mike" McNab Bunn; Renate Aschaffenburg Christensen; Phoebe Hall, CC's Office of Communications; Harriet Bassett MacGregor; Margaret Park Mautner; Joy Anderson Nicholson; Anna Pluhar; Ann Sprayregen; Lynn Ward White; Natalie Bowen; Judith Chynoweth; Joan Onthank; Gloria Jones; Lois Sessions Sprately; Pamela D. Vose and Bonnie K. Yarrington. I had the privilege of meeting twice with Dr. F. Edward Cranz, international Cusa scholar and Frances' major professor for her senior work at Connecticut.

Within the Nevins/Tenney family circle I am indebted to Frances Waters Nevins Tenney, mother of Frances Nevins, for letters, photographs and lessons in courage when faced with a terminal illness. I am also grateful to Mrs. Barbara Nevins Ford, Frances' aunt. I visited her in England, and she, too, provided family pictures and letters. Included in the family circle is Paul Cawein, Frances' husband. He was unfailingly kind and helpful. When we both lived in Washington, D.C. we met for a meal occasionally. He reminded me that he taught Frances how to cook. Other family support to my writing efforts came from Deana Waters Lyman, Ted Lyman and Mrs. Charles Tenney (Lederle Stearns Tenney). Annamarie Pluhar, Frances' godchild, is a refreshing challenge to my ideas about contemplative life from her contemplative corner of Vermont.

To Greta Valuski for her leadership of the Berkshire Print Shop team (Galynn Barcher, Kathy Holt and Jean Haywood). I offer gratitude for their expertise and good-natured encouragement.

"For those who believe in God,
no explanation is necessary;
for those who do not believe in God,
no explanation is possible".

Franz Werfel
"Song of Bernadette"
1941

PROLOGUE
CARMELITE CIRCULAR LETTER

After Frances died, the Schenectady Carmelites sent to the other 65 monasteries and to friends of the deceased a more or less official document called "The Circular Letter". It is a chronological account, orderly but not sentimental, of her life from birth to death. The letter was helpful to me in organizing other information drawn from journals, letters, and pictures that served to expand the basic presentation.

The Circular Letter [2]

CARMELITE MONASTERY
428 Duane Avenue
SCHENECTADY, NEW YORK 12304

SISTER CHRISTINE MARIE OF THE HOLY SPIRIT, O.C.D.
1930-1980

Sister Christine (Frances Nevins) was born in Springfield, Massachusetts on August 17, 1930, the daughter of a Catholic father and a Protestant mother. She was baptized a Catholic in infancy, but was brought up in the Protestant religion. When she was twelve years old, her father died. Her mother married again.

As a child she was piously inclined, having an attraction for things of faith and religion. When she asked her mother about the Catholic Church (she knew her father had been a Catholic and that she had been baptized a Catholic), she was told that it made no difference which Church one attended. Thus the issue of her Catholic faith was evaded and eclipsed.

After graduation from college, Frances began teaching. Through the associations made in her work, she met a young man to whom she became greatly attracted. His piety, uprightness and his interest and love of religion, (he had thought of studying to be a minister), found their complement in her. They were married and lived happily together for about a year and a half. During that time, in the course of a European tour, they visited Rome and had an audience with the Holy Father. This event was the turning point in Frances' life. She experienced a strong

-ix-conviction that the Catholic Church was the only true Church. Thereupon she seriously investigated the matter, becoming more strongly convinced of its undeniable truth.

In order to find out what was to be done that she might become a practicing Catholic, Frances went to the Jesuits for assistance. The outcome was, of course, that since she was a baptized Catholic, her marriage would have to be blessed by a priest and her husband must promise to bring their children up in the Catholic faith. This he absolutely refused to do, as he felt that no religion had the right to demand that they be "married again" and in conscience he felt that he could never promise to bring the children up as Catholics.

Thus Frances was faced with the only alternative – to obtain a divorce and begin a new life as a Catholic. At first her husband was adamant in his refusal to consent to a divorce. However, he finally yielded for the sake of her happiness. It was a great ordeal for her, but she went through it courageously. She obtained an annulment, which left her free and her former husband went to Canada to continue his teaching profession. Since that time she embraced the Catholic faith with intense fervor and found in it the deepest happiness.

Five years of intense and persevering spiritual activity ensued for Frances. She felt as though she had "come home" at last. Daily Mass, Holy Communion, prayer, spiritual reading occupied a good part of her time. From the time she came into the Church she began to experience a great desire to enter Carmel. She confided this attraction to her spiritual director. However, considering her unusual background and also her excellent teaching ability, he advised her to enter an active Community where her God-given talents could be employed for God's glory and for the service of the Church. She thought this was a sacrifice God wanted of her, to relinquish her strong attraction to the contemplative life, to serve Our Lord in the souls who needed her assistance.

Therefore, Frances entered the Convent of the Good Shepherd Sisters. She made a valiant effort to embrace their generous way of life. Frances' worth was recognized by her Superiors, who were very fond of her and most *anxious for her to persevere if it was God's Will. As a postulant she was given the obedience to teach not only the young girls there, but the Sisters in the Community as well.*

However, it became all the more evident to Frances that she was not in the right place. She felt a great need and desire for solitude and silence which could be had only in a contemplative order. After much prayer and consultation with her Superior and her Spiritual Director, Frances decided that it was not God's Will that she sacrifice what was most fundamental in her spiritual life, her desire for Carmel, with the opportunity it would provide for living the purely contemplative life.

Frances left the Sisters of the Good Shepherd for these reasons. The Sisters could not speak highly enough of her; they would have been only too happy if God had destined her for their Community. They gave a fine recommendation.

On December 8th 1960, she entered the Carmel of Schenectady and embraced all aspects of the life with great enthusiasm. She maintained sufficient health for the postulancy and novitiate. However, after Profession, she began to suffer from a circulatory ailment which, little by little withdrew her from Community activities. By the time of her death, she lived in almost complete solitude, a life style that corresponded with her inner attraction to the eremitical life.

Although her health was poor, the coming of the Angel of Death was swift and unexpected. On the morning of December 5th, Sister Christine did not answer the signal for rising. It was discovered that her bed had not been touched and a light was burning in an outdoor hermitage. To our shock and dismay, we found her on the floor of the hermitage, comatose and icy cold. The initial diagnosis was hypothermia (her body temperature was 80°), but by 8:00 P.M. a hemorrhage in the brain was discovered and immediate surgery was performed to release pressure. However, Sister Christine never regained consciousness and Our Lord came for her on Tuesday, December 16 at 9:30 P.M. She had just passed the twentieth anniversary of her entrance into Carmel.

The funeral was on Friday, December 19 and after the Liturgy, Sister Christine was laid to rest in the Monastery Crypt.

NOTES

2. The author of the Circular Letter is unidentified in keeping with the Discalced Carmelite custom.

◆ PART I ◆

The Call

1

The Early Years: Only the Governess Took Good Care

Born in Vermont, grandfather William Nevins moved to Springfield, Massachusetts and prospered with his printing and binding business. In addition to being a prominent businessman and public citizen, he was a life-long practicing Catholic. He saw to it that his children were raised as Catholics. Following the rules that a Catholic should marry in the Catholic Church and the children be baptized as Catholics, his son, Jerome Nevins (a Catholic) and Frances Waters (an Episcopalian) were married at St. Patrick's Cathedral in New York City. Their only child, Frances Nevins, was baptized as a 1-year-old at St. Michael's Cathedral in Springfield; William Nevins was a godparent. The fact of this baptism will emerge as a significant matter later in Frances' life at the time of her marriage.

As for Jerome, he attended Yale, followed his father in the printing business, kept a yacht off the Connecticut coast, drank too much, and died at the age of 42. A picture of father and daughter on the yacht seems to indicate that they were close. Frances was 12 when her father died suddenly of a heart attack. Not much is known about the relationship between mother and daughter. What is known is that when Frances was two years old, a decision was made to bring into the household Miss Ethel (Mil) Miller from Vermont to care for her.

Mil was born February 12, 1886 in Malden, MA. She graduated from Baby's Hospital, City of New York in 1919. Her first job was with a wealthy family on Park Avenue, NY. She had asthma that forced her to recover in Vermont. Meeting a person in the Nevins family, she was hired to take care of Frances in the Nevins family home in Longmeadow, MA in 1932. She was a mother substitute for Frances during her childhood and pre-boarding school years. Frances always kept in close contact with Mil and members of Mil's family. In 1958 she went to Duxbury, VT where Mil was dying. With the permission of the family, Frances baptized her. Long after Mil's death, she would say sorrowfully, "Mil loved me but she died".

Fact gathering about Frances' early years was difficult. Her mother chose to provide information with newspaper clippings and school information saved in a large scrap-book. Frances' aunt, her father's sister, lived in England for most of Frances' life. We enjoyed scones and tea while she said quite proudly that she was Frances' Godmother. Mrs. Barbara "Bardy" Nevins Thomson Ford divorced, remarried and joined the Anglican Church. She was sympathetic toward Frances' life choice as a nun. While aunt and niece always kept up a correspondence, "Bardy" supplied very little information about the early years. I also interviewed Mil's sister, Ermina Miller. She was cautious about criticizing Frances' parents while making it clear that her sister provided the parenting that Frances needed.

Before Frances was sent off to boarding school, she was transferred back and forth from one country day school to another, eventually being settled into the nearby public school in Longmeadow. The location depended on what was happening in her parents' turbulent lives at the time. From all this upset she absorbed the profoundest feelings of abandonment and being unloved that were not healed until the very last days of her life. She would name it the deepest poverty. Retreat notes and journal entries witness the dreadful legacy of this parental chaos.

Three entries from roughly the last year of her life are reminders of the pain she continued to feel:

9/28/1979 Retreat Notes

> In this age of broken families, there will be many who are paralyzed as I have been. Jesus - I sense that I may not receive a total healing of this weakness, but only "treatments" till the end. It keeps me very small and conscious of my poverty in the midst of all Your riches - and it draws Your loving mercy to me like a magnet. You have told me that this need makes a special bond between us.

I am so clearly that one in Ezekiel whom
You found lying in a field not cared for
(spiritually) by her own parents and whom
You took for Your own, and loaded with gifts.

11/1/1980 Journal Entry

"We are the children of Saints:" said
Tobias, and if this is not very applicable in
the natural order, still it is absolutely true in
the family of heaven.

Boarding School: Turbulent Years 1945-1947

What goes on in the classroom usually gives valuable
clues to a person's development. After completing the 10th grade,
the principal of Classical High School in Springfield reported:
"There is nothing but good to say of Frances Nevins. She is an
attractive, interesting girl, who does good work and has good
manners. We shall be sorry to lose her". [3] The impending loss
referred to her mother's plan to have Frances attend The Masters
School (aka "Dobbs") in Dobbs Ferry, New York, beginning in
September of 1945. Dobbs was a boarding school for young women
from wealthy families. Frances was accepted but quite soon ran
afoul of certain rules and practices. To complicate matters, she was
in an auto accident in November of her first semester at Dobbs.
To fill in the picture about the School, a retrospective paragraph
describes the Headmistress and the program this way:

"Charlotte Welles Speer, who succeeded Miss
Pierce as Headmistress in the fall of 1945, was the
widow of Northfield-Mt. Hermon's former Headmaster,
Dr. Elliot Speer, and the daughter-in-law of Dr. Robert
Speer, a popular Dobbs speaker since 1928. Before
coming to Dobbs, she had been Headmistress of the
Ethel Walker School in Simsbury, Connecticut.

A gentlewoman of somewhat unearthly beauty, she tried to continue the traditional religious training at Dobbs, while opening up some of the earlier restrictions. During her administration, the rigid Communication Rules, changed their name to Study Rules.

Dobbs was still known, however, as a strict girls' boarding school. And one of its rigid rules was neatness in the dormitory rooms, which were open to inspection by housemothers at any time of day. On each girl's desk, attached to its spotless blotter, was a weekly chart for tidiness comments. One alumna remembers a particularly cryptic remark by her housemother who had written in the appropriate space, 'Happy Birthday. Hair in comb.'[4]

Students still had to stand before the school at Friday Assemblies and answer 'Perfect,' 'Nearly Perfect,' or 'Imperfect,' as delineated in the Honor System, and many of Mrs. Speer's written chapel talks seem weighed down with discouragement at the number of 'malefactors,' unless the subject was foreign missions, in which she took a lively interest...." [5]

In the 1940s boarding school faculty wrote voluminous reports about and to students and to their parents. The reports about Frances were near unanimous about her high intellectual ability:

> "...Frances' work is as nearly perfect as could reasonably be expected: [yet] she is a passive member of the class when she should be a leader. She seems to have a sense of futility; if true this is unwarranted...as she has real ability". [6]

And a faculty consultant observed:

> "...It is very difficult to find out very much about Frannie as she is so silent and standoffish in her manner. She seems to have a chip on her shoulder and resents being corrected by the faculty or girls. She seems to have no interest in the school or in school affairs, and is just enduring the year as a basis for something further on....Her eating habits are very poor and she diets foolishly – at least

she does this at table which makes it very difficult for both girls and staff as that makes for nagging by the staff to get her to eat". [7]

Disobedience was very serious business. At one point, suspension or even dismissal was considered. Outside the classroom, trouble began soon after admission. Frances was caught smoking with a group of girls. She came under school censure and was confined to campus for an extended time. The penalty process eventually included a long and dreaded interview with Mrs. Speers, the headmistress, and also a letter to Frances' mother. The latter's response to the Headmistress is worth noting because it gives some insight into the mother-daughter relationship. Mrs. Nevins recognized that there may be good reasons for the failures in citizenship and the inattention to some of the rules at Dobbs:

November 14, 1945

My dear Mrs. Speer:

I have your and Miss Steen's letter of November 10. I am quite concerned over what you have to say about Frances's attitude toward her daily routine and, also, her carelessness in complying with the house rules. I have not, as yet, taken up this matter with Frances, simply because of her accident. I feel it would be unwise at the present time.

I am almost sorry that I did not send her away to school this past year, as I feel the fact that she has had one year of High School makes it harder for her now to re-adjust herself to community living [at Dobbs]. Also, the fact that Frances is an only child is not favorable to her. In other words, I think it might serve to make her chafe at rules and regulations a little more than she would ordinarily if she had been brought up with brothers and sisters. However, I am very sure she is a law-abiding girl and I will discuss it with her before she returns to school.... [8]

Most Sincerely,
Frances W. Nevins

What the Dobbs faculty did not know was that Frances' mother was about to marry Charles Tenney who was involved in a messy divorce. In order to marry, both Frances and Charles moved temporarily to Reno, Nevada, since the marriage could not be legalized in Massachusetts until his divorce was finalized. In Springfield and suburban Longmeadow, both the Nevins and Tenney families were prominent. Tenneys, in particular, had major holdings in the power and light companies, the banks, and had, along the way, founded the Longmeadow Country Club. As a consequence, this embarrassing situation was discussed widely among the many who knew both families, which caused strain for everyone involved, including the young Frances.

Toward the end of her senior year at Dobbs, the following report was sent to Connecticut College for admission with the class entering in the fall of 1947. It includes the assessment of her high intellectual ability, comments on her infractions of rules and her punishment, and gives an analysis of her behavior as a student. There is also an interesting comment about her genuine interest in religion:

> As the American Council percentiles and the Scholastic Aptitude Test results (taken junior year) as well as her record of achievement all indicate, Frances is a superior student with high intellectual capacity. Frances shows real mental alertness and open-mindedness, a high degree of intellectual curiosity, excellent study habits and purposefulness, and ability to work independently; she has a good deal of imagination and originality, is well above average in mental maturity and has both the appreciation and power of analytical thinking, the latter to a considerable degree. Unfortunately, Frances does not have as strong a record as a citizen. She is a strong individualist, living in a world of her own and she found it rather difficult to adjust to boarding school life and regulations. She is naturally retiring and self-conscious and seems to feel some gulf between herself and her group, partly because she is superior in academic achievement. Furthermore, she has allowed herself in some instances to come under the influence of the wrong group. For all of these reasons, the girls tend to distrust her and on several occasions she has definitely broken rules of the school or of the Student Council. Early in the fall she came

under school censure and received a severe penalty as a result; since then, her misconduct has been of a less serious nature, more an accumulation of small infringements. Because of self-consciousness, she has seemed to be less interested in people and seems to resent correction. During the second semester, however, there has been a noticeable improvement in her general attitude in the group; she is more outgoing, pleasant and friendly although her influence and leadership are still very much limited. Her teachers have no question whatever of her integrity and find her very responsible, cooperative, courteous and considerate, the latter quality shown particularly by her patience with students far less able than herself. In the classroom she has shown good judgment and emotional stability. For the first time she seems to realize genuinely what her responsibility is as a member of the community and to relate to her daily living the standards which she has for her academic work. She is genuinely interested in religion and we believe now is awakened to the realization of its bearing on her general conduct. We have given you this entire picture in order to be completely honest. While by temperament Frances may never be an outgoing, contributing member of the community, we believe that she has the potentialities certainly to develop into a very steady, quietly influential member and that the improvement begun this year should carry over into college. There is no doubt but that she is a superior student and should have the advantages for development which a fine college can give her. While she was home on a week-end last year, she was in an automobile accident and was badly shaken up. Since that time she frequently has severe headaches. In general, her health is good. Her father is dead and her mother is cooperative with the school". [9]

Academic Dean

Perhaps even more important to Frances' future at Connecticut College was a letter from the Academic Dean, Maude-Louise Strayer, to the Director of Admissions at Connecticut College:

For the sake of the record, I am putting into writing the gist of my telephone conversation with you this morning.

It seems only fair to include in the record the fact that Frances Nevins was more upset by her mother's re-marriage than she has been willing to admit. She feels that her mother will be happy but Frances, herself, does not like her step-father. As I told you, I understand that his divorce is not accepted in the state of Connecticut and until it is, they must live outside the state. Frances has been very much humiliated by all of this experience and upset by the change in her life which this involves. Her greatest salvation will be getting into a good stiff eastern college where she can make her own adjustment aside from the family and where she can be stimulated by the academic challenge which will call forth her best effort and forget her personal problems.

Her actual record in citizenship has been creditable during the second half year and she has gained in responsibility, cooperation, consideration and has attained a certain objectiveness about herself which is a sign of maturity. Had this not been true, we could not have permitted her to graduate with Honor, even though her academic ratio jumped during her senior year to 3.52 from 3.19 junior year. During the second semester, she gained a little and raised her rank from fifth to fourth place.

As I said over the telephone, I feel that Frances will not be anti-social or upset your community. Just how far she can go in her personal development as a constructive, socially-minded citizen, it is hard to say but we have great hopes for her.

I do hope that it will be possible for you to accept her at Connecticut since it has been her first choice. As I told you, she has already been accepted at Mount Holyoke and by this time may have decided to go there. Even so, it would mean a great deal to her to hear favorably from you. [10]

Sincerely yours,

Maude-Louise Strayer
Academic Dean

This letter from Dean Strayer is the first written recognition by faculty that troubles at home play a part in the way Frances Nevins deals with school work and her peers. Dean Strayer sets the record straight. She rightly states that Frances is an honors student; that she will make a contribution at Connecticut College; and that she has real and present personal family problems from which she needs to free herself. Dean Strayer gained her clear understanding of what was going on with Frances by taking the time to interview her:

> "I had a long and very satisfactory talk with Frances Nevins about her citizenship and I think that at long last she has seen the light and means to be a good citizen. She herself is astonished that up until very recently she never thought of citizenship as a matter to which to apply her intelligence or as a field to which to relate her religious feeling. The only explanation she can offer is that she never really listened to anything that was said about citizenship.
>
> Her religious feeling I think is genuine. No girl is going to take the initiative in asking permission to go every Wednesday to a seven o'clock service in an unheated church, unless she is serious. Frances says that she decided to do that as her way of keeping Lent and that she finds that doing so 'helps with problems'." [from a handwritten note]

At the conclusion of the Dobbs years, the 1947 Masterpieces, the Dobbs Yearbook, shows a lovely, somewhat melancholy young woman. In her copy, there are many messages from classmates written in the over-heated prose of the time...Dearest Frannie, etc., etc. Many of the messages include a reminder to her to "take care of Jack". Unfortunately, no further information was provided about Jack.

NOTES

1: The Early Years

3. William C. Hill, Principal, Classical High School, April 26,1945.
4. The Masters School Retrospective, 1877-1977, p. 52.
5. See Ref. 4, p. 11.
6. Faculty Report, American History, The Masters School, 1947.
7. Faculty Consultant Report, The Masters School, 1947.
8. Letter written by Frances W. Nevins (Frances' mother) to Mrs. Elliot Speer, Headmistress, The Masters School, November 14, 1945.
9. Summary report prepared by Miss Maude Louise Strayer, Academic Dean, The Masters School, prior to Frances' graduation 1947.
10. Letter written by Maude Louise Strayer, Academic Dean, The Masters School to Dr. Robert Cobbledick, Director of Admissions, Connecticut College for Women, May 1947.

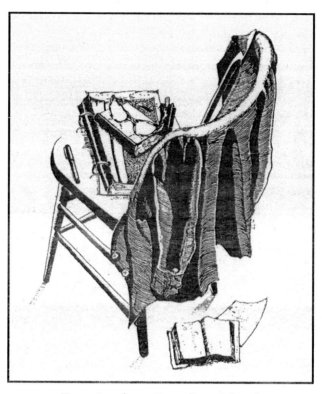

Drawing from Boarding School
(Dobbs) Yearbook 1947
Example of Frances Nevins'
Artistic Ability

2

The Passionate Years: Learning About Learning
1947-1952

Connecticut College for Women

Experienced advisors to college students hope two things happen with their advisees: that the students make a connection with someone, and that the students find their passion during their four years in college. When Academic Dean Strayer at Dobbs wrote her letter of recommendation for Frances to Connecticut College, she had the same hopes in mind. She wanted Frances to go to a "good stiff eastern college" where she could make her own adjustment away from her family and where she could be stimulated by the academic challenge.

And it all happened. Frances made a connection with Professor Edward Cranz, who mentored and challenged her passion for the intellectual pursuit of truth in the environment of Connecticut College, where she indeed met a stiff, academic challenge with stunning success.

Cranz was born in Germany; educated in the United States, he earned a doctorate from Harvard in medieval studies. Many years later and after he had become an internationally recognized scholar, he remembered Frances this way:

> "My main recollection of Frances Nevins is that she was the most brilliant student I encountered in a lifetime of teaching at Connecticut College. She was full of goodness, and by the time she had graduated, she had achieved a remarkable concentration of the self in things intellectual".

Cranz added that:

> "...Early in her time at Connecticut College, I recognized the nice CC girl, though of course, much smarter than most, but my memory is that it was only in her Junior year that she began to come to my office to discuss what she was studying. The turning point was her decision to do an honors study....She gave up the pleasant trivialities of her early college life, and she turned to an almost undivided concentration and

allegiance to things intellectual, notably as she saw
them in Augustine and Nicholas of Cusa. But this new
allegiance was in no way an abandonment of the self
or submission to what is beyond or other; indeed, it
was in some way an assertion of the self, though now
at a higher level...." [11]

Gertrude E. Noyes '25, who was then dean of freshmen,
has described the array of academic honors Frances earned: she
was the class' Winthrop Scholar, won departmental honors in
history, and also shared the History Prize for Understanding and
Originality of Thought in the Study of History. Her honors paper,
directed by Professor of History F. Edward Cranz, was entitled "The
Relation Between Christianity and Philosophy in St. Augustine
and Nicholas Cusanus". [See Appendix a: Nicholas of Cusa: 15th
Century Cardinal/Theologian/Writer.]   Dean Noyes points out
that Winthrop Scholar is the top academic honor at Connecticut
College. Frances was named first in her class of 175, and though we
don't use the term, she could be considered the valedictorian or, at
any rate, the "top-ranking student".

One of the honors accorded to an outstanding student as
graduating senior was addressing the student body with an original
"Chapel Talk". Professor Cranz wrote:

> "My recollection is that I wasn't too
> impressed with it at the time, but I was too young and
> too intellectual and not serious enough. Frannie was a
> good deal younger but also a good deal more serious.
> Now it seems to me a splendid statement, and I am
> particularly impressed with its 'quietness'." [12]

CHAPEL TALK

Frances D. Nevins
Connecticut College, May 2, 1951

***It seems to me that to anyone who turns to
Christianity with a desire to find out what it's about, the
first thing it has to say is found in the Gospel of Matthew:***

Ask, and it shall be given you;
seek, and ye shall find;
Knock, and it shall be opened unto you:
For everyone that asketh receiveth;

and he that seeketh findeth;
and to him that knocketh it shall be opened.

(Matthew VII 7-8)

Much of the rest of the Bible and the Christian tradition may seem incomprehensible and incredible, but this is clear; and in a sense it is an introduction to the incomprehensible and the incredible, for it warns us that the answers aren't found on the surface, nor are they easily understandable at the beginning. It tells us to be cautious about what we condemn as "not so," because it tells us there is something to look for which we don't yet see. This seems to me to be a pretty big step in the right direction, for I think we get a sense in college that Christianity is something that everybody knows about. If we think that we know what it means and it isn't exciting then we are probably mistaken, and we are blocking any understanding we might get---but if we accept the fact that we don't know what the Christians were talking about and we'd like to, and that the seeking may be a fairly long process which takes time and effort, then the question is where and how to go about it.

The answer for those of us who don't belong to a specific church which takes over the task of teaching us seems to be so bound up with the process of education that the best place for us to look for an understanding of religion is probably at college. Here we run up against a number of ideas which are flatly anti-religious and a number of others which don't seem compatible with religion as we have known it. And if we're going to find for ourselves a religion which we can hold honestly and talk to other people about, it will have to come face to face with these other ideas and argue with them.

In another sense college is the place to do this because education which is more than superficial seems to end up asking religious questions. If education takes, it should give us an idea about the meaning of life in general and the life of each of us in particular. There are all kinds of partial meaning that education can give to life, from learning techniques that we can use after graduation, to the objective which most modern theories of education set forth---to make responsible citizens. But the techniques are not going to do us any good in time of trouble, and nobody can be a really responsible citizen unless he's made a kind of peace with himself. If education is to give a total meaning it ought to give us a way of thinking about God and the world and ourselves---which amounts to saying that education should be religious.

This works two ways---it means that once this way of thinking about education makes sense to you, you begin to see that everything you study throws some light on the basic questions you are asking. And the answers you find give importance to all the things you study, which unless you have an awfully strong intellectual curiosity sometimes seem pretty meaningless if we look them in the face and ask what is the use of doing it anyway.

Religion tends to be thought of as something to consider alongside of the other areas of life, running parallel in thinking, and in environment with economics, history, biology, etc. On the other hand, thought about in this way, all education, not just one area of it, is religious. Because everything fits into the search for meaning somewhere, everything contributes to it. At one time or another it will probably include the study of the religious ideas of the past, but biology and English poetry will be part of it as well. To speak of education as religious isn't so much to change the subject matter as to change the way of thinking about the subject matter.

Some of the reasons for thinking about education and religion together this way are different depending on what kind of a person you are and some of them are the same for all of us because we're all people asking questions and looking for a purpose in life. For the believer it seems as though particularly in our time religion needs education in order to keep itself going. It can never survive the attack of the anti-Christian ideologies if it can't meet them on the most high powered intellectual level. Nor can it keep itself going long even among sympathetic people without some good intelligent support. The real force behind the great religious personalities of the past was never intellectual, but was something which was common to the most ignorant peasant and the most learned teacher. But the most important transmitters of the Christian tradition since St. Paul have been highly educated people who have been able to argue for their point of view against all kinds of heretics who were often pretty subtle intellectually.

But probably the most important reasons for seeking religion in education are those that have to do with all of us simply because we're people in a world we don't know very much about, and not knowing the reason why. Pascal has said this pretty strongly, in talking about what he called "those who pass their life without thinking of the ultimate end of life";

And how can it happen that the following argument occurs to a reasonable man?

> *"I know not who put me into the world, nor what the world is, nor what I myself am. I am in terrible ignorance of everything. I know not what my body is, nor my senses, nor my soul... I*

find myself tied to one corner of this vast expanse,
without knowing why I am put in this place
rather than in another, nor why the short time
which is given me to live is assigned to me at this
point rather than at another of the whole eternity
which was before me or which shall come after
me...

"As I know not whence I came, so I know not
whither I go....Such is my state, full of weakness
and uncertainty. And from all this I conclude that
I ought to spend all the days of my life without
caring to inquire into what must happen to me."

(Pensées, #194.)

The situation he describes gets even more acute in time of war, and one of the basic reasons for making an effort to find out what we believe is because of the feeling of futility of so many people around us and the sense of meaninglessness that the people have who are going to war.

But to say that we ought to think about religion to get us out of the unhappy state we're in is only half the story. The best reason I know for thinking about it pretty hard during college is that sooner or later it makes the whole world look better and everything in life seem more important.

The statement of this is found in the text from Matthew quoted in the beginning. It applies to both ends of the search; it urges us to undertake it and it tells us there is something to search for. But perhaps the most important thing to those who are in the process, it offers itself as a provisional faith. To accept it is a kind of gamble; you start out on a road that you can't see the end of. But to accept it is also to have faith that the end is there and that if we start it's impossible that we should not succeed. Saint Augustine said what I'm trying to say much better than I could:

"Now we must treat the matter this way, not as though
we now understood, which is impossible; but as
though desiring that we should sometime understand.
For if truth or wisdom is not sought with all the mind
and heart, it will never be found. But if it is sought as
it is worthy to be sought, it can never withdraw or hide
itself from those who seek it. This is what is meant
when it is said:

"Ask, and it shall be given you;
seek, and you shall find;

-17-

Knock, and it shall be opened unto you:
For everyone that asketh receiveth;
and he that seeketh
Findeth; and to him that knocketh it
shall be opened."

Recollections of Classmates
at Connecticut College

After her death I wrote an essay about Frances that was published in the Connecticut College Alumnae Magazine (Fall, 1982).[13] In response, some of her classmates wrote their recollections and also came to the CC campus for a gathering to reflect together about her.[14]

"I was her roommate at Dobbs and, of course, knew her at Conn. I remember her mother bringing her to Dobbs. She (the mother) seemed 'hardened'. She would take us to New York. We went to the Stork Club and to shows. Frannie adored her father. She had a big 8x10 picture of him on her dresser. Frannie had the reputation of being the smartest kid at Dobbs - even smarter than that kid who graduated from Yale at 14. And it was almost a 'ritual' or a ceremony when she came to say 'goodbye' along in her junior year. She brought me a stuffed animal and she had made up her mind to be a scholar - from then on she was totally in the library - and totally into her academic work". (Gloria Jones)

"I never knew her well although I went to summer camp in New Hampshire and Connecticut College with her-we were always in different groups. When I first knew Frannie, we were in our early teens (12-13) but I remember her as being very well liked and (I remember) dumb things like how cute she looked when we persuaded her to cut her hair. It was naturally curly and looked adorable cut short. She thought it great, too. Am I reading too much into this, now with mature eyes, to get the feeling she had not been around a bunch of girls very much before, (and) led a solitary sort of life? Four years later we arrived as freshmen at CC. Again, we were assigned to dorms on opposite ends of the campus and never changed, sticking (probably) with the girls we were first assigned to live with (I know I did). But we (Frannie and I) would meet and talk sometimes, particularly our Freshmen and Sophomore years, because of our past association at camp. We were never in class together. But my feeling is that because of her brilliance she grew more and more remote from campus life, and, although always friendly and polite, rather solitary. Only at night would you see her walking around campus to see a professor or so for her independent study programs. She was so far ahead of everyone else. She worked almost always independently, and grew farther and farther withdrawn from campus social life". (Lois Sessions)

"Fran, Mike (Mary McNab), and I were among a group of 13 or 14 members of the class of '51 who started out together in North Cottage as Freshmen, moved as a block to Blackstone for our sophomore year, and then to Mary Harkness for our junior and senior years. ...Fran withdrew a bit from the group in our junior year. ...Here's a photograph of most of us. Fran is dressed as she always was...most of the rest of us, too; it was our undergraduate habit...blue sneakers, white socks, man's white shirt with tails hanging out, and cuffed dungarees (as blue jeans were called then). I don't remember her in any other clothes". (Natalie Bowen)

"Frannie and I were not classmates or even close friends but were history majors, and I shall always remember the awe and respect she inspired in all of us as 'the smartest girl on campus'...studying her history sources in the original language, for example".
(Judith Chynoweth)

"Frannie and I first met at Conn. College in 1947. We became fast friends. Her intellect never ceased to amaze me, but I think I worried some about her sensitivity and vulnerability. We spent many a night discussing 'life' into the wee hours....I watched the transformation of an extremely attractive young woman in our freshman year, tall, very thin, long painted fingernails to a totally intellectually committed recluse over the next 3 years. She remained open and friendly to all, but had a small coterie of friends who shared the enthusiasm for Augustine, Cusa, etc....I remember that during a wonderful trip to Europe in 1950 with classmate Joy Anderson Nicholson, Frannie spent hours arguing with several young Jesuit priests about the meanings of the parables. She had read the New Testament in Greek, of course!

As to Fran's proclivity for the cloistered life showing up at C.C. - you bet! She had many friends, loved us all but loved God more. She was more than an intellectual - much more." (Mary "Mike" McNab)

Frances Nevins to Joy Anderson

As part of the European trip, Frances left the group and went alone to Heidelberg for several weeks in search of primary source material about Nicholas of Cusa, her senior honors project at Connecticut College. Joy saved this letter for 30 years.

Europe
September 15, 1950

It is 6 A.M. and the Genoa R.R. station is very uninspiring. However, the time schedule all worked out like a Chinese puzzle, so I am very lucky. Cusa was wonderful. Was glad I went when I did as it seemed like a fitting end to the summer (and I couldn't have spoken a word if I'd gone earlier). It's little and peaceful and has hills all around and really quite medieval. Don't remember how much I told your mother about Cusa's hospital - 6 Sisters and a Rector in charge. Sweet people, all very proud of Cusa. The Library was very exciting. Lots of his unpublished things as well as his own books - Bible, Aristotle, Augustine, etc. - the hand-written books are almost unbelievable - all look like they were done by masters of the craft with such loving care, letter by letter (sort of the same impression as the Cathedrals with all the beautiful detail - what energy the people must have had then!) One Biblical Dictionary with beautiful blue and gold birds all over the margins. Wish you could have seen it. I was glad to have seen Cusa's home.

Somehow it did make it all more real - when I pick up the books now I'll think of how quiet and nice the Mosel River was....Incidentally found the cheapest place of the summer there - $2.50 to eat and sleep for 3 1/2 days!

Felt pretty homesick for Germany for a couple of days....Came out the most on trains, I think....Now I just have a thank-God-for-the-whole-summer feeling and excitement about seeing everybody again. (Stood in the Am. Express in Paris for a few minutes to try to get used to the American atmosphere - think maybe the boat'll be a transition)....

Spent the last 3 days in Paris in the B.N. [Bibliotheque National] doing a microfilm job for Dr. C. [Connecticut College Professor]. Good in lots of ways - good practice trying to find the books and kept one busy after just having left Germany - Paris was an amazing change. Probably a lot of it was coincidence but all the time I was in Germany, in cheap cafes, 3rd class trains, etc. I didn't come across an obnoxious, even slightly fresh, man. The minute we got across the French border, I spent the night fighting with a French soldier - (good-naturedly that is, he was very cute but still that Frenchman attitude). Taxi horns in Paris most annoying....

I have the Durer cards for you - glad people like it as I'm so fond of it too. Protestants (especially we self-styled ones) have so little symbolism that really does make sense to us (i.e. in contrast to the Catholics) that seems to have been particularly done for us. Do you have Durer's 4 Apostles? You would like some of his other things, too, I think. Will keep the cards till I get home and then send 'em.

Radcliffe/Harvard 1951-1952

Radcliffe, as the sister arm of Harvard and prestigious women's college, was established in 1879 under the name "Harvard Annex" as an alternative to women who were denied access to Harvard. It wasn't until 1943 – with Harvard's men off fighting in World War II – that Radcliffe women were allowed to take classes at Harvard.

It is hard to characterize the Graduate School of Radcliffe of the 1950s. It was large, one of the largest for women in the country, with 289 students enrolled in full-time study, coming from the United States and 22 foreign countries. In 1952 about 11% were studying history, and 59 MAs were granted that year. All the teaching was done by Harvard professors.

There was no graduate center or common room at that time, and probably little group experience. Students lived in scattered accommodations. Frances rented a room with Mrs. George Waring on Walker Street in Cambridge. "I am very pleased with it," she wrote to an inquiring Dean. In answer to the financial question about payment for the program, she wrote: "by trust fund – as much as needed."

Frances makes clear on the application that her interest is more focused than it was before beginning her honors work at Connecticut. Originally, she was seeking to come in contact with basic elements in the Western tradition. Now, she is not only honing in on the Renaissance and medieval history, she is edging closer to the special field of Theology. At this point, her intention was to study the history of Christian thought – intellectual history rather than church history.

Frances wrote this statement as part of her application:

> "I am interested in the history of Christian thought, especially during the Renaissance and Reformation. This interest seems to lie on the borderline between history and Theology. I feel that it falls more within the provenance of intellectual history as I am interested in the relation of Christian thinking to other

developments in Western civilization and the course of study which I would like to follow is not in any sense limited to Theology. The following is a very general statement of what I should like someday to study in this field and connection with it. Part of this work will doubtless have to be left till after graduate school but I should like to do as much of it as possible in the next two years.

My field of concentration would presumably include the intellectual developments preceding the Reformation as well as the Reformation itself, with special emphasis on Luther. This would involve a knowledge of the intellectual history of the Middle Ages. I should like if possible to take some courses in New Testament and early Christian Theology at the Divinity School. I feel that a knowledge of the Greek language and Greek philosophy as well as the modern developments in philosophy would be useful in connection with my work. Upon completion of my graduate work I hope to teach in college. I did my seniors honors work on the relation between the thought of St. Augustine and Nicholas Cusanus. Eventually, I hope to do some fairly intensive work on Cusanus." (April 30, 1951).

An example of her work on Cusanus submitted to Radcliffe/Harvard follows.

Nicholas of Cusa - 15th Century Cardinal/Theologian/Writer:
An Analysis by Frances D. Nevins[101]

The fall of man was theoretically a fall from a state of harmony with both the world and God; the corollary to the idea of original sin is a prior state of nature in which God, man and the universe all existed in a right relation to each other and in which the whole creation had a purpose. The punishment for sin was not existence in the world but blind attachment to and involvement in the processes of the world. Hence Christian theology implies that a fulfillment of God's original purpose would include a harmony between man and the world rather than an irreconcilable conflict between the two. However, this idea has received little development among theologians, with the notable exception of Nicholas of Cusa; a theory of such a harmony appears in his *Idiota* of 1450. It is what might be termed a Christian idea of nature; if Cusa's people are like Adam, it is because the Christian God dwells with them, and not because they are the products of Nature in either an Aristotelian or an eighteenth century sense.

The mainspring of Cusa's theory is closely related to the first chapter of *Romans*, verses 19-22:

...that which may be known of God is manifest in them; for God hath shewed it unto them. For the invisible things of him from the creation of the world are clearly seen, being understood by the things which are made, even his eternal power and Godhead; so that they are without excuse: Because that, when they knew God, they glorified him not as God, neither were thankful; but became vain in their imaginations, and their foolish heart was darkened.

To Cusa the invisible things of him are still clearly seen, and he uses this insight as the nucleus of a way of thinking in which faith in God and knowledge of the world are simply two aspects of the same reality, which reinforce each other.

The ideas are set forth by the *idiota*[1], a carver of spoons, who claims to have no knowledge of philosophy or theology as it is taught in the schools. There is no adequate English translation of the term *idiota*; it had several connotations in Medieval terminology, but the most relevant seem to be that of "layman," as opposed to one who holds an ecclesiastical office, "unlearned", especially with relation to the art of grammar,[2] and simply "common man."[3] In the *De Sapientia*

I the spoon-maker talks to an orator who has not found the summum bonum in his literary studies. He is told that sapientia dwells more naturally in the books of God than in those of man, that it actually shouts in the marketplaces;[3] that God has made Himself clearly recognizable to those who will sincerely see Him.[4]

To return to the passage from Paul, Cusa puts comparatively little emphasis on the foolish hearts which are darkened (though the orator and the philosopher of the third book evidently fall in this category.) Blindness is indeed interminable torture,[5] but it is natural to see, and the reader has a very strong sense that evil and sin are a sort of unnatural mistake analogous to a plant which somebody forgot to put in the sun, or in Cusa's own terms, a horse which is by nature free but constrained to feed upon that which is not its natural nourishment.[6] Cusa's conception of the Christian experience is not the revelation of God after long search to those who have reached humility through weariness of following dead end roads to blessedness. To him, God's traces in the world are so compelling that if, one can be brought to see them, the perception itself will bring humility. Once man has seen his true treasure whose image is present everywhere in the creation he will gladly sell everything and buy the field in which it lies.[7] The process of separation from attachment to the finite is rather a simple turning to something better than a slow and painful extraction of the soul from its temporal web.

Sapientia or the *Verbum Dei* is the true home of the soul; at times it is borne toward it as iron toward a magnet.[8] In these moments of intuition, of freedom from the world of sense, it feeds up the true source of life, has contact with the essence of all existence. But the uniqueness in Cusa's thought is that this perception is not of another world, but in a sense a closer contact with this world that can be attained through the senses. There is here a danger of making the infinite finite and of making God world. But God is not world, since He is triune.[9] Similarly the infinite is in no way finitized, rather the finite becomes nothing but an appearance of the infinite suspended in space and time. Hence the place of the mystic intuition is not over and against everyday existence, it is at the silent center of everyday existence, working through the active life and giving it meaning.

The enjoyment of *sapientia* is immortality, which to Cusa is as natural to man as humanity itself.[10] Just as milk is the natural nourishment of a child and so he has a foretaste of it, so we have a certain indelible notion of *sapientia* which makes us unable to rest except in it.[11] In it the soul finds its source and goal, the very truth of itself.[12] Hence since only immortality is the fulfillment of its nature its existence on earth is motion, a constant ascension.[13] There is security without fixedness.

The orator perceives early the spoon-maker's purpose in the discussion, Cusa's idea of the purpose of all intellectual activity: "For this seems to be your intention: that the cause of our being, by which, in which, and from which we live and move be experienced by us as *principium, medium,* et *finis.*"[14] In the third book of the *Idiota,* the *De Mente,* the spoon-maker talks with a philosopher whose life is devoted to the precept 'know thyself,' in order that he might discover his mind to be joined with the divine mind and therefore immortal.[15] The spoon-maker replies with a description of his conception of the function of mind in the world. The reason for all activity of the mind is so that it might know itself; that by action in the world and analysis of that action, it might be brought to recognize its nature as described in the *De Sapientia I.* This inspiration is both source and object of Cusa's theory of knowledge-the discussion begins and ends with the question of immortality.

The philosopher's desire to understand the relation of our mind[16] to the mind of God is early fulfilled. They are in the same relation as *videre* is to *facere.*[17] God's mind contains the truth of all things; our mind an approximation to the truth. God's thought is the creation of things, and to understand is to re-think, as far as we are able, the thoughts of God.[18] Thus we form notions of things, which are rather conjectures than true ideas, since true forms are obscured in the variability of matter. (Knowledge of mathematics, as we shall see, and abstract forms of which the mind has true knowledge are an exception.)[19]

The human mind is the nearest likeness to God that we know. Its image character consists in the fact that it is the *complicatio* of all its imperfect notions of things, while God is the *Complicatio* of everything in the truth of its being. The concept of *Complicatio* and *explicatio* is one of Cusa's key ideas and may perhaps be better understood by description than by definition. The nearest, though still imprecise, English terms are probably "enfolding" and "unfolding." God is the *complicatio* of all things because in Him everything exists as one in the truth of its being. It is important to realize that the essences of the separate entities are not discrete in God. *Complicatio* is not *collectio* (this is where the term *enfolding* is misleading) and all *complicationes* are unities. The universe is thus the *explicatio* of God. Here plurality occurs, but a plurality in which nothing is found but the original essence differently expressed. Thus "one" is the *complicatio* of number and number the *explicatio* of "one." The mind is simple and one yet can contain in itself many notions of things, just as the polished surface of a cut diamond reflects the images of the things which appear before it.[20] Since it is in this way the image of God, it can have approximate conceptions of what "the things which are made" really are.[21]

The mind attains a knowledge of truth in two ways: first, in an attempt to discover the nature of separate things, it comes to realize that the essence of any given thing is unknowable and that the essence of all things is one---that by penetrating into any single creature it does not come to an end except in so far as it finds the infinite at the source and center. Just as the mystic intuition is not conceived as in opposition to the temporal life but rather at its heart, so the perception of the infinite is reached by penetration farther into the finite. The knowledge that the essence of all things is one and unknowable is not another kind of knowledge than the lower, less precise recognition of the appearances of things, it is simply a higher result of the same process. Secondly the mind uses itself, abstracted from the world, as a means to the intuition of absolute truth. By considering its own simple nature as *complicatio*, it understands by analogy how all things can exist simultaneously in God who is infinitely simple. The mind's understanding of its own processes is thus a method of theological speculation.

Since the mind's notions are approximations to the truth of things, Cusa calls that power by which it forms these notions the *vis assimilativa*. In a sense the mind actually becomes like the object of its knowledge; it is like a piece of wax, imbued with intelligence, which forms itself into an imitation of whatever is presented to it.[22] This is the measuring quality which to Cusa is the prime function of the mind.[23] Only God and man can measure, and to measure means to create order, proportion, harmony, discretion, integrity, even plurality---the plurality of things as it exists apart from our mind is only a modus intelligendi of God.[24] The *vis assimilativa* is not thus a passive mirror quality on which images of entities existing outside the mind are impressed. God, by conceiving of things, creates them; we, by conceiving of them, recreate them. The things are not there as we know them until the mind names, defines and terminates them. The conception of the world as existing apart from mind is an impossibility, since it has its being from the fact that it exists in the mind of God. (Theoretically without mind there would be only a confused mass of solidity.)[25] So the things about which we make conjectures really exist, whether we see them or not, but not as a collection of independent entities. If God stopped thinking of any part of the world it would simply cease to exist.

The mind works by using certain indispensable concepts as instruments (not ordinarily consciously.) We have seen that the divine mind is the supreme *complicatio* of all things. Our mind is the most exact image of this and in its turn it contains other images of *complicatio*, or simply *complicationes*, as they are usually termed. These are simple unities which cannot be found in the world, but in terms of which everything in the world receives form as we know it. Apart from its existence as simple essence, the universe exists in God's mind also in number, magnitude and motion and in this form we are meant to understand it. However there can be no understanding of number without one, of motion without rest, of time without the present, of magnitude without the point; number, time, motion and magnitude are *explicationes*.[26] It will be seen that none of these has existence "in act." *One* is an idea which comes from the mind, not things; there is no object which because of its nature can be called 'one' since all things can be divided into infinite parts and themselves may be conceived as parts of other indeterminate wholes. Similarly the point exists nowhere in the world—neither point, nor line, its extension, nor surface, the extension of line, can exist anywhere but in the mind. The representation of a point which we make on paper is not point but solidity: it is impossible that it should not have three dimension if it has material existence.[27] Neither can rest nor 'the present' actually occur.

These *complicationes* serve a double function. First, they point to the way in which everything in the world is dependent upon a simple *principium*, since there can be no complexity without prior simplicity, no motion without rest, etc. The *principium* of all finite appearances is then not attainable by the finite but is behind and in and through it;[28] it appears in time and space contracted within certain limits, just as the uncontracted and simple "one," "rest," and "present" appear in the world in complex form as number, motion, and time. Secondly, these *complicationes* are the instruments by which the mind recreates the world. The concept of 'one' is crucial, since mind can do literally nothing without number---number and mind are so closely related that at times Cusa speaks of the mind as being a "certain divine number" or more exactly, as a simple unity causing number to rise out of itself.[29] The importance of number as an instrument of mind stems from the fact that it is an image of the creative principle of the universe. Because the universe could not have been formed by the putting together of parts,[30] the creative principle must have been analogous to our number, since it is the only thing we know which is composed of itself (i.e., nothing is found in 'three' but the repetition of 'one' three times.) Number is the cause of proportion;[31] forms appear in the world only when matter is proportioned to them. Hence number is the reason for the *delectation et pulchritudo* in the creation.[32] God, wishing to make His concept sensible, acts upon indeterminate matter as a musician who organizes his chorus to conform to the harmony in his mind.[33]

The point is another key instrument for the understanding of the world. Just as in the mind, with respect to number, was a simple unity creating number out of itself, so with respect to magnitude it seems almost to become the point. The terminations of things are lines and surfaces (simple the extensions of the point) which define the integrity of a thing, i.e., the truth of its being as it exists distinguished from all other things.[34] In reaching the integrity of a triangular object the mind acts as a kind of lead pencil whose point traces three sides and three angles. The triangularity is thus not a property of the object as such, but of the minds of its Creator and its observer.

The mind is an image of God not only as *complicatio* but because it can receive the divine sapientia. Man's mind becomes a kind of incarnation of sapientia (always incomplete and partial.)[35] It participates in the truth not by passively reflecting certain 'truths' but by receiving the very power of truth within itself, so that it becomes a living criterion for judging everything with which it comes in contact.[36] Admiration of the world is a precondition for the awakening of this power[37] (the orator remarks at one point that it seems to him that admiration is the incentive for seeking to know about anything whatever.)[38]

We have noted that Cusa's idea of purpose of knowledge of the world was so that we might come to understand our own nature. So in the last chapter of the *De Mente* he shows that all the principal ways of thinking about the mind which he has hitherto outlined point toward immortality. The totality of things is divided into 'measured' and 'measuring.' God is the absolute Measurer, He who set bounds to all things in His creation and decreed that motion and time should be their masters. Viewed in one light, man's perception of immortality is the perception that he is not subject to these masters—that he stands apart and watches their activity. The attainment of this perception is the object of all his specific operations in the world of things; he eagerly measures all the other parts of the creation in order that, seeking his own measure among them, he may see that it is only found in Him in whom all things are one.[39] The new astronomical instruments were concrete testimony to Cusa that man alone besides God sets limits to motion. Motion is the cause of all dissolution; it is then impossible that the mind should be dissolved by that which is terminated by it.[40] Man alone in the created universe understands its processes and appreciates its beauty. He uses the finite, the passing, to read the thoughts of God in images and shadows. God tears up the pages but the reader remains.[41]

The argument for immortality ends on the note on which it began in the *De Sapientia I*. The mind which has received within itself the actual communication of sapientia will live beyond the body for it is resplendent with incorruptible truth.[42] Since the truth is also absolute goodness it is impossible that it should ever withdraw itself, just as it is impossible that days, which have their being from the shining of the sun, should ever end until the sun itself shall pass away.[43]

* * * * * * * * *

The *De Sapientia I* is rather more religious than philosophical. Some of its roots are deep in the writings of Paul, and though it has within it the beginnings of the philosophical theory of the *De Mente*, its interest is in the relation of the soul to God rather than to the world. The first and last books of the *De Mente* tie up the philosophical theory to its religious origins. The *De Mente* begins with the problem of the philosopher who would attain to the spoon-maker's certainty of immortality, and ends with a reference to the same belief in all the religions.[44] The purpose of the *De Mente* is to show the philosopher that the faith of the spoon-maker cannot be refuted but is rather substantiated by his kind of knowledge. The most important philosophical idea in the *De Mente* is the idea of *complicatio-explicatio*, which is capable of extremely broad application and also lies, as has been intimated, at the basis of Cusa's theory of the universe. This idea may be viewed as a development out of the Christian conception of God as the I AM THAT I AM, the completely infinite and unknowable, and yet apart from whom there is no substance. Paul had said of the Christian God: "For of him and through him and to him are all things to whom be glory forever."[45] God as *Complicatio* is a translation of this into philosophical language.[46]

So Cusa perhaps has an answer to the problem implied in I *Corinthians*---the problem of the reconciliation of the wisdom of this world and the foolishness of God,[47] of making "He who seemeth to be wise...to become a fool"[48] so that he might believe. Cusa would not ask the wise to deny his knowledge but only to follow it to its conclusion: *Vera scientia humiliat*.[49]

NICHOLAS OF CUSA
FOOTNOTES

1. Idiota has been translated into German as de Laie and into French as 'le pro-fane.'

2. Cf. Docta Ignorantia I, II where Cusa emphasizes matter instead of art, and Faber Stapulensis' preface to the 1514 edition of Cusa's work: "Talis est Cusae stilus, talis est. dicendae character: in quo potius intelligentia quam sermonis flos requiri debeat. . .Catholicus est potius quam oratorius sermo."

3. Nicholas of Cusa, Idiota de Sapientia I, 1450, in Nicolaus von Cues, Texte seiner philosophischen Schriften, ed. A Petzelt (Stuttgart, 1949), I, 301.

4. Ibid., "absque curiosa inquisitione affectum"

5. Ibid., p. 306.

6. Ibid., p. 300.

7. Ibid., p. 308.

8. Ibid., p. 307.

9. Cusa's idea of the Trinity is not directly relevant in this connexion and so will not be discussed here.

10. Idiota de Mente, XV, p. 369.

11. Idiota de Sapientia I, p. 307.

12. Ibid., "veritatem suum esse."

13. Ibid., p. 304.

14. Ibid., p. 305.

15. De Mente, I, p. 322.

16. Mens is perhaps nearer the German Geist than either mind or soul. It is the entire intellectual nature, that which inhabits the body and gives it life.

17. De Mente, VII, p. 341.

18. Ibid., III, p. 330.

19. Ibid., VII, p. 343.

20. Ibid., V, p. 335.

21. Ibid., III, p. 330.

22. Ibid., p. VII, p. 342.

23. Ibid., I, p. 324. "Mens quidem a mensurando dici coniicio."

24. Ibid., VI, pp. 338-339.

25. Ibid., IX, p. 349.

26. Ibid., IV, p. 331. These may be taken as the principal complicationes which the mind uses. They are by no means a hard and fast group and the idea is applied to anything which it seems to fit. Thus at times tempus explicat aeternitas, not praesens, compositio simplicitas, motus momentus, etc.

27. Ibid., IX, p. 350.

28. De Sapientia I, p. 303.

29. De Mente, VII, p. 341. "Unitas simplex ex sua vi numerum suum exerens."

30. Ibid., VII, p. 337.

31. Ibid

32. Ibid., VI, p. 339.

33. Ibid., p. 338.

34. Ibid., X, p. 353.

35. Ibid., V, p. 335.

36. Ibid., IV, p. 332.

37. Ibid., V, p. 335.

38. Ibid., p. 321.

39. Ibid., IX, p. 352.

40. Ibid., XV, p. 367.

41. There are several other arguments for immortality which relate specifically to the main characteristics of mind as previously discussed, the most important being the conception of mind as image of the divine "Complication." It is the nature of all "complicationes" to be simple unity not found in the finite world, and never to be exhausted by "explicatio"---(thus the universe does not fully express God, but He exists above and apart from as well as in and through it.) The mind, as "complicatio" of motion and time, is also freed from both, (De Mente, XV, pp. 367-68) and as "complication" of incorruptible number must also be incorruptible. (p. 367.)

42. De Mente, XV, p. 368. The attempt to put this into adequate English is here even more unsuccessful than usual. Cusa very often uses words like "reluceat" and "resplendeat" in this connexion which should be seen in the Latin context in order to get the full force of the thought

43. Ibid

44. Ibid., pp. 368-369.

45. Romans 11:36.

46. De Sapientia I. Cf. especially pp. 302-303: "...per quod, in quo, ex quo..."

47. I Corinthians I:18-31.

48. I Corinthians III:8.

49. De Sapientia I, p. 300.

AUTHOR'S NOTE:

Interest in Cusa's ideas has risen among philosophers and Church leaders. Cardinal Avery Dulles, one of America's premier Catholic theologians, cites Cusa's work as useful in searching for guideposts to understanding Muslim, Christian tensions. (see John Allen, "Seeking insight from Muslim/Christian history", *National Catholic Reporter*, November 3, 2006): p. 10. The 20th Anniversary of the Paulist Press Series (1999): *The Classics of Western Spirituality* included for the first time in one volume in English, the spiritual writings, translated and interpreted by H. Lawrence Bond. The text brought to the fore this outstanding 15th century figure whose work anticipated modern problems of ecumenicity and pluralism, empowerment and reconciliation, and tolerance and individuality. See also: C. Bellito, T. Izbicki and G. Christianson: *Introducing Nicholas of Cusa, A Guide to a Renaissance Man* (NY: Paulist Press, 2004).

After one year of full-time study, Frances completed the requisite course work at A level. More than half of the courses were in Church history. She earned the Master of Arts degree from Radcliffe/Harvard in June 1952.

Frances Nevins to Joy Anderson
Mid-way in the demanding Radcliffe/Harvard Master's Degree program, Frances writes to a Connecticut College friend affirming the value of setting time aside for contemplation.

Cambridge
January 1, 1952

It came to me over the vacation that it seems to be as much of a duty to sit and be quiet or look at the sunset or something, to help restore the soul as to do the active tasks that are required - I never really thought of it this way, but the one somehow gives you power to do the other.

NOTES
2: The Passionate Years

11. Letter written by Dr. F. Edward Cranz to author, December 15, 1993.

12. See Ref. 11. Of interest, Dr. Cranz, an internationally recognized scholar, had saved a copy of Frances' "Chapel Talk" for 42 years.

13. Joan Ward Mullaney. "Frances Nevins, '51: Friend, Scholar, Wife, Nun, Mystic." The Connecticut College Alumni Magazine, Vol. 60, No. 1, Fall, 1982. pp. 14, 15.

14. See Ref. 13, p. 15.

3

Marriage: Happy, Unexpectedly Short

Not long after completing the Radcliffe program, Frances became more directly involved with the Episcopal Church. She described herself as a church worker and accepted an assignment counseling college students in Athens, Ohio. It was not surprising that she would be drawn to some kind of Episcopal Church membership. Her mother had brought her to services now and again. Apparently her father was an inactive Catholic Church member. Dobbs, always distinctly Protestant, had, as its Chairman of the Board of Trustees, the Rt. Rev. Henry Knox Sherrill whom Time Magazine called the "No. 1 Protestant Churchman in the U.S". He was still active on their Board while Frances was a student at Dobbs. And, of course, while at Connecticut College not just her Honors project engaged her strong interest in ideas related to religious personages. She and her friends discussed church issues often and passionately.

In the course of her church work in Ohio, she met Paul Cawein from Hamilton, Ohio. He was beginning preparation for the Episcopal priesthood. Their mutual interest in the Episcopal Church led to a mutual interest in each other. They were married in Athens, Ohio on February 5, 1954. A few weeks later, Paul wrote to a friend sounding like a very happy husband:

20 March 1954

Dear Joy [Anderson]:

My lovely wife is ironing. It's quarter till seven and a friend (one of the ushers from our wedding) is arriving from Youngstown for dinner at eight. She needs an apron and I a white shirt. But lest you get the idea that Fran is not changed at all by marriage, I will add that the roast is in the oven and plans have been made for dinner today and tomorrow. We spent about two hours this afternoon rearranging a couple of tables and pictures in the living room, and that is the cause of our being behind schedule. We've really been having an awfully good time in our first "house". Though, I'm not a little surprised with the way the business girl has turned to the "joys" of housekeeping. When I get home in the evening from the office the dinner is ready and she is ready to report on the things she has done. Of course, occasionally she breaks down and slips back to bed after I leave in the morning, but so far she has never failed to be up at six-thirty to get my breakfast. Not that she's very happy about it; and my cheerful nature in the morning doesn't seem to help any.

Gosh but we are very happy. I just read back over the letter you sent to me before our wedding telling me of the fine wife I was getting. When I read it the first time, I thought that you were right, but now I can only say amen. Thanks go to you for any help you have been as her good friend in making her such a good person.

Very sorry that it isn't working out for you to visit us here in Cleveland. Hope perhaps you can get out "West" sometime later in the spring or summer. I'm really anxious to meet you and your family. Nick sounds like a real fine fellow, and the children. Hope to know you all well, soon. It'll be a while before our plans for the next three years (seminary) are set, but if it works out that we get to Cambridge, I expect you'll be seeing a lot of us.

Till then if not sooner,

Paul

Pregnancy and Miscarriage

To accommodate Paul's seminary studies at Episcopal Divinity School, the couple moved to Cambridge, Massachusetts. After getting settled they took their delayed honeymoon trip to Europe during July and August, 1954. It was not, however, without severe difficulty. On board ship, Frances miscarried in her third month of pregnancy. They went first to England and her aunt Barbara Ford, her father's sister. Recovering sufficiently to travel, she and Paul went to France and Italy.

Frances Nevins to Mary "Mike" McNab
Frances filled in some of the travel details at the end of her honeymoon for a friend from Connecticut College.

London
September 2, 1954

> *Am trying to write this in the car,*
> *hence it may not be readable at all -*
> *seems hard to believe this is our last day*
> *- we leave London at 3:30 tomorrow.*
>
> *After I last wrote we flew to Frankfurt*
> *- (a big, business-like city which we didn't*
> *like too much) - rented a car and drove to*
> *Heidelberg. It was nice to see it again,*
> *tho it was bigger and more touristy than*
> *I'd remembered - I guess I just ignored*
> *them last time.*
>
> *In a restaurant in Salzberg we*
> *watched a group of (American) fellows*
> *(very white shoe) picking up some*
> *American girls, and sort of taking over*
> *the place to do it. Amusing, and made us*
> *feel very old.*
>
> *After Heidelberg, went down thru*
> *Munich to Salzberg, and stayed in a little*
> *town outside. In some ways, we liked*
> *this best of all - right in the mountains,*
> *quite high ones, and on a beautiful lake.*
> *The houses are just like the little alpine*
> *cottages you see in pictures - with over-*
> *hanging roofs, and upstairs porches with*
> *flowers growing over them - and the*

*people are so friendly and cheerful. We
found a very nice room in a house a little
out of town - the windows looked right
out on the lake, and the room was large,
with painted Austrian furniture - only
kerosene light - altogether charming.
After a couple of days we found that
the people who ran it were a Herzog
(Archduke) Godfrey and his wife, a very
lovely Frenchwoman. I guess they were
in the position of much royalty nowadays
- very little money, so they rented out their
house in the summer and were living with
their 4 children over the garage. It was
really delightful to be there - the food
was the best we've had all summer, and
excellent wine. There was only a very
young hired girl, and I think a cook to
help, so the H's wife did much of the work.
They were both terrifically gracious; the
Herzog making a rather self-conscious
little bow to you when he left you - though
very genuine, not affected. He fixed the
car one morning when it wouldn't start -
they asked us in to the "Salon" one night
(just a living room) and we played cards
with the kids. They were such unusually
nice people. I think that's why the whole
thing sticks out in our minds.*

This trip was the second for her, the first for Paul. At Assisi
she was strongly attracted to St. Francis and his story. So much
so, that when she returned to Cambridge she plunged into the St.
Francis part of modern Church history and began searching out her
own background. Her search moved very quickly. In the latter part
of 1954, she sought instruction in the Catholic Church. Perhaps
she was more surprised than others at the turn of events. In the
Cambridge Star market, Anna Pluhar met Frances after 2½ years of
never seeing her. Frances was Anna's "senior-sister" at Connecticut.
Out of the blue, Anna asked: "Are you Catholic yet?" – a move
Frances was contemplating but hadn't told anyone. Pluhar was
instrumental in directing her to Boston College and Jesuit Father
Charles Reardon. He instructed Frances in the Catholic faith.

Reardon met her at 10:00 on Saturday mornings in an office on the Boston College campus for nearly four years. When they began instructions, he had been a Jesuit priest for 27 years, having prepared in philosophy and theology during his 12 years of study for the priesthood and Jesuit life. He was up to the task of dealing with her questions. The fact that he came from Vermont didn't hurt, either. It was a link to Grandfather William Nevins whom she credited with the Catholic connection in the first place. It also didn't hurt that Reardon had a sense of humor. When remarks made to him raised doubt that a Jesuit could (actually) come from Vermont, he assured one and all that Vermont was not overrun by Indians and vast herds of cows and that Rutland was half Catholic and, of all things, half Democrat.

Frances never thought of herself as a convert; indeed, she strongly protested the label. In her own mind, she was catching up with knowledge and information she should have known. Consequently, she paid serious attention to Reardon's teaching about the Mass, sacraments, prayer, saints, and particularly about the spiritual life itself.

The decision to return to the religion of her baptism would cost Frances her marriage. Roman Catholic canon law at that time required that a baptized Catholic could contract a valid marriage only when married in the Church, i.e. by a priest. Paul, by this time studying for the Episcopal priesthood, felt that he was already validly married and, therefore, refused. Nor would he agree to bring up any children in the Catholic faith. [See Appendix b: Frederick R. McManus, D.D., J.D., Commentary on Roman Catholic Law Governing Marriage Annulment.]

Annulment and Divorce

Following due process, the Catholic Church granted an annulment on June 7, 1955. Frances had set her conscience, accepting the rules as she understood them to be. These months were a great strain as they continued to live together in their apartment at 52 Garden St., Cambridge, Mass. When the annulment was finalized, Frances moved to nearby Chestnut Hill.

Jesuit Robert Drinan, then Dean of Boston College Law School, was instrumental in securing legal counsel. Drinan went on to become a well-known Congressman and author. Fifteen years after the divorce, I met Fr. Drinan at a social justice gathering in New York. Without any catch-up conversation, he asked: "How is Frances?" and "How is Paul?"

A Civil Decree of Divorce was not final until May 23, 1958. It took lawyers time to reconcile the usual reasons for divorce with the reasons for this divorce. Eventually, the third judge to hear the case accepted the fact of irreconcilable differences. Frances and Paul had lived together only a little more than a year. "I remember when I had to leave Paul I was sometimes harsh in speaking of it to others, so that they thought I had no feeling or didn't love him - but at the time I somehow had to be that way because the thing was so hard for me". Father Reardon saw pain and sadness on both sides. "I saw tears from both of them right up to the end". Paul would remarry and divorce again. Frances became a nun, and that path, too, would not be an easy one. He would not forget her and often told her mother that he could not. Frances did not forget him, either. In a light moment with some Sisters, she wondered if she might call out Paul's name when she was really sick.

Some ties also remained between Paul and Frances Tenney. He visited her frequently over the years, particularly when she began to lose ground to bone cancer. In 1965 Paul and Bess [Paul's 2nd wife] visited her on their wedding trip. Paul talked to Mrs. Tenney's doctor. "Thank God for his attentiveness," Sr. Christine wrote in a letter to me at the time. When Frances Tenney died, she remembered Paul in her will.

He did not see Frances again until her burial service at the Carmelite Monastery in 1980. Part of the drama of that day was the bringing together of Father Charles Reardon and Paul. There was her husband and the priest who had instructed Frances talking quietly together after 25 years. Reardon said: "My heart went out to Paul...It was strange meeting him after all these years...and, a strange meeting for the two of them after all these years. I recall some of the tearful sessions I had with him when the final steps were being taken...the years have brought him much suffering, but I have the feeling he was reconciled at the end".

4

Commitment to Catholicism

When asked if she was a convert, and she was denying it with some indignation, what questioners had observed in Frances was the excitement, energy, and single-mindedness that she was pouring into a search for Truth.

Father Reardon was giving her detailed instruction in the Catholic religion in an orderly, systematic way. Outside the "instruction room," she was quickly beginning to re-configure her life. Soon she was living with Catholics, attending Catholic services regularly, teaching in a Catholic institution, and taking courses at a Catholic college.

She not only moved out of the Cambridge apartment she and Paul shared, she moved to a resident house for Boston College students, all of whom were Catholic. The house was owned by William and Katherine Duhig. Active in St. Ignatius Parish, Katherine had survived a terrible automobile accident and never ceased thanking God for her life. Catholic life was her life. The routines of the house followed fast days, feast days, meatless Fridays, and Monsignor Fulton J. Sheen at 1:30 on Sunday afternoon TV. I was one of the Boston College graduate students in the Duhig household. What brought us together was the remarkable fact, as we saw it, that Frances was teaching Good Shepherd students in Boston, and I had recently been supervisor of social services at the House of the Good Shepherd in Albany, New York.

Frances Nevins to Joan Mullaney
Preparing for a summer trip to visit shrines in Europe, Frances wrote a "reminder" letter.

Boston
1957

> *Sister Glorita said we must not miss the Scala Sancta (that should really ruin the knees for good and all). We must get a guidebook to Rome.*
>
> *One of the reasons I was concerned about books (I will keep after the Daniel-Rops) is that I still persist in the notion we*

should read up or refresh our memories on the people and places. I thought I would bring the Chesterton on St. Francis, then I bought the short autobiography that Ignatius wrote, which I could bring, tho it is hard cover. Also bought a thing on Bernadette. Wish we had something small and light on St. Joan (on whom I am very hazy).

I wrote what I hoped was a most ingratiating letter to L'Hotel Montalembert yesterday, so I hope they will welcome us with open arms. I ought to hear from them before we leave.

If I forget that clock, I think I will jump overboard and quietly sink.

Since Frances was no longer a church worker for the Episcopal church and had no job, she followed Fr. Reardon's suggestion and located a job with the help of the Boston College Alumni office. She began teaching at the House of the Good Shepherd. Located in a rough neighborhood of downtown Boston, it was a large Catholic institution run by the Sisters of the Good Shepherd that accepted girls and women in trouble with the law or their families. She had a sizeable workload, teaching six classes Monday through Friday. As things turned out, she taught in this program for three years. At some point after Frances was hired, Alice Welch, Grandfather Nevins' secretary, remarked that the Nevins family had a connection with the Sisters. They came to his office now and again for donations - and they would have long talks and much laughing.

Assessment of Frances' work was positive, not only by the Sisters and other teachers but also by the students. At the end of the three years, the senior administrator commented:

"No one ever speaks of Miss Nevins except in the highest terms. Principals, teachers and our girls have never found her anything but devoted, I might also say dedicated, in her work and she has the respect of all. Quiet, but not retiring, she well deserves the reputation she has

earned as an excellent disciplinarian and is kind, but fair, in her dealings with the pupils. In teaching religion, I think her own spirituality does as much to teach the lesson as her words". [15]

More important to her than where she lived and worked was the change in church life. She became a fully participating member of the Catholic Church when she made her first Holy Communion in the Convent of the Cenacle, Brighton, MA. Father Reardon was the celebrant of the Mass. The Cenacle, a retreat house for women in many countries of the world, was not far from Boston College and became a favorite place of retreat for Frances while teaching at the House of the Good Shepherd. The date, June 11, 1955, is significant because it was only four days after her annulment was granted. She writes: "…since that date I have been able to go to Mass and Communion every day and Confession once a week, to make yearly retreats and practice mental prayer daily".

Prayer Schedule

While at Radcliffe, she had begun to visit the Cowley Brothers [Anglican] Monastery in Boston for her "church time" as she called it. Four years later, in 1956, her "church time" was the part of the day around which she tried to schedule everything else. She used the time for quiet reflection, meditation, and spiritual reading.

Before she left the house at 6:30 a.m., she had spent about three-quarters of an hour in prayer, followed by Mass and approximately 15 minutes of thanksgiving at St. Ignatius Church, or, on weekends at St. Mary's Chapel on the Boston College campus. At the end of the school day, depending on teachers' meetings, or other professional duties, she would plan on a half-hour or so of church time on the way home. At the end of the day, she would spend at least an hour in prayer.

She had also begun to try hard to keep her prayer schedule wherever she was. When something unavoidable came up, she attended to it, then made every effort to move back to her regular schedule or make up the time. Father Reardon provided a structure by providing instructions and spiritual direction. She trusted and valued his priestly ministry and demonstrated that respect by protecting her 45-minute appointment with him on Friday evening at 7:00 PM as carefully as she protected her other prayer time.

When Frances visited at home, her mother was aware that her daughter would go to the local Church in Enfield for Mass. Her mother had always liked Paul and did not understand the reasons for the divorce, but she seemed to make an effort to keep in contact with her only child, even though visits were strained and not too frequent. Visits increased as Charlie Tenney became ill and died of cancer in 1956. He was buried from the Calvary Episcopal Church, Suffield, CT. Frances stayed with her mother a week or so and then returned to Boston. Frances Tenney employed a cook, a chauffeur, and a married couple to take care of the house, otherwise she was pretty much alone.

More than many people, Frances Nevins had tried for some time to resist the rush of modern life as much as possible. For example, only with reluctance did she give up the bicycle that had done the job of getting her around Cambridge. The eventual choice of a convertible Plymouth with a cream top was a reminder of earlier days, particularly when she returned to her mother's house where there were many expensive reminders of a life very different from the one she was now living. It is fair to say that Frances was now in a totally different environment – physically, socially, and spiritually – than she had thus far ever experienced in her life.

Wrong Convent: Right Transition
A Religious Woman Becomes a Woman Religious [15a]

It was not surprising then, that she began to think about a deeper involvement of herself in the life of the Church and about the possibility of a vocation as a Sister in a religious community. At that point, she had come to know, like, and respect both the Sisters of the Good Shepherd and the Sisters of the Cenacle. Distinctly different in their work, both were well established and esteemed. When she began to think seriously about applying to the Sisters of the Good Shepherd in 1958, she explained that ever since she could remember:

"I have had a desire to serve
God, to devote myself to the service

-43-

of God and my neighbor, especially those most unfortunate and needy, though I knew nothing of the religious life. I tried to fulfill this as best I could in the sect in which I was brought up by becoming a full-time Church worker. However, I realize that I never could have understood the meaning of my vocation until I had begun to live and believe as a Catholic. The desire to be a Religious (Sister) came to me in 1955, a few months after my first Holy Communion which was in June of that year....Since that time the desire for the religious life has deepened and grown stronger and, I believe this is the means of consecrating myself to the service of God and of souls which I have been seeking all my life."
(Frances Nevins, November 25, 1958.)

After three years of instruction and spiritual direction, Fr. Reardon was supportive of her entering a religious community. He had offered no encouragement until her civil divorce had been granted. When Paul had not contested it and the matter was completely settled, Reardon encouraged her to go ahead with an application to the Sisters of the Good Shepherd. As he saw it, she had already completed three years in one of their programs and had already caught much of the spirit that motivated their work. He considered that the Sisters of the Good Shepherd, like the Jesuits, combined the contemplative life and the ministerial life. He was not surprised by her interest. "From the very start, I have been aware of a soul that might be called to religious life at some time".[16]

Entrance, however, into the Sisters of the Good Shepherd, Peekskill, New York, was delayed for some months because of their nervousness about the grounds for her annulment. The confusion was cleared away by the Boston Archdiocesan Marriage Tribunal. Fr. Reardon would come to realize that he may have misjudged her readiness to join a cloistered order. While she did express that preference, she chose to follow his judgment, and she became a postulant of the Sisters of the Good Shepherd on September 8, 1959.

The reports indicate that she did her best. However, "...she finds recreation and 'God Be Blessed Days' [special feasts] in the refectory very difficult and expresses the need and longing for more silence and solitude". Despite everything, her wit did not desert her, even as health problems presented a new concern. Frances wrote from the Good Shepherd Convent on October 27, 1959:

Last week we had a little play for Mother Michael's feast in which I had a 2 or 3 line part as Columbus - same part is being transformed into Alice in Wonderland for Mother Provincial. Flexibility is an asset.

I work clumsily in the Refectory washing various things, sweeping, putting out food, etc. I am a very bad slowpoke about everything - something peculiar has happened to my system. All that nice powerful nervous energy has disappeared (probably with the advent of coffee-rationing) and I can hardly even keep up with other people when <u>walking</u> - can you believe it? Am among the last at table, and various other manifestations of this phenomenon.

Noon reading is <u>All for Jesus</u>, Fr. Faber. Being read to at meals is one of the joys - others look forward to "God be blessed". I, per usual, to silence. I remain a somewhat frustrated Sr. Elizabeth[Sr. Elizabeth of the Trinity, Carmelite mystic].

The Office is beautiful - (3 times a day for 1/2 hour). Even with our type of voice, it isn't too hard to follow along, as of course it is pretty much on one note - once you find that, you're O.K. Doing it alone will be another matter - but that doesn't come for a year or so and, as Sr. Elizabeth of Boston says, moment by moment.

I have lived by her words this month. It's remarkable how many of the thoughts

*and inspirations, etc. that came to us over
the past year are coming into their own,
so to speak. I thought I had understood
them and tried to live by them over
again day by day. Ordinary things like
group life I find rather difficult - though
it shouldn't be. And, as time goes on, I
think it will not be, as there is so much
unfeigned charity on everyone's part.*

Mother Michael (Kennedy), a wise and experienced Novice Director, recognized by Christmas of 1959 that Frances had a vocation elsewhere. When Fr. Reardon came and recommended continuing with the Good Shepherd Sisters, the Sisters and Frances agreed. She was teaching in their House of Studies, and the extra time would benefit everyone. In May, 1960, just eight months after entering the Good Shepherd community, Frances left.

*"She gradually found that there was
too much activity. If it hadn't been for that
kind Mistress of Novices, she probably
would not have stayed as long as she
did....At this stage, when she mentioned
Carmel, I was more than slow....I could
just imagine, appearing at the stile (turn)
asking for admission and saying that
she was married, divorced, etc. As we
found out later, it was no easy task to get
through those stiles." (Reardon letter
11/25/81).[16]*

There was a tearful, sad goodbye. As a sacrifice, Mother Michael and Frances agreed not to write. They would keep that promise; but they would not forget one another. Frances often credited Mother Michael with helping her get ready for Carmel. Mother Michael never forgot her remarkable postulant; she would come to Schenectady for the burial.

The Good Shepherd Sisters were kind and thoughtful when Frances was leaving their Order. Mother Hildegarde, the Provincial, contacted her counterpart Mother Florence Murphy, the Superior of the Cenacle Retreat House in Mt. Kisco, NY, about 40 miles away, explaining that Frances needed accommodation until she could enter Carmel. Frances immediately accepted their offer of board, room and some light duties in the gift shop. Because the Cenacle Retreat Houses are similar in the United States, Frances easily adapted to the Mt. Kisco Cenacle, even though the building was large and in a relatively rural setting. The chapel was close by, with Mass and a resident chaplain available. The Sisters even arranged for one of the neighbors to locate a small second-hand car for her use. As events unfolded, she definitely needed the car.

There was a seamlessness about Frances' move to the Cenacle. "Just down the road" was comforting. She was, after all, still Frances Nevins who was once again without any particular place of belonging.

Frances lived a semi-secluded life at the Cenacle. It was neither in the everyday world that so many experience, nor in the seclusion that she had recently left. She was free to come and go after her gift shop and office duties were completed. During those seven months, she visited her friends in Boston and Washington. She visited her mother monthly. Frances accepted the Cenacle's hospitality with gratitude although she settled in lightly and did not plan to stay long.

Examined in more depth, this transition in which she found herself was not that of a person waiting somewhere for a problem to resolve itself. Passivity would not help the major questions confronting her:

> How was the experience with the Good Shepherd affecting her?
>
> What would her role be (as distinct from her Spiritual Director's) in applying to Carmel?
>
> Was she ready for the kind of silence and solitude that she has sought so long?
>
> And, arguably most important, how was her own approach to prayer holding up?

A transition of sufficient length to answer these questions required the full eight months as Postulant and seven months as Retreat House resident. Over time, positive developments in her readiness to enter Carmel began to emerge. Testing her desire to enter a convent, Frances had become more convinced than ever that she belonged in a Carmelite convent. This conviction was strengthened, not by rejecting the Sisters of the Good Shepherd, or by their rejection of her. Rather, she absorbed their prayerful ways and guidance generously shared with her even as she was leaving them for deeper silence and solitude.

The decision to leave the Good Shepherd convent also gave her confidence in her own decisions. As required by Church law, Frances participated fully in the decision to stay or leave. By doing so, she became better prepared to engage in the application for Carmel along with her priest advocates, Jesuit Father Reardon and Carmelite Father Bourke.

The Cenacle required only very limited duty in the office and gift shop, so that Frances followed a schedule of her own design. A benefit of the transition was the opportunity to test her tolerance for long periods of uninterrupted prayer, the solitary life and her own way of praying: "I ask Him to help me see the situation as He wants me to see it, and to produce in me the dispositions He wants me to have toward it". [See Chapter 5 for complete text of her method of prayer].

Overall, the Cenacle was a heaven-sent interlude when Frances used her freedom to take stock of all aspects of her life in an atmosphere of kindness and support that did not intrude or build obligations to itself.

This pre-Carmel period had real potential for unsettling her. A sample of letters to me shows that it did not. To the contrary, she is humorous, hopeful and characteristically trusting that God is taking good care of everything. The letters convey a cheerful alertness as she expands her life as a religious woman toward becoming a woman religious. During summer, 1960, Frances wrote to me about her Cenacle duties, temperament and solitude, an application interview with the Flemington, NJ Carmel, and the children's retreat among other things.

...My driving assignments - though fewer and farther between - have included trips to Manhattanville - about 15 to 20 minutes away - i.e. Pius X music school at which a very important liturgical somebody from Solemnes is holding forth this summer. I have not seen him - nor anything beside the outside of several buildings - got lost, of course, on the first solo flight and was put back on the track by three young laborers with the thickest brogues I ever heard.

The filing is not bad and so far I have made no major blunders - I try to appear like a competent old file clerk from way back - tho alas, I am ignorant of basic filing lore like how to get the drawers in and out of the cabinets, the staples in and out of the stapler, etc. I am now ensconced in the big office, as the rooms are all taken for the 5-day Retreat.

...Enclosed find 2 pamphlets - one by your friend Miller [Jerome]. I'm sure all contents are old stuff to you - but I read them over this afternoon and they started me thinking a little. It is rather fascinating to try to fit oneself into these categories (I seem to be an obvious sanguine - along with mon pere, I guess - with some choleric overtones? What think you?) - and also, I think it might help the problem of where I am as to desire and need for solitude. At first thought, I would say that mine is not temperament (this doesn't belong to poor sanguines) and, as a matter of fact, large doses of it, such as I am getting now, can be extremely trying to nature, I am finding. On the other hand, I do seem to have that "deep need for intimate contact with God

in solitary prayer, a need which constitutes the peculiar vocation of the contemplative soul." (Merton, <u>Silent Life</u>, p. 130). But this would seem to be supernatural rather than natural. A third complicating factor in all this is, as p. 2 of larger pamphlet points out, that temperament can be influenced by environment - Hence in my case the natural extrovertedness (even talkativeness!) of the sanguine temperament has been modified by early experiences - so that we are sometimes shy and silent, etc. But this is not, I think, what basically causes the need for solitude, since it disappears when we are really comfortable with people. (As you well know!)...

P.S. The other day I found this little exchange in the file - we had sent a little note to an individual re: some unclear point about his order and as usual the heading Ave Maria was in one corner - Reply came back - Dear Ave Maria: How's that?

Cenacle
August 4, 1960

During the A.M. prayer break this morning I took your letter to the outer corridor for reading purposes and was detained there several minutes due to laughing. The clipping is just about the best yet - every time I read it the laughing comes on again. I shall take it to tomorrow's luncheon engagement as my offering to the festivities.

Today a kindly little note came from Mother Flemington [Prioress, Flemington, NJ Carmel] (her typewriter seems to have brown type!) welcoming me on the 18th. Good-o.

The children's retreat is on in full force and the house is not exactly bathed in silence at present. The corridors are resounding with "what kind of soap did you bring?" "Is the water hot?" and similar little fervorinos. There was such a mad rush for the Confessional tonight I thought I might be crushed underfoot as an innocent bystander, and I could not understand this mass attack of penitence till I observed that the Father was quite young and attractive....

P.S. I am re-reading Merton's pamphlet Praying the Psalms - Do you have a copy? I think it is excellent.

Cenacle
September 9, 1960

I have laboriously arranged this little cell for writing operations - maximum efficiency of writing requires that extension cord is applied to lamp, top drawer of chest be cleared out and contents filed - (45 minutes at least) a coffee be produced to avoid last night's difficulty. Also that Little Flower be ensconced atop the chest, to supervise the proceedings.

Now for a run-down on yesterday's activities. I stopped in Nassau [NY] for a second Mass - the longest sermon I believe I ever heard. It went from the Magdalenes (of whom he approves and from whom he buys vestments) to missing Mass, slacks in Church (disapproves), the Bishop's letter (which he claimed the Bishop didn't write), to working on Sunday - a rather unique approach but not altogether bad as it was all quite pastoral....

Am reading, and loving, St. Paul at last. What a tremendous consciousness

*of the meaning of the supernatural life
and how completely unmodern he is. No
wonder we do not take to him right away.*

In a significant letter dated October 2, 1960, Frances describes two momentous events that occurred the day before. In the morning she was interviewed in Boston (MA) by Fr. Albert Bourke, Definitor General of the Carmelites; and, in the afternoon, by the Prioress and Mistress of Novices at the Schenectady (NY) Carmel. Prior to these interviews, Fr. Reardon provided both parties with detailed information about Frances' marital status in light of Roman Catholic canon law. Beyond the legalities, however, was the profound question: "At this time does Frances Nevins have a Carmelite vocation"? Fr. Bourke answered readily and affirmatively; Schenectady was cautious, but willing to learn more about this applicant.

*Cenacle
October 2, 1960*

*...I think the little car and I must have
made some sort of record for mileage
since Friday night - and, Thank God,
it performed admirably. Even had oil
change in Sc'y at interview time.
     The upshot is that though they
were quite non-plussed and leery of the
whole affair, they did not say absolutely
no - and will talk it over and pray, and
especially consult with Fr. Albert [Bourke,
Carmelite] the Brookline Father I saw this
morning. He is the brightest star of all in
this picture, as he actually said he would
help us, and try to convince them at Sc'y
that it would be a good idea to give me a
chance - and if they don't agree, he will
present my case to other Carmels till we
find one that will take me - and he doesn't
seem to have much doubt that there will
be such a one. It is almost hard to believe
this beautiful act of Providence after so
much seemingly fruitless endeavor - just*

imagine his being so positive and helpful.
Father Charlie [Reardon] must have done
a wonderful job presenting the situation
as he was very well disposed before I said
very much at all. He [Father Albert] goes
to Sc'y to give their Retreat on Tuesday.
Meanwhile I am supposed to be writing
them a letter, after having seen him. (To be
done mañana - auspicious day). [October
4, Feast of Francis of Assisi.] Rev.
Mother said she couldn't give me much
hope, as she doubted it would ever pass
Chapter - but that I had come at a very
opportune time on account of Fr. Albert.
So now it all depends on the Holy Ghost,
The Blessed Mother, The Little Flower,
and how much weight the nuns give to Fr.
Albert's opinion.

Tomorrow I will write more re:
impressions of the visit - in general good
- tho in some ways rather different than
our other experiences. Surprisingly
enough, they have just completed a new
monastery, which is hiding behind the old
one - and are already living in it. There
seems to be only one factory neighbor and
it's a discreet looking factory at that.

On this day, particularly with Fr. Bourke's assurance that there would be a Carmel somewhere for her, Frances Nevins, for the first time, sees the likelihood of entering Carmel. The day was suffused with hope. The tide had turned.

'Above all Frances Nevins finds in her
experience both an answer to prayer and a felt
recognition of truth. She has long been praying. She
believes she knows the contemplation to which she is
called. With longing she describes it.'[16a]

The rightness of this longing became clear after Frances Nevins became Sr. Christine. "The mystery of my life brings me to the frontier, the threshold of the 'unsearchable wisdom of God'." (Journal Entry 5/29/1980)

4: Commitment to Catholicism

15. Letter written by Sister Mary of Francis Xavier R.G.S., Administrator, Convent of the Good Shepherd, Boston, Massachusetts to Mother Hildegarde R.G.S., Provincial, Sisters of the Good Shepherd, Peekskill, NY, January 6,1959.

15a. The phrase, 'A religious woman becomes a woman religious" is credited to my copy editor, Sr. Jane Morrissey, S.S.J.

16. Letter written by Charles Reardon S.J. to Mother Hildegarde R.G.S., Provincial, Sisters of the Good Shepherd, Peekskill, NY, March 5, 1958.

16a. In beautiful words, Sr. Morrissey summarizes the transition and its resolution by explaining its deepest meaning.

PART II

The Call to Carmel

Love Is Repaid By Love Alone

Baroness Adé Bethune (1914-2002), renowned
liturgical artist and consultant in church architecture,
designed Schenectady Carmel's circular altar and
surroundings.

5
Carmel

Most Discalced Carmelite Monasteries in the United States followed widely-published guidelines for judging applicants. According to the best source book of the time describing purpose and qualifications, the Discalced Carmelite nun is distinguished from other Sisterhoods by:

Purpose:	The life of a Carmelite nun is both contemplative and apostolic. By her prayers, sacrifices, and penances, she atones for numerous sins committed against the Eternal Father. Her apostolic life is spent in supplication, praying for the needs of the Church, sanctification of priests, the salvation of souls and the conversion of sinners. Although a great deal of time is spent in reciting the Divine Office in Choir, meditation, and other pious exercises, the remainder is allocated for household work and other occupations.
Qualifications:	The basic requirements for a Carmelite nun are: A love of silence and manual labor, a strong desire to lead a contemplative life, (strict enclosure is observed according to the Rule established by St. Teresa of Avila).
	Sufficient health to assume the obligations of fasting, sound understanding and good judgment. [17]

Definitor General Acts

Each Carmel Monastery seeks to limit its community to 21 members. Widows may be considered for acceptance by a community such as the Sisters of the Visitation. In general, requirements for the Sisterhood did not take into account that an applicant might have been married, despite the fact that founders of religious communities (e.g. Elizabeth Seton - Sisters of Charity and Cornelia Connelly - Society of the Holy Child Jesus) had been married. Also those over thirty-five were not encouraged to apply.

Like the initial uneasy response by the Good Shepherd

Sisters to her marriage status, the Carmelites, too, were hesitant to invite Frances to join them. During the summer of 1960, with Father Reardon's help, several Carmelite Monasteries were contacted. She was interviewed at the Carmelite Monastery, Danvers, MA; Carmelite Monastery, Concord, NH: Carmelite Monastery, Flemington, NJ; and the Carmelite Monastery, Barre, VT. None encouraged entrance.

Father Reardon, however, continued to write references and make phone calls. Only after the fourth Carmelite Monastery turned her away did he try something else. He sought help from a priest friend who had been a Carmelite. "Brendan, how do I get a girl into Carmel?" Brendan's answer was: "Go to Father Albert (Bourke)". "Father Albert was the Definitor General of the Carmelite Order and lived five blocks away, literally, in my backyard!"

In his turn Fr. Bourke later wrote:

> *...No doubt Fr. Reardon has in his notes how I came into the picture. He had prepared the way for the only meeting I had with Frances Nevins. That (meeting) was very final when she accepted the direction to enter the Carmel of Schenectady which I think was very providential because I do not think she would have received the consideration which was given to her in the Schenectady Carmel. I do not think the nuns ever questioned my judgment of her fitness, of her vocation. At that time the big question in my mind was that she would have no canonical impediment which, of course, Fr. Reardon had taken care of.*
>
> *I would say that Sr. Christine (Frances Nevins) had a superior intelligence and was very capable. God seems to favor her love of prayer in solitude by giving her poor health that keeps her away from Community life pretty much. When I would go there and all the Nuns*

would talk with me, Sr. Christine would
come for about 20 minutes then depart.
We all accepted her limitations. While
she was increasingly drawn to prayer
and solitude, she took her share of work
which she liked to do alone. In that only
interview we had, I told her that her
constitution would be her penance.

She was always grateful to me for my
role in getting her settled in Carmel. She
did not say much but I just knew that she
was grateful and I had my special niche
in her life. [18]

Frances' reaction to Father Bourke was very favorable:

"He was really wonderful –
understanding and easy to talk to – I
talked very freely to him and he with
me, about Carmel in general and about
Schenectady. He wanted to know if I
could get along without intellectual
activity and companionship, as he says
there is not much of it there – but he
seems to quite admire their spirit – says
it is a good Carmel, and I would be very
fortunate if they took me. I somehow got
the feeling from my interview and from
Fr. A. that there is a very genuine and
pure Carmelite spirit there..." (FN letter
to JWM 10/4/1960)

Shortly after Father Albert began to participate in her
application process to the Schenectady Carmel, the traditional
activities required by Church law and the Carmelite Rule were
satisfied. Letters, references, health assessment and an interview
with the entire Carmelite community proceeded in an orderly
fashion.

"My own scattered impressions: not
as sophisticated as most of the others, but
much kindness. I was greatly consoled
by the fact that they asked if I had a great

love of silence – said this was necessary and mentioned that they lived alone in the cells as much as possible – a hermit life, etc." (FN letter to JWM 10/4/1960)

The key reference letter from the Good Shepherd Sisters was written by Mother Michael as Novice Mistress. It was very positive:

October 22, 1960
Mother Mary Magdalen of the Holy Ghost, D.C.
Monastery of Discalced Carmelites
428 Duane Avenue
Schenectady 4, New York

Dear Reverend Mother:

I am writing in answer to your request for information regarding Frances Nevins, who was a postulant in our community from September 8, 1959 until May 15, 1960.

While with us Frances was in good health. She had a great love for the work of the Good Shepherd, but felt she had a contemplative vocation. Frances experienced many doubts about her vocation as a Religious of the Good Shepherd from the month of December on, but these doubts did not interfere with any of her religious exercises or novitiate duties. During the month of December, Frances definitely felt the contemplative life was where God wanted her, but she made no decision. She sought the advice of her director, Father Reardon, who visited with Frances at this time. Father told her, he did not doubt the possibility of a contemplative vocation but felt she could combine the active with the contemplative and make use of her teaching ability. Father advised her to give this life a fair trial, and this she did. Frances did not leave until May 15,

*1960, and then only after fervent prayer
and on the advice of her director.*

*Mother, while Frances was with us
she was very edifying and was striving
to be a good religious. She was humble,
obedient and very docile. She was
gracious and kind in her manner and was
loved by all of us. She was very generous
and showed a great interest in the smallest
duty given her and did her very best.
Although she experienced this longing
for more solitude and silence, she did
not complain or make herself singular in
anyway. Frances is a very sincere person
and has common sense. During these
months of doubt, she seemed to grow in a
greater trust and confidence in God.*

*Reverend Mother, we hope this
information will be of assistance to you
in forming your decision in regard to
Frances.* [19]

*Sister Mary of St. Michael R.G.S.
Mistress of Novices*

Carmelite Monastery Accepts

With a breathtakingly swift and confident decision, the
nuns at the Schenectady Carmel accepted Frances Nevins. The
letter of acceptance from the Prioress dated November 14, 1960,
suggested entry on November 21, 1960. Not a moment to be lost
or wasted. Mother Magdalen D.C. combined enthusiasm with a
reminder about practicalities like money and art work materials in
her letter of acceptance:

My dear child,

*We just received your permission.
Today is the feast of "All Saints of
Carmel" so it looks as though your new
family in Heaven is taking you into their
keeping. May God be praised!*

Frances, I forgot to tell you when you were here, that $200.00 novitiate expense money is required, besides the dowry stipulated by Canon Law.

Mother Mistress would like you to come on the 21st. I hope you can be ready on such short notice. A warm welcome awaits you, our dear Frances. [20]

Yours humbly in Our Lord,
Mother M. Magdalen of the Holy
Ghost, D.C.

As eager as she was to be on her way to Carmel, Frances needed to visit her mother, Mil's family, Father Reardon and several friends. December 8, 1960, was agreed upon as her entry date.

On that date she began the day by attending Mass celebrated by Father Reardon in the Boston College chapel. Several of her friends from Boston were there. She and I then drove to Schenectady arriving about 5:00 PM. Sister Alberta opened the door, saying: "Praise be Jesus Christ". Frances answered, "Now and forever".

Standing at the monastery door, what did Sister Alberta and Frances see, and, perhaps sense, as they exchanged their short, profound greeting? Sister Alberta saw a tall, attractive woman in a nicely tailored black coat who was quiet but not frightened or uneasy. She also had red eyes and a bright red nose. The red eyes resulted from intermittent tears; the nose, a fierce head cold. Frances saw a smiling nun with a touch of Boston accent wearing the brown habit and scapular of Our Lady of Mt. Carmel, black veil and white guimpe.

Each woman wonderfully symbolizes in clothing and demeanor who she is. Sister Alberta represents nearly 400 years of Carmelite tradition. Indeed, the Schenectady Carmel is a direct descendant of the Reform of Carmel by St. Teresa of Avila in 1562. Lives of austerity and prayer are the daily role of the Discalced Carmelite nuns who belong to one of the strictest orders of the Roman Catholic Church.

Frances came to the door with her own traditions, customs

and way of life. In 1960 she was 30 years old. From a material point of view, she had many assets. Born and raised in a wealthy, distinguished New England family, she graduated with honors from an elite boarding school, was first in her class at college, and capped this unusually strong academic career with a Master's degree in History at Radcliffe/Harvard. But the other side of the ledger was written in loneliness and sorrow. Both her parents drank too much, living a social life that did not allow much of a place for her. The adored father died when she was 12. The much less adored mother went on to a new marriage. Only "Mil", both governess and housekeeper, was there for Frances. Having found Paul, her husband, only to lose him is hardly fathomable using ordinary logic, or even rules of the heart, perhaps most particularly, rules of the heart.

At this point in her life, old stereotypes might still be pulled off the shelf to explain why she was entering Carmel. An unhappy childhood and the end of a marriage are often spoken of by family and friends who find the whole matter perplexing, disturbing even. For Frances herself, however, she has arrived at the monastery door with a clear conviction that this Carmelite life, as hard as it is, is right for her. "For me, I have to be here to be. It's who I am".

She had prepared as well as possible for beginning her new life. The months with the Good Shepherd Sisters and with the Cenacle Sisters had accustomed her to a seriously routinized religious schedule. She had six years of concentrated instruction in Catholic doctrine and five years immersion in the sacraments and their effects, particularly Confession and Communion. Perhaps most important of all, she had found her own way of praying that governed everything she did.

In a remarkable letter written in 1958 to Father Reardon, she provided a step-by-step explanation of her approach toward making choices about the events in her life within the context of her primary relationship with God:

> *"...I thought I ought to write to try to explain to you my way of dealing with my difficulties and temptations, and how it often seems to be that God makes things clear to me at these*

times. Whenever I have any difficulty or perplexity or temptation, small or large, I present it all to God, drop it at his feet, so to speak, and I tell Him that I am sorry for all my wrong attitudes in this situation – be it fear or repugnance or uncharity or discouragement or whatever – and I accept all the trials and hardships to myself involved. I ask Him to help me see the situation as He wants me to see it, and to produce in me the dispositions He wants me to have toward it.

At the same time, if it is a perplexity of some kind that could be helped by reasoning or studying, I either reason it all (sometimes on paper) or read whatever I can find on the subject but all the time asking for light to understand what I read as God wants me to understand it, or to reason correctly.

Sooner or later there generally comes to me, either when I am reading or praying, or even when I am doing something else, a time when the difficulty seems to be resolved. On the surface there still may be some sadness, fear, etc., but this is all under control now, and the peace is what dominates. The beginning of this is usually rather sudden and definite, and then it grows until it takes possession of me, and if it is a situation in which there has been a great storm of feelings (rebellion, despair, etc.), there comes a great calm. Along with it I seem to be aware of an increase in my love for God and my determination to do His will no matter what it costs me". [21]

5: Carmel

17.   Thomas McCarthy C.S.V. *Guide to the Catholic Sisterhoods of the United States* (Washington: The Catholic University Press, 1958), pp. 24, 25.

18.   Letter written by Fr. Albert Bourke O.C.D., Definitor General, Carmelites to author, March 3, 1982.

19.   Letter written by Sister Mary of St. Michael R.S.G. Mistress of Nov- ices, Sisters of the Good Shepherd to Mother Mary Magdalen of the Holy Ghost, D.C. Prioress, Carmelite Monastery, Schenectady, NY, October 22, 1960.

20.   Letter written by Mother Mary Magdalen of the Holy Ghost, D.C. to Frances Nevins, November 14, 1960.

21.   Letter written by Frances Nevins to Charles Reardon S.J., March 25, 1958.

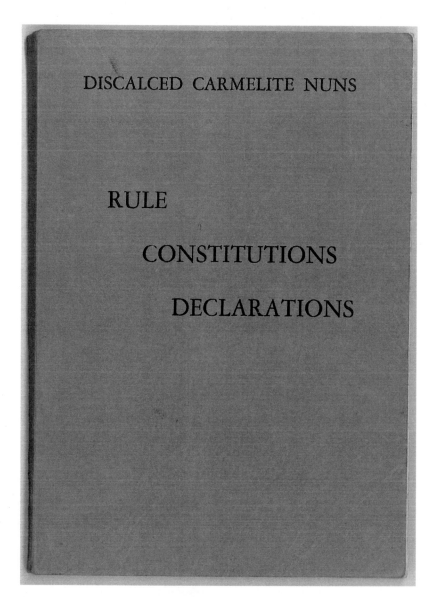

DISCALCED CARMELITE NUNS

RULE

CONSTITUTIONS

DECLARATIONS

The original rule was formulated by
St. Teresa of Avila in 1562

6

Early Years in Carmel

Traces of History: Order of Discalced Carmelites

Carmel, a Hebrew word meaning "garden," has been used to describe a lifestyle begun more than 700 years ago when Carmelites lived as hermits on Mount Carmel in the Holy Land, following the way of life of the prophet Elijah and living under the patronage of the Blessed Virgin. In the Old Testament its majesty and beauty are extolled. While on most mountains in Palestine there is hardly a tree visible, Mount Carmel has trees and shrubbery. The climate is moderate. Contrary to its name, it is a chain of mountains. Since time immemorial, however, Carmel has been considered a Holy Mount...a sacred temple where the deity is revered. [22]

In the 21st century Carmel is also a general term that can be used as shorthand for the life within a Carmelite monastery itself, or for Carmelite communities. A Carmelite with the initials O.C.D. after her name is a member of the Order of Carmelites Discalced. [23]

Carmel displays features of the east and the west. Clothing, prayer and work follow the example of hermits in the desert. The traditional Carmelite habit is similar to the garb required by Islamic law to be worn by women in public. Indeed, the veiling ceremony that is part of professing Final Vows is rooted in the Moorish or Islamic invasion of southern Spain. Veiling the face was a custom of the time. Work is to be performed, as far as possible, not in common rooms, but by each nun in her own room.

When the initial seed of the Discalced branch of Carmel was planted in Spain in 1562, St. Teresa of Avila (1515-1582) little thought that four centuries later there would be more than 1000 monasteries with over 15,000 Discalced Carmelite Nuns and more than 4000 Discalced Carmelite Friars scattered over the face of the earth in almost every nation of the world. Discalced Carmelite Nuns came to the United States in 1790, establishing a Monastery at Port Tobacco, Maryland.

Four years later, Carmelite nuns in France are killed. Poulenc's famous opera, "Dialogues of the Carmelites", immortalized the tragedy. In "Dialogues of the Carmelites", the year is 1794, the high tide of the French revolution's Reign of Terror. Suddenly it has become a crime punishable by death to live in a religious community and devote your entire life to prayer. On June 22, 1794 in the French city of Compiegne, 16 Carmelite nuns, who had already been banished from their convent, were arrested, charged with counter-revolutionary activities and shipped off to Paris for trial. They were sent to the guillotine July 17, 1794. One of them, Sister Charlotte, was 79 years old. If they had managed to survive another 10 days, the nuns might have been spared; on July 27, 1794 Robespierre was struck down and the Reign of Terror reached its violent end. The conclusion of "Dialogues" is even more dramatic. It begins with 15 voices, eight sopranos and seven mezzos, singing a hymn, "Salve Regina" ("Hail Holy Queen"). After 10 measures, the sound of the guillotine is heard (represented in the vocal score by an arrow pointing downward), and one soprano voice is stilled. A mezzo voice drops out after the next descending arrow, and the chorus shrinks, one voice at a time, until the voice of Sister Constance, the youngest nun in the convent, is cut off in the middle of the word "Maria" then the voice of Blanche, the timid one who had escaped, is heard, "a bit slower and extraordinarily calm," singing "Glory be to the Father and to the Son" as she emerges from the crowd of onlookers and marches up the scaffold to join her companions. Her voice is cut off just before she can finish singing "Forever and ever, Amen". There are not many operas that have a more dramatic conclusion, and probably no other where the key question - will Blanche find the courage to accept martyrdom? - is left unanswered until a few seconds before the final curtain. The true story of "Dialogues" was fictionalized in a novel by Gertrude von Le Fort and rewritten into a film script by Georges Bernanos. The film was never made, but Poulenc revised the script into his libretto. The opera adds a fictional character to the 16 whose names are recorded in history: Blanche. [24]

Carmelite Monastery of St. Teresa, Schenectady, NY. The Carmel of Schenectady was the third foundation made by the Mexican Carmelites exiled from Quertaro during the Civil war. The nuns settled first in Grand Rapids, Michigan; then in 1920, a foundation was made in Buffalo, New York. At the invitation of the Most Reverend Edmund F. Gibbons, Bishop of Albany, New York, eight nuns of the Buffalo Carmelite monastery of Our Lady of Mount Carmel and the Little Flower of Jesus arrived in

Schenectady, New York on Monday, August 13, 1923. In 1925 Bishop Gibbons broke ground for the new chapel that would adjoin the large house the Bishop had bought earlier for the nuns. It was not until 1959 that the construction of a permanent monastery was begun, on the same property as the original old mansion. In 1964 The Schenectady UNION-STAR, May 2, 1964 reports completion: "Bright, cheery rooms greeted visitors during a three-day open house in the new wing at the Carmelite Monastery, observing completion of a two-phase $513,000 building project. The cloistered quarters will be closed to outsiders forever at the conclusion of the public visitation tomorrow at 7:00 p.m. Sisters in the monastery are from Troy, Albany, Brooklyn, Herkimer, Rensselaer, Amsterdam, Philadelphia, and Massachusetts. Some of the nuns at the monastery when it was established in 1923 still participate in the daily life within the cloistered walls".

Ten years after the monastery renovation, the chapel was remodeled under the direction of Adé de Bethune. Sr. Christine wrote to a Boston friend that she was surprised to hear that de Bethune had visited and drawn the plans:

> "She thought of everything - a round
> (!) altar so that the priest can face either
> the nuns or the people, or kitty-corner.
> The presider's chair is to be in the back
> right corner, and the Bible enthroned
> where the tabernacle used to be. The
> tabernacle will be against our choir
> grate - a 'tower' (Adé's idea) with a little
> roof over it. She took great pains with
> everything - you could see it was a labor
> of love, not just a job".

Every Roman Catholic was affected by the changes mandated by Vatican II, the historic Church Council convened by Pope John XXIII in 1962. In the 1960s Catholic Americans were ushered unmistakably from the closed and confined limitations of the previous century into an era that bore only a fragmentary resemblance to what had gone before. The changed situation, however, was in transit quite some time before Vatican II, allowing that the latter gave further impetus in that direction. [25]

Encouraged by the Diocesan Liturgical Arts Commission, the Carmelite nuns contracted with Adé Bethune for a visionary reworking of the altar and sanctuary. Baroness Bethune, gifted and broadly skilled, was highly sought as liturgical consultant to church architects. In addition to her artistic interests, she was also closely associated with Dorothy Day and Peter Maurin of the Catholic Worker movement.

In 1964 Sr. Christine reacted rather merrily to the change from Latin to English:

> "I will have to stop having thoughts in Latin or I will be out of step with the Church. I don't know what I will be like when and if we have the Office in English. Apparently the new translation for one of the Antiphons for Our Lady of Sorrows is 'Strengthen me with raisin cakes and refresh me with apples for I languish with love'. (The first phrase to be intoned by the Versicler alone.) I wonder who could manage that? However, all things are possible and, I really do approve of the vernacular".[26]

Not Easy, But Right

Sr. Christine never put aside her scholarly habits from Connecticut College days. She kept excellent notes in clear, precise sentences. Even when she was suffering or very busy, she was thorough and precise. The almost lost art of correct punctuation was not lost with her. As a consequence her written record is a valuable documentation of 20 years as a Carmelite nun. Daily activities, conversations with God and other struggles come alive in a unique way. Like her contemporary, Trappist Thomas Merton, Sr. Christine wrote both journals and letters that provide insight into the issues of the times in which she lived. She entered Carmel when the Catholic Church was on the cusp of radical change that would affect even the most cloistered nuns. About the same time, 1968 or so, the prodigious writer and monk Thomas Merton chronicled in great detail monastic culture and practices at Gethsemani Monastery, Bardstown, Kentucky. While it is not useful to take

Sr. Christine's measure against him since they are quite different people, it is useful to consider his description of monastic life at that time. Doing so places Schenectady's daily schedule in some perspective, and also frames the remarkable spiritual growth of Sr. Christine. It is possible this growth occurred, at least partially, in spite of what was going on in monastic training in United States monasteries. Merton explains:

> "... We knew that we were getting into something hard, even unreasonably hard. But we also knew that this counted for very little in comparison with something else which in our case was decisive. We believed that we were really called by God to do this, to entrust ourselves to Him in this peculiar form of life, to enter into it believing in His word and in His promise; that this was one way of being a completely dedicated Christian, taking up one's Cross and living as a disciple of Christ. It is true that we were told absurd things, made to behave with a stupid and artificial formality, and put through routines that now, as we look back seem utterly incredible. There is something deeply unchristian about the way in which the monastic life is sometimes interpreted and 'enforced'." [27]

Even when no point-by-point comparison between the Trappists and the Carmelites, or Thomas Merton and Frances Nevins is made, we can be absolutely sure that they asked exactly the same thing from their monasteries: "Give me a chance to do my very best".

Like any successful organization Carmel sets goals, provides means to achieve them, and holds to benchmarks that let everyone know whether there is progress or not. Between 1960 and 1965 Frances moved through the usual stages new members must complete successfully: receiving the habit and her new name, "Sister Christine of the Holy Spirit" (October 7, 1961); making First Vows as a Carmelite Nun (October 8, 1962); making Solemn Vows as a Carmelite Nun (October 8, 1965); and doing the Veiling Ceremony, as the last part of making Solemn Vows (October 9, 1965).

Horarium

The Schenectady Carmel (and all Carmels at that time) required all members, including their newest, to follow a demanding daily schedule. The Liturgy of the Hours (called "Divine Office") is a central prayer of the Roman Catholic Church and forms the core around which much of every day revolves. As with the Eucharistic Liturgy (The Mass) the prayers are universal and said around the world by monastic communities, priests, sisters and laity. In the Carmelite Monastery in Schenectady, NY, Frances' life was directed by this Horarium.

5:00 am	Rising
5:25	Lauds
5:45	Coffee
6:00-7:00	Prayer
7:15	Mass
*8:00	Tierce - then manual labor until
11:00	Sext and Examen
11:15	Dinner (and dishes)
*12:00 pm	Recreation
*1:00	None
1:15-2:30	Time of silence - rest, pray, work quietly - also read for 1/2 hour during this time
2:30-4:30	Manual labor
4:30	Vespers
5:00-6:00	Prayer
6:00	Supper - then dishes and recreation 'til
7:30	Compline - then time of silence 'til
*9:30	Matins

She noted "Most of us go to bed around 10:30 or 11:00. Things marked with an * I don't go to at present on account of the ailment". [28]

In 1970 or thereabouts, Sister Christine was allowed to say certain hours of the Office privately. At this time she had been hospitalized briefly at St. Clare's Hospital, Schenectady for symptoms that included severe dizziness, weakness and trouble breathing. The diagnosis was "vasomotor instability". The treatment included more protein and much more fresh air. Work assignments now included driving the lawn tractor and peeling potatoes in the monastery basement 'cool and solitary'."The last few Sundays I have been the cook(!) - a couple of us are trying to relieve the Sunday cook so she will have one day off a week - as you know I was always rather helpless in the kitchen but 'nothing is impossible with God'. I find it quite different trying to cook for 14 than for two".

NOTES

6: Early Years in Carmel

22.   Francois Jamart O.C.D. *The Spirit and Prayer of Carmel* Translated by E.J. Ross (Westminster: The Newman Press, 1951).

23.   Mary Jo Weaver. *Cloister and Community, Life Within a Carmelite Community* (Bloomington: Indiana University Press, 2002). An appealing text and Glossary.

24.   Washington Post, Opera Section, "Dialogues of the Carmelites" Two Hundredth Anniversary," July 17,1994.

25.   J.T. Ellis, "Transitions in Catholic Culture-The Fifties", U.S. Catholic Historian, Vol. 7, No. 1 winter, 1988 pp. 134,135.

26.   Letter from Sr. Christine to the author, September 9, 1964.

27.   Robert E. Daggy. *The Road to Joy, The Letters of Thomas Merton* (NY: Farrar. Straus. Giroux, 1989) pp. 112, 113.

28.   Letter written by Sr. Christine to her friend, Lorraine (Mrs. Sydney) Stewart, July 3, 1972.

Pope John Paul I
August 25, 1978 to September 29, 1978
"The Smiling Pope":
Sr. Christine's favorite

7

Influential Priests: Four Directors-One Direction

Surprisingly, the Billet, or Carmelite Letter about Sr. Christine after her death, includes only a passing reference to a priest, and that without naming him. Priests, of course, are important to all Carmelite monasteries both for celebrating the liturgy and administering the Sacraments as well as linkage with the wider Church and human support in general. And, among Carmel's highest priorities is unceasing prayer for priests themselves.

When Frances Nevins entered Carmel in 1960 Fr. Owen Bennett, O.F.M. Conv. was the Confessor available to the sisters. After completing his doctorate in Philosophy in 1943 at Catholic University he was assigned in 1945 to Carmel as Confessor. Between 1965 and 1980 he was retained as Extraordinary Confessor coming to hear confessions four times a year. In 1965, following the new emphasis coming out of Vatican II that encouraged choice of confessors, the Monastery invited other priests from time to time. Father Albert Bourke, Discalced Carmelite, came occasionally from Boston. Father Henry Tansey, from the Mill Hill Missionaries was also included. At different times other priests from parishes in the Albany Diocese and various religious communities acted as retreat masters and provided spiritual direction and support.

Among this group of visiting priests four are important in understanding Sr. Christine's life as a Carmelite: Charles Reardon (Jesuit); Albert Bourke (Discalced Carmelite); Owen Bennett (Franciscan); and Henry Tansey (Mill Hill Missionaries). Each priest was a member of a well respected, large, international religious community that had clear differences in its formation and work. As a consequence, each community recruited a different kind of membership, while, at the same time, all were profoundly Roman Catholic in their beliefs and practices. Adding natural differences in personality and temperament to the differences among the religious groups themselves, the monastery made available to its sisters a diverse group of Confessors and Spiritual Directors, particularly after Vatican II.

Fr. Reardon and Fr. Albert contributed significantly to Frances Nevins' preparation for Carmel. Their help is described in some detail earlier in this narrative. Both priests continued their interest in Sr. Christine's spiritual growth and visited her from time to time. Fr. Reardon gave the homily at her funeral Mass.

Owen Bennett O.F.M. Conv. (Franciscan): Confessor/Spiritual Director 1960-1974.

Fr. Bennett (or Fr. Owen as the Sisters called him) was the homilist for Sr. Christine's Veiling Ceremony at Final Vows October 9, 1965. In a 1981 conversation he recalled being impressed by the love of the Holy Spirit she brought with her to Carmel.

> *"Very unusual", he said. "She could quote long passages by heart from the 'Sanctifier' by Archbishop Martinez.* [29] *It was as if Martinez was so alive to her that he was a kind of Spiritual Director. We used to discuss his ideas because she would be so steeped in what he said. And, Elizabeth of the Trinity. She came to Carmel with a great love of Elizabeth. She wrote only one note to me in all those years. She thanked me for a pamphlet I sent, and then alluded to her favorite quotation from Elizabeth: 'I must be wholly filled with Him. Then my prayer will be all powerful because it will be like offering God to God.' "* She wrote: *"This sentence was the deciding factor in my vocation to Carmel".* Fr. Bennett said: *"Frances Nevins was "genuine", "her dedication perfect" and "prayer for priests was truly her spirit". "She lived the quote (of Elizabeth)".* [In 1981 he still had her note from 1968.] *"...In any direction I recall giving to Sister Christine Marie I needed to do very little beyond assuring her that she was following a safe path. I was soon convinced that her religious name was well chosen: she was completely open to the interior light and direction of the Holy Spirit. At times, as with all contemplative sisters, I would answer some questions on some point of theology which was pertinent to her prayer".* [30]

Fr. Bennett was successful in smoothing tensions between Sr. Christine and her mother immediately prior to Final Vows scheduled for October 8 & 9, 1965. Frances Tenney had been diagnosed with bone cancer. The surgeon forecast a 50-50 chance of successful surgery if done promptly. Three times during July and

August Fr. Bennett visited Mrs. Tenney in East Granby, CT. While she ultimately made a decision against surgery, she sent a telegram that lifted an enormous weight from her daughter's shoulders. Dated September 3, 1965 the telegram read:

> *My darling daughter, thank you for your beautiful letter and its contents. I really do understand better now and can only wish you complete happiness for the rest of your life starting October 9, 1965. I will be with you in spirit. All my love....*

In Sr. Christine's letter to Fr. Bennett dated the same day, she writes...

> *Truly, it fills me with awe, to see grace working that way - and with gratitude to God and to you, because I never would have dared to write to her in that vein if you hadn't advised it. So - magnificate dominum meum.* [31]

Fr. Bennett's generous, effective human support to Sr. Christine, her mother, and the Carmelite community at a critical time exemplifies how a priest-confessor helps in many ways beyond those formally prescribed by the Church.

The Hermitage Struggle

Fr. Bennett mentions counseling Sr. Christine about her exploration of the hermitage aspect of Carmelite life. In his letter of 12/13/1981 he writes:

> *"...I counseled her in the matter of making a practicable adaptation of her eremitical desires. She did succeed - with the help and permission of her Prioress - in becoming a Carmelite "hermit" within the community; and she did this in a way that never separated her in spirit from her sisters. The Schenectady Carmel has a deep love for and appreciation of their "hermit".* [32]

Bennett refers to her eremitical desires. That term means hermit and implies a degree of solitude different from cenobitical or community life. There is a large body of literature about the distinctions between the two forms of religious life. In the 20th century Cistercian Thomas Merton had a well-published struggle with his Abbot and Rome about his wish to enter upon a hermit life, if not in the Carthusian Order then in some adaptation of the Holy Rule at his Cistercian (Trappist) Monastery in Kentucky. The latter did work out, and he began living in a small cement block house not far from the main building of the Monastery. He was required to maintain certain obligations about saying Mass, The Divine Office, teaching etc. as conditions for using the hermitage.[33]

Between 1969 and 1974 Sr. Christine began to have a longing for greater solitude and described her reasons in some detail. What would a move in this direction entail? Ruth Burrows O.C.D., an experienced Discalced Carmelite prioress and well-respected writer, provides useful information about what is involved in this serious and contentious issue. In: *Fire Upon the Earth, St. Teresa's Teaching on the Life of Deep Union with God*, she writes:

"...Teresa did not establish an eremitical structure as she might have done, rather she established a community life with eremitical elements, but with a spirit that is totally eremitical. Her nuns are called to be 'not merely nuns but hermits', detached from everything, totally exposed to God. Teresa grasped that, in order to be thus exposed one must be purified and mature. For this we need others absolutely. There is no other means of purification than learning to live with others. We could live in physical solitude and be exposed, not to God, but to ourselves. Is it ever allowed, I wonder, considering the absolute need we have of others, to take the initiative and choose the eremitical vocation?...(I believe) the vocation to the eremitical life must, of necessity, be very rare, and, in my opinion, must in some way be forced upon us....Incidentally, it is worth mentioning here that the deeper our prayer, the more real it is and the more truly we are exposed to God in it, the less it is possible to spend long hours at it. It is literally impossible and if it were possible it would be destructive. The pressure of God is too great. In my opinion, only someone endowed with 'light on' already sanctified, is fitted for the purely eremitical life, and even then, safeguards are needed and some social contacts".[34]

In a later book entitled: *Carmel, Interpreting a Great Tradition*, Burrows devotes an entire chapter to eremiticism [the state of being a hermit] in a Teresian Carmel. In it, however, she treats the issues of solitude and community with a broad brush recognizing that while different temperaments respond differently to the creative tension between the solitary and communal aspects of Carmel, all are required to bring the same wholehearted generosity and fidelity to the ordinances of solitude and silence. [35]

While observing the Holy Rule's directives, there were adaptations that Schenectady Carmel instituted. According to Sr. Mary of Jesus and St. Joseph:

"We always had an oratory right behind the tabernacle and you could go there. It was also in the tradition of Teresa to have a hermitage on the property. You could retire there in total solitude. You couldn't sleep there but for your "hermit day" you could be there all day. That was always a goal. Even before the Vatican Council, different Carmels had built their hermitages. When I entered in 1949 and was on retreat, you came to the full Divine Office but you could start your prayer in your cell and then finish it with the community. Actual development of physical solitude began with the Vatican Council. But it really did begin with Sr. Christine at Schenectady - probably for her health, but mainly her inner spirit. She asked if she could make prayer in solitude. We would begin in Choir - everybody in Choir. She asked if she could leave so that's where she was really like a pioneer. Once she did that, she was voicing what was in many people's hearts. Some people, of course, would always want to stay in Choir in the presence of the Blessed Sacrament; others would want to go to the garden or their cells. That was all part of the renewal. What evolved - and we did discuss all this and get permission for all this - was that finally you didn't have to be in Choir to begin. You could be at your place of prayer for the full hour. When the bell was rung, then everyone came to the Choir and then went to the Refectory with a Psalm. So she was instrumental in that change". [36]

With her rock-solid practicality, Burrows always signals what is healthy general practice in the Carmelite community. Nonetheless, she always allows for the rare person, the "Light On" as she describes someone with remarkable gifts.

In the early 1970s the Schenectady Carmel was the epitome of fervor, great love and sacrifice, according to Sister Mary. Another witness to this genuine Carmelite zeal was Sr. Clare Joseph. Together with Sr. Christine, all three sisters, and perhaps others, were attracted to a more fully developed option of a hermitage. Sr. Christine and Sr. Clare Joseph studied the Primitive Rule of Carmel, looking for additional possibilities in the early usages supporting hermitage life within Carmel. Meanwhile, private retreats and "hermit days" were permitted more frequently for those who felt drawn to solitude. Sr. Clare Joseph writes: "Unity in diversity balanced the previous emphasis on uniformity and for a long time we (Christine and I) both believed that our 'call within a call' (solitude within Carmel) would be fulfilled...". That was not to be, however, when the Superior General of the Discalced Carmelites turned back the suggestions. As if proving the theorem about "unintended consequences of purposive action" all three Sisters' lives changed dramatically in a short time. Sr. Christine became more and more a "hermit" because of her seriously diminished health; Sr. Clare Joseph transferred to the Barre, Vt. Carmel; and Sister Mary founded a new religious community with Diocesan approval that used hermitage as its foundation.

Sr. Christine was intensely human. Her sanguine temperament (with a sliver of choleric) would assure intensity and quickness even apart from the effects of emotional ups and downs of her vivid life. She was neither cold nor indifferent, particularly when loss was involved. Understandably, she was deeply saddened by Sr. Clare Joseph's transfer to the Vermont Carmel in 1975. They had shared a lot beginning with vestment work and ending in a quest for new conditions for prayer. They shared common goals and a kindness toward one another and the rest of the Community. Sr. Mary's departure was also a loss. "Mother let me say goodbye to everybody, after being there 28 years...Sr. Christine didn't really understand. Nobody really did. She said she knew that I was following my conscience. She knew that she had done the same thing. So we had a bond...." [37]

Prior to 1969 only hints about Sr. Christine's need for more solitude show up here and there. "I am a scavenger for solitude. Why does it have to be this way?" Beginning with Retreat, August 1969, she expressed more concern about solitude, community and how to live the ideal that is becoming clearer to her.

8/6 and 8/11/1969 Journal Entries

What I hope for:
It seems to me I must find ways of living this more hidden, silent recollected life, without failing in my responsibilities to Community. To do this in great prudence, so as not to rouse more opposition than necessary. Are these possibilities? Greater use of hermitage (2 days?) Feast Days? Sunday? 1-2:45? 8-9? Should review St. Teresa on this for authentic tradition.

Things that work against this:
half conscious preoccupation with others' opinions
guilt feelings caused by disapproval

How to surmount this:
To be more sure of my ideal, my being called to it
To freely and openly admit - to myself and others - that He calls me to a way that is somewhat different - and to ask leave to follow it?

In 1970 and 1971 Sr. Christine cries out against incursions into her space for prayer. "De profundis clamavi ad te, Domine. Lord, why do I suffer so when solitude is violated? Because my solitude is a sanctuary, alive with the Divine presence, and it is the experience of a kind of profanation." She ponders about Bernadette, the remarkable Saint of Lourdes and links herself with her: "We both have something which makes us special - you, your memories and I, my inner experience - neither one is communicable."

Christine's retreat journals in the early 1970s suggest that availability of a spiritual director was on the thin side. She turns again to Archbishop Martinez and his text *"The Sanctifier"*...."The experience of Arbp. Martinez helps me as perhaps nothing else could because my own, although unique, is like his. His acceptance and confidence seem so natural and spontaneous. This book at the right time is another precious grace. It sets my own grace in context." Nonetheless, she misses the help of a priest and spiritual director...."Jesus - sometimes I am afraid that without a human guide I will somehow wander and fail to please You as I ought - yet it is only through You that they could give me any help in the past. Therefore, I trust Your wisdom - the Lord has given and the Lord has taken away."

Even in 1974 she still reaches out for guidance from Martinez, and now for guidance about a very serious matter indeed. The idea of hermitage away from Schenectady Carmel has begun to form:

6/11/1974 Journal Entry

> ...Jesus - to live and grow in this love and intimacy is all that matters. Fr. Martinez - lead me forward if it is His will. Could this be done more perfectly in a different mode of life...is there something between my everyday life here and my way of life in Retreat, which would foster this intimacy more perfectly? This is the great and only issue for me - Do You even want these questions re-opened? During these past 4 years I have come to appreciate and cherish the community aspects of life (real community: growing together in mutual love and understanding and forbearance as never before). But is it in the right proportion? Fr. Martinez: as my spiritual director, I commit my question to you.

At this point, Sr. Christine is sure that hermit life, no matter whether settled in a new configuration at Schenectady Carmel or elsewhere is closer to the Carmel ideal.

10/1/1974 Journal Entry

> The hermitage seems the only way to maintain the sacred atmosphere which is the environment of this life - in solitude everything is sacred - it is deep interior liturgy

of praise and reverence and thanksgiving for all the creatures around us - a life of total awareness.

A few days later, during this October, 1974 Retreat, she pulls together all the strands of her longing for a hermitage:

10/10/1974 Journal Entry

> What a difference for me to be living a truly religious community life with the blessing and approval of the Church - not on the fringes and by way of dispensation. I have completely hidden and buried my charism under this veil of humiliation, all to Your will - but it is ready to come forth at Your words, Jesus - I believe that if You want it, it will take place, as long as we put no obstacle...Your action, so far has been so sovereign and decisive and independent: placing me in solitude; my health improvement; the contact with Sr. Clare Joseph; Mother's (Dolorosa) favorable attitude. You will complete what You have done for us if this truly is Your eternal design unfolding. Only grant me enough light to cooperate perfectly with Your actions.

The Superior General's Denial of the Request to Establish a Hermitage Vocation

Sr. Christine's journal and retreat notes do not include a copy of the proposed Rule sent to the Superior General of the Carmelite Order. According to Sr. Mary, "Once the General said that there was no way, then Christine knew that (the proposed change) was not for her. So it took another form." [38] Already, in early 1975, Sr. Christine turned her prayer toward change about hermitage possibilities where she was, rather than elsewhere... "to beg and pray and hope for a place for hermits in Carmel".

It is important to keep in focus what she is trying to do by pursuing a hermitage. Now in her mid-40s she is utterly single-minded about doing everything she can to keep herself free and clear for a unique illumination that leads to whatever God's plans are for her. She is protecting the conditions for God to do His work, and nothing must interfere.

Once again, English Carmelite Ruth Burrows walks us through what is going on with Sr. Christine. Burrows' "light on" and "light off" paradigm shows the way

> "The 'light on' experience is not the mystical grace itself, it reveals it. It seems we must say that it is supernatural in the strict sense, that is, that it is of God and not, in itself proper to the human experience of God in this life. That being so it is wiser to leave it in its mystery and concentrate not on its nature but on what it does. What it does is precisely to illuminate the mystical happening which of itself, is secret....What we have to grasp is that this gift, puts a person in a class apart - their experience is fundamentally different from ours. It is a very rare gift and all of us would do well to take for granted we are 'light off' no matter how great our psychic perception and consequent 'spiritual favours'....Inevitably the 'light on' person lives in great loneliness once they have begun to realize that others do not share their vision." [39]

Henry Tansey M.H.M. Mill Hill Missionaries: Confessor/Spiritual Director 1977-1980

The most influential priest in Sr. Christine's life was Fr. Tansey. He turned her extraordinary intellect much more toward scripture, and, at the same time, expanded her generous heart to include his priestly work with all sorts of people.

'Mill Hill Missionaries' is the popular name for St. Joseph's Society for Foreign Missions. The Society was founded by Cardinal Vaughn in 1866 at Mill Hill, a suburb of London, England. The Mill Hill Missionaries are an international group of priests and brothers whose work is exclusively missionary. Their mission fields are in Africa (Kenya, Uganda, Sudan, Darfur, Cameroon), India, Pakistan, Philippines, Borneo and South America. In the United States houses are located in New York, Missouri and California.

Henry Tansey was born in Ireland and ordained by Cardinal Griffin in 1948 in London. He was sent to Malakal, Sudan where he worked until 1958. Then as now, the weather and the politics were equally dangerous. "I put up with swamps, snakes and crocodiles in Africa. I guess California won't be that bad," he joked with a reporter before he was to leave on assignment outside Los Angeles. In that same interview, he spoke about the 'deep roots' he had in the Albany Diocese and how leaving would be like going to the dentist to have a tooth pulled. He had worked with thousands of people in the Charismatic Movement, Marriage Encounter, The Cursillo Movement, Ancient Order of Hibernians and with many families and individuals. Ken and Gerrie Goewey, co-directors of the Marriage Encounter Movement spoke about Fr. Tansey's work in Marriage Encounter:

"...He was the most accepting person I ever met," Mrs. Goewey said. "He knew what walking with Jesus really meant. He gave Encounters all over the country, and, after every weekend, he called each of the couples. He'd see them if there were any problems he could help them with. He was an excellent counselor." [40]

"He seemed to be everywhere. Troubled child. Troubled teens. Troubled marriage. Baptisms. Hearing confessions. Visiting the sick. He'd open that day planner of his and find a date and time for you." [41]

Tansey had a variety of contacts with the Schenectady Carmel. He had shown slides of mission work in Africa and given a series of talks to the Community about changes arising from the Vatican II Church Council regarding rights of Sisters, etc. At some point he was given a three year assignment as a confessor/spiritual director to Schenectady Carmel as one among several priests available at that time. Sr. Christine made an unswerving choice of Tansey as confessor/ spiritual director in the latter 1970s. "Between then and 1980 I saw her every 2 weeks for 45 minutes in the confessional room separated by a grille. She would write out what she wanted me to read between visits. Her amazing growth was possible after the 'anointing', that is, the 'healing of memories'. After that, she was able to delve into scripture much more, to use it, and to grow. She had also begun to teach the novices the monastic view of Mary. She enjoyed this teaching very much, and her 'students'.

"I delayed until the last possible moment telling Sr. Christine I had been assigned to California. I was prompted to tell her about these plans when I did because the 3rd Order Carmelites were giving a farewell party for me and I didn't want her to hear it through the grapevine. I think that Christine's constitution just couldn't take that kind of news." [42]

Indeed Fr. Tansey's prophecy proved to be accurate. Sr. Christine was stricken with her last illness just two days later- December 4, 1980.

Incredibly, Fr. Tansey was killed in a car accident January 21, 1981, about six weeks after her sudden death, and one day before he was scheduled to leave for California. He was delivering his bicycle to a family of eight children.

At his huge wake and funeral, many had their own affectionate story to tell about him. Sister of Mercy Cecelia Guckian knew Tansey well. As cousins, they both came from Keadue, Roscommon, Ireland. She told this story:

"An Albany family had two sons. One son had been gone from the family for a long time. Fr. Tansey was instrumental in bringing one son back to the family through the power of prayer it is thought. With all the focus of attention going to the first son, the second son left the family and was not heard from for several years. At Fr. Tansey's wake the family entered the funeral parlor to find the son kneeling at Fr. Tansey's casket. The family experienced the reunion of the family there." [43]

NOTES

7: Influential Priests

29. Luis M. Martinez, Archbishop of Mexico. *The Sanctifier*. Translated by Sister M. Aquinas O.S.U. (NJ: St. Anthony Guild Press, 1959) Arguably, Frances Nevins' most preferred text about the Holy Spirit.

30. Letter written by Fr. Owen Bennett to the author, December 13, 1981.

31. Letter written by Sr. Christine to Fr. Owen Bennett, September 3,1965.

32. Letter written by Fr. Bennett to the author, December 13,1981.

33. Lawrence S. Cunningham. *Thomas Merton and the Monastic Vision* (Grand Rapids: William B. Eerdmans Publishing Company, 1999). Well researched, highly readable examination of key issues in Merton's life including his considerable interest in the eremitical life. Also see: Patrick Hart. *Survival or Prophecy? The Letters of Thomas Merton and Jean Leclerq* (NY: Farrar. Straus. Giroux, 2002). A profound exchange of letters about monastic life, particularly Merton's quest for a hermitage; and Leclerq's humane, measured response as a Benedictine scholar to his Trappist friend's special vocation.

34. Ruth Burrows O.C.D. *Fire Upon the Earth, Interior Castle Explored, St. Teresa's Teaching on the Life of Deep Union with God* (N.J.: Dimension Books, 1981), pp. 96, 97.

35. Ruth Burrows O.C.D., *Carmel, Interpreting a Great Tradition* (London: Sheed and Ward, 2000), p. 54.

36. Interview with Sister Mary of Jesus and St. Joseph, H.O. Carm. by author on December 13,1981.

37. See Ref. 36.

38. See Ref. 36.

39. See Ref. 34, pp. 48, 49.

40. Sr. Mary Ann Walsh, R.S.M. "A Last Farewell to Father Tansey", Evangelist, February 5, 1981.

41. Letter written by Michael Finn to the author, December 15, 1981.

42. Conversation with Fr. Henry Tansey, M.H.M. by the author, January 14, 1981.

43. Conversation with Sr. Cecelia Guckian, R.S.M. by the author, July 3, 1981.

Picture of Our Lady:
a favored image referred to by Sr. Christine
in teaching the novices

8

Teacher for the Novices: A Loving Heart and a Well-Stocked Mind

Novices Judge Their Teacher

Mother Mary John made an inspired choice in the late 1970s when she asked Sr. Christine to teach the Novices the monastic view of Mary. Everyone was pleased with the outcome. Sr. Christine was unusually well prepared to teach the Novices. By 1978 she had 18 years of lived experience as a Carmelite nun judged by a succession of Confessor/Spiritual Directors to be genuine and full of growth. Before entering Carmel there was a successful teaching experience with the Sisters of the Good Shepherd, years of rigorous academic study of Church related subjects as well as her own thorough search for understanding of Roman Catholic doctrine and practice, including the important role of Mary. Shortly after Sr. Christine's death, each Novice described her experience in the class.

1. Letter written by Sr. Therese

1/18/1981

Mother,

Since you asked for a few impressions of our classes with Sister Christine for Joan, I'll try to do my best. It is a little hard because my love for my dear "big" sister and my impressions of her as a person are so deep in my heart. Well, simply here are my impressions.

I found Sister Christine to be a fantastic teacher. She was more guide than teacher though. Our classes with her were very simple and informal. She mainly shared with us her own personal reflections on a particular topic she wished to tell us about. Her class was not a "rap session" and her sharing didn't take away from the fact that she had a very definite point to make and an end in view.

She was kind of like someone who takes friends on a treasure hunt, she herself knowing all the while where the treasure is. Instead of dumping the treasure in our lap, so to speak, she gave us hints and clues as to where the treasure was hidden. To her it meant more if we discovered the treasure for ourselves. So we kind of worked as a team with her as coach.

She had a great love and enthusiasm for the topics she shared with us. She would take a topic and have us look at it together from different angles and different aspects of it. She would make a reflection or a comment and ask, "What do you think?" or "How does it strike you?" or "What do you see?" and we'd share our thoughts. If one of our thoughts were kind of fuzzy or not in line with sound theology, in her great kindness and delicacy, she had a way of inviting us to look again and her own thought on the subject would make it clearer. We never felt "turned off" when she pointed out fuzzy thinking or a mistake.

To our surprise and hers too, our topic would so develop that before we knew it her point was made and we stumbled on the treasure together. It was all so simple like close friends speaking together about what they love most. One could easily see in her classes the fruit of her own prayer and deep reflection. She gave something to us that no text book could give (though she used books a lot to make a point or enhance something) she gave herself. In some of the classes, I'd say she gave of her deepest self, her very soul. I learned a great deal from Sr. Christine, perhaps

more from her wonderful example than
from words. I am forever grateful to God
for this soul.

I am afraid, Mother, I have expressed
myself poorly, but I pray it will be a little
help!

As a "post-script" dated November 11, 2008, Sr. Therese
wrote: "I do remember one thing she said about Our Lady which
impressed me at the time and which has stayed with me over the
years: she encouraged us Novices to cultivate the motherly heart of
Our Lady in our own hearts; as a true mother Our Lady loves all
souls and earnestly desires their salvation, and, as Carmelites, we
should have that same love and desire".

2. Letter written by Sr. Mary Joseph

1/18/1981

Re: Sister Christine's Classes

Sister would always begin with
a prayer and a few moments of silent
reflection. Then usually she read a few
lines from a book, often A Woman Wrapped
in Silence about whatever feast we had
just celebrated or were going to celebrate.
Often she would ask our reflections on
the readings, sometimes giving us her
own, but usually after us. As you know,
she always spoke quietly and reflectively.
I never doubted what she said was an
overflow of her prayer. When we gave
our comments or reflections she would
sometimes nod her head if we seemed to
have really penetrated the thought and
this with a little smile, if we had not, she
would sometimes ask a question or add
further questions for clarification. She was
always quick to say she had not thought of
a certain aspect. If a comment was made

*in something of a different idea, often
almost non-verbally urging us to always
probe more deeply these sacred truths or
thoughts. She would read further if the
discussion lagged, always there was a
sense of peace and calm.*

3. Letter written by Sr. Paul

1/18/1981

*Sr. Christine was one, who above
all, had a deep love and devotion to
the subject she taught. (The role of the
Blessed Virgin Mary in our Carmelite
life). She was simple and straight forward
in her approach and was always open
to questions, discussions or reflections
on our part. Her classes were built on a
solid foundation, i.e. Holy Scripture, the
teachings of the Church, the Pope, and
our Rule, Constitutions and Declarations.
Her classes always reflected her deeper
prayer life and her earnest desire to
impart to us a greater awareness of the
important influence of Our Lady in our
way of life. She was a teacher who strove
to live what she taught.*

Teacher Judges Her Novices

Still feeling the aftermath of Mother Dolorosa's death and
dying [former Prioress], Sr. Christine's class met at its usual time.
Written after class, Sr. Christine's journal entry captures her gentle
caring about her teaching "duty" and how closely it is tied into her
own contemplative life. For her, it is really not a class, it is a calling.

7/3/1980 Journal Entry

Mary - My little task with the Novices
is to light a flame of love in their hearts for
you, to hold you up before them for their
admiration and appreciation and delight.

They must look at you first from one angle, then from another, so as to fall in love with their own ideal - this Marian life of Carmel, which means continuing your very self in their own persons. You have blessed my little efforts all these months out of all proportion to anything I have done. Each time, the Spirit seems to organize my thoughts, quietly inspiring one insight after another for me to share with them. It is You who want to be close to them - You are simply using me as Your instrument to make You known. This is a humble and hidden work with a handful of Sisters - but I would like to make You known to the ends of the earth.

And only the week before she was stricken, Sr. Christine praises the Novices as only a Master-Teacher can; that is, by making a confident statement about the future of her students.

11/27/1980 Journal Entry

Jesus - what a joy it is to share my vision of Mary with the Novices - to see them absorb it with love, and make it a part of themselves.. "...A sower went forth to sow..." I am a very humble sower but these precious children of Yours are good soil, the best - so why shouldn't these seeds bear fruit?

The study of the monastic view of Mary, or its Marian character as it were, is central to the tradition of Carmel.

Carmelite legislation states:

"The Discalced Nuns of the Blessed Virgin Mary of Mount Carmel belong to a religious family, endowed with its own proper charism for the purpose of fulfilling a special mission in the Mystical Body of Christ...The beginnings of the Order, the title of the 'Blessed Virgin Mary of Mount

Carmel' and the earliest spiritual traditions provide ample evidence of the Marian character and prophetic spirit of our vocation. By choosing the Blessed Virgin Mary as mother and patroness of the Order, we place ourselves in her safe keeping and we look to her lifelong union with Christ as an ideal model of faithfully-lived consecration." [44]

It is not surprising that each novice made reference to Sr. Christine's use of books. *A Woman Wrapped in Silence* is the profoundly contemplative prose poem to which Sr. Mary Joseph referred. It has a strong biblical base and provides an excellent structure for discussion. It is likely Sr. Christine also drew attention to *The Sanctifier* by Archbishop Martinez and the book-length essay, *Carmelite Spirituality* by Paul De La Croix, O.C.D.. In April, 1980 she wrote to me that she was using *Our Lady Speaks to her Beloved Priests*. "This is an unusual book and would not be everyone's cup of tea, surely, because of the very strong Marian aspect, but the spirituality seems very solid, somewhat a la St. Therese in simpler and less flowing language."

The Novices were encouraged to find in Scripture both the questions and the answers needed to sort out the monastic view of Mary. Christine, too, plunged deeply into the scriptural texts particularly when Father Tansey was her Confessor/Spiritual Director. Like the Novices, she was on a treasure hunt and it brought her joy.

9/6/1980 Journal Entry

"Let everything you do have the word of God for accompaniment." (Rule of Carmel).
Lord, this meant nothing at all to me until recently - but now everything I "do" in my inner life, everything I think, is indeed accompanied by some word of Scripture which Your Spirit brings to my mind. This gift blossomed in me without my knowing how - it is precious, habitual inspiration of His inner teaching. As He forms the thoughts in my mind, He reminds me that St. Paul or St. John said the same and helps me find the

passage if I do not know by heart. We search for the translation which fits best with the thought He gave me, or sometimes go to the Greek, where the agreement is closest of all. This has become so habitual that I hardly realized what I was doing. Today He is helping me to examine lovingly this gift, so as to be more thankful.

Sr. Christine ended this entry with a quote from her favorite of favorites, Sr. Elizabeth of the Trinity: "Mary was the only creature who never lost a particle of the divine gift. Jesus - this is the grace I ask of You at the end of these days - not to lose a particle of this serene, secure confidence in Your love that You have given me".

The Novices' outline for each session includes a prayer at the beginning. Many people associate two prayers with Mary: "The Hail Mary" and "The Magnificat". Novices commit both to memory. Roman Catholics learn "The Hail Mary" as children. "The Magnificat" is part of the Evening Prayer, or Vespers, of the Divine Office and is said daily in Carmel. Christine teaches the meaning behind the words of this ancient prayer. During her own Retreat, she re-examines this prayer of faith in a new way.

8/30/1980 Journal Entry

"The Lord has established his Throne in heaven, and His kingdom rules over all". (Psalm 103)
Lord, this is a deeply consoling word, when we understand it right. All of Mary's Magnificat proclaims that "our God reigns". He reigns through the lowly, and in their favor - He reigns by lifting them up at the proper moment.
Lord, this view makes the Magnificat fit together and make sense for me as never before. It is all a praise of "Your ways with us", of which the Incarnation is the chief example. "He has looked upon his servant in his lowliness" (poverty, dependence, openness); "He who is mighty has done great

things for me."

Lord, show me Your ways that I may find favor with You," said Moses. "They are a people of erring heart, and they do not know my ways." (Invitatory Psalm) Mary is the "highly favored one" the one full of grace - she 'knows Your ways' better than any other, and witnesses to them in her Song of Praise.

At this moment she sees Your ways prophetically, but at other times she had to cling by faith to what she had seen. An immaculate faith, strong and resolute, but one that was tested and tried as no other. Mary was the strong one, the valiant woman. Faith is the only strength, for it relies on Yours.

Lord, the scholars endlessly discuss and dissect her song, but it is easy now for me to see how these verses of Scripture could have come spontaneously to her lips, when they come so readily to my pen. "The Holy Spirit... will remind you of all I have said to you." He filled her heart and reminded her of what the God of Israel had said to His people, all through their history. She who understood His meaning better than any other.

Another foundation for life in Carmel mentioned by Sr. Paul, was the Pope. Understandably, she did not specify which Pope because, in 1978, there were 3 Popes in one calendar year: Pope Paul VI; his successor, Pope John Paul I; and, after 31 days, Pope John Paul II. There were qualities in John Paul I that Sr. Christine particularly admired. He insisted that faith is not 'a stroll through pleasant gardens' but a journey that is sometimes difficult, often dramatic, and always mysterious. He could relate the Gospel to everyday things with a skill and perceptiveness that are rare. And he greeted 'the suffering, the sick, prisoners, exiles, the unemployed, those down on their luck'. He was a smiling, reconciling Pope. 'Gianpaulo' as Sr. Christine called him, was a trusted guide for her Novices. [45]

The "Classroom" and the "Teacher's" Health

Totally absent from the Novices' letters is any comment about their "classroom", or the physical condition of their "teacher". Nor does Sr. Christine comment on either issue in any journal entry directly related to the Novices. She does, however, make an occasional reference to her extremely poor health. She learned Yoga to strengthen her breathing and circulation. "I am now teaching Yoga - in a very amateurish way - to the Novices on Sunday and must say it is fun. I don't mention the inversion postures to many people since I find that some have difficulty with the idea of a nun standing on her head - nonetheless it helps!" She could no longer sit in a chair. Instead, she sat on a low bench Sr. Bernadette made for her use. Only in sharp cold or with the windows open wide was she able to breathe. Dizziness made it difficult to get around. She went to recreation for about 20 minutes and quietly left. As a consequence of this severe debilitation, the Prioress allowed Sr. Christine the use of a place of solitude in the basement and a hermitage in the back of the property. The grounds had a small, cement block house Sr. Christine was allowed to use. Noting Sr. Christine's great need for fresh air and cold, the Prioress asked that the Novices go to Sr. Christine in the basement hermitage every two weeks for her lectures on the Blessed Virgin Mary. [46]

9/1/1979 Journal Entry

> The importance of lowly work and constant unremitting austerity - heat, cold, dirt, lack of modern conveniences etc. In my tiny hermitage, You have created for me an extreme simplicity of life I could never have dreamed of - everything I need to live all my waking hours in a 6' by 8' cubicle with no furniture but mats and wooden crates. This simplicity is home to me as nothing else could be - it is somehow the external expression of my inner emptiness, poverty and recollection, and Mary is there to give it beauty and grace.

The Novices may not have written any comments about the surroundings in which they met because they were not asked to do so, or because it was not among the reasons for being in the hermitage. Not commenting upon such obvious frugality goes beyond mere politeness. For these Novices, from their earliest days in Carmel they were taught to observe the Rule in letter and spirit.

Teresa's Constitution states:

> The sisters must never possess any kind of private property: such a thing must not be allowed them, either in food or clothing. Unless they have duties in the community, they may have no box, drawer, chest or cupboard, nor any other private possession: everything they must have in common. This is very important, for the devil uses small things gradually to undermine our perfection in poverty. So if a sister is seen to be attached to anything, the Prioress must be very careful to take it away from her, whether it a book or a cell or whatever else it may be. [47]

Summing up, the Novices write about the friendly exchange of ideas with Sr. Christine. According to Sr. Therese, it was not a "rap session". The atmosphere, the texture of the classes could be expected. Christine has a gift for friendship and a sense of kindness that builds community life.

9/5/1980 Journal Entry

> Jesus - There is more joy for us when You let us help each other - when You weave us into each others' lives and more joy for You, in looking at the pattern.

NOTES

8: Teacher for the Novices: A Loving Heart and a Well-Stocked Mind

44. Discalced Carmelite Nuns, Rule, Constitutions, Declarations (Roma: Curia Generalizia O.C.D. Corsa Italia 38, 1977). p. 54.

45. Peter Hebblewaite. *The Year of the Three Popes* (Cleveland: Collins Press, 1979).

46. Conversation with Mother Mary John of the Cross O.C.D., Prioress by the author, December 6, 1980.

47. See Ref. 44.

9

Friendships, Part One: A Sample of Letters 1960-1980

Sr. Christine wrote swiftly and with a good deal of openness and self-revelation. Her writings are engaging in a most personal way. Father Reardon said that her letters were little masterpieces because she always wrote as if she was right there with you. And the truth of it was that she did not forget her friends when she went to Carmel. Nor we, her. Many years of wonderful letters back and forth prove the point. A book of letters even apart from her retreat notes and journals would be a stunning accomplishment.

Ruth Burrows, the English Discalced Carmelite, favors friendship and maintaining contact with friends.

> "...We may be fortunate in our former relationships which continue after we have entered the monastery. We may have to wait and look to God to send us the friends we need but this means being open to recognize one if sent...Perhaps we are being invited to give closer attention to our companions in the monastery and value more the diffuse but staunch and faithful friendship they afford us. What matters is a realistic acknowledgment that we are not self-sufficient either as individuals or as a community. We need others as they need us." [48]

Sr. Christine wrote letters to friends and benefactors of the monastery and, with permission and at specified intervals, to her friends and relatives. Approximately 125 letters that Frances Nevins wrote were still in their possession 30 years later.

Frances Nevins to Joan Mullaney
First Christmas in the Monastery

Carmel
December 25, 1960

Here we are at last with all our Christmas wishes - it was so good to have your letter to read today - and then all the surprise packages. The books

*especially are lovely - today or tomorrow
(I think) the Professed are coming to
visit the Novitiate (i.e., Mother Mistress
and me) and Our Mother (that is Mother
Prioress) has said they can all have a
good look at the books then - and next on
the agenda for me after letter writing is
to sit down and enjoy them. How's that?*

*Before I get any further, you will
wonder what has come over our writing.
No, we are not weakened by fasting (in
fact, not exactly fasting - coffee and
cookies at 3! Very temporary and only for
me) - nor have we suddenly become very
lowly and small, rather it is this monastic-
type pen which takes a bit of getting used
to. Remember St. Therese said she never
felt her letters would do any good unless
they cost her something - so I trust you
will profit by our ineptness.*

*Where to begin - with the building,
I guess. It is something you would have
thought up - all walls just off-white,
and everything else in different lovely
shades of brown. (Except a little colored
tile in lavatories.) It is so peaceful and
recollected and just what one would have
dreamed of. The Refectory is especially
glorious with the big brown cross at one
end, brown tables and benches, gray
(earthenware?) dishes, and our friend
the skull (which one gets used to fairly
easily) at the head table. We sit two-
by-two, with a nice space between. In
fact, nowhere do you get that smothered,
closed-in feeling - there is room enough
everywhere for the body and plenty for
the soul, which is the main thing, I guess,
that produces that sense of space and
lack of tension. Rather hard to verbalize,
but you know what I mean.*

*Everything is lovely. There is
a beautiful rhythm and dignity and
simplicity to the life, which seems to be
what we have been reaching after all
along - and at the same time, recreations
are now a joy and at that time it is really*

like a family - all talk together (not all at once) which is very pleasant and relaxing. And we get out for a little walk every day (I think this is special, postulant treatment) alone. There are the little sacrifices (as well as the big, separation ones) but the sources of strength are all there, so we could not ask for more. God is very good. And even though we have only made a tiny beginning of the life, you feel you are starting to be a part of something very important and wonderful in the Church, which is a great happiness. So pray that we will be able to do our little part well, and take each new thing as we should.

I'm glad we spent those trying times seeking quiet shoes; everything is so quiet that noisy ones would have been a real trial to all. Speaking of clothing - we have a long brown dress and cape - dress can be put up in back a la Good Shepherd habit - and white beguine (beg-win) [hood] like the extern postulant. This is quite monastic garb after the little black outfits. Loose and comfortable.

Christmas was beautiful - a procession with candles at 9:45 p.m. (I think this part is in <u>My Beloved</u>) then Matins, at which I had to chant one lesson solo, shaking vigorously from head to foot - then Mass, Lauds, a hot drink with <u>marshmallows</u> (most unusual fare), and bed.

Christmas A.M. our alarm clock was the Community singing carols. Their voices are sweet and clear and quite angel-like (till I join in). We had dinner together in the Recreation room <u>with</u> talking and it was delightful with much laughing. How nicely all these things fit into the life when there is enough solitude, so that one is not always longing for it.

And - we have a little tabernacle of our own in the Choir, which at Benediction times (we can't see what's going on in the chapel, of course) our

Mother opens, so that we can see the Blessed Sacrament which is always exposed in a little Monstrance inside.

So there are some of the main features of our new regime and I will tell you more when I see you. Am waiting now for word about the visit as it seems we have no grille at the moment - it is in the process of being moved about.

In this life where there is much silence and looking to the interior, one's nearest and dearest seem often very present - you are receiving more praying than every before. Is it coming through on the internal phone?

Sr. Christine to Joan Mullaney
Final Profession. A special invitation.

Carmel
August 23, 1965

A quick note to let you know the ceremony is set for Saturday the 9th at 9:30. Tell that University they have to let you come because you are the family of the bride! (I hope you will sit there permanently and give me moral support like last time.) [10/7/1961 - receiving the habit and her new name, Sr. Christine Marie of the Holy Spirit.]

Sr. Christine to Joy Anderson
Detailed description of the Final Profession ceremony. Sr. Christine adds a compassionate update about her former husband whom Joy had known. Joy is a classmate from Connecticut College

Carmel
September 21, 1965

My biggest news is that I have been received by the Community for my final profession which I will make on Oct. 8th. As you probably know, there are various stages in the process of becoming a full-fledged Carmelite - first there is a Novitiate, then a temporary profession (that is, you take vows for a period of three years - this is a very wise arrangement, of course, in case the Sister or the Order should change (her (their) mind) - but it makes you anxious for the day when you can add "until death" instead of "for three years". So now that day is coming and I am peacefully and intensely happy, and wonder how God could have been so good to me.

The Profession itself is a private ceremony with just the Community present but the next day there is a public veiling ceremony (Mass and sermon and the Bishop's delegate officially confers the black veil which is the sign of one's new status) and afterwards I go to the grate to meet those who have come. This is really my big day and I would love it if you could be here. Also, this is one of the rare occasions when we could see each other. But on the other hand, there wouldn't be much chance to really talk (or perhaps, any at all) because, since it's a public ceremony, there will probably be quite a few people (even many who don't know the Sister personally come to ask prayers, etc. on that day). Also, of course, it's such a distance for you, and at 9:30 A.M. So I'll leave it all in the hands of God and feel sure you will be with me in spirit at least on both the 8th and 9th (I'll make my Profession about 8:00 A.M. on the 8th). I'll count on that and it will add much to my joy!

Dave has probably told you that Paul was married in August to a girl who taught in the same school where he teaches. To me this was a tremendous answer to prayer, as I was longing for him to be happy, and I was afraid for awhile that perhaps he would never settle down and have a family when I knew how much

he wanted one. Now I am happy because
he is - truly God makes all things work
together for good, as St. Paul says, if we
can only be patient and wait - though
that part can be hard sometimes.

Please pray for my mother - she has
cancer of the mouth. My heart aches for
her since she is so alone and yet I know
deep down that giving up my vocation
would never be the answer and somehow
I think she knows it, too, as she seems to
be much more reconciled to my being here
and even sent me a beautiful telegram
a couple of weeks ago saying that she
understood better now and wished me
complete happiness, etc. I think she is
planning to come to visit soon. Pray
that I will somehow be able to help her
to realize that I really do love her very
much and that my life here is for her
sake, too. I do hope and trust completely
that God will bless her and take care of
her - and I'm grateful that her friends are
so attentive - (if you write at Christmas
or anytime, please - no mention of her
sickness unless she tells you).

This whole letter has been about
me and my affairs. I guess if I am your
psychiatrist-by-mail, I'm the silent
listener kind. But maybe even this can be
of help sometimes, I hope. And I do listen
with as much interest and concern as the
best of them! I hope your trip to the Cape
had the desired relaxing effect. There
is nothing like that salt water and sun,
and the sight of the ocean stretching out
and out without any boundaries to make
everything within you calm down, or so it
always seemed to me. What a beautiful
image of the peace and constancy of God
there is in nature, if only we can be still
enough to see it.

Observations about the world-wide Church; spirited description of an Irish custom; and, a serious reflection about the poor of this world

Carmel
August 14, 1972

Greetings for Paschaltide - I had meant to be sending them sooner - at least by a few days, but Providence just did not provide the moments. As you say, it is a beautiful season. More and more, I seem to grasp that the whole spiritual and theological renewal is saying that Easter is totally central - or rather is all - in the Faith. So your instincts must be from the Spirit. Apropos of this, I'm reading a book (2 small vols) by a Charles Augrain, S.S. called Paul, Master of the Spiritual Life. It is by far the best thing I've come across on St. Paul. The author seems to have gotten right inside him to think his thoughts and then has a way of making them make sense with the fewest possible words of his own. Obviously based on very sound scholarship, but this does not intrude itself at all. It's most readable and almost lively, a la Paul himself. If you ever get a yen for such like - it's Alba House, Daughters of St. Paul publication.

God reward you for the little book on our Cesar [Chavez]. I haven't had a chance to get much into it, but at quick perusal it looks very sound and sensitive to the real person - and the illustrations are most welcome. I smiled most happily at its arrival as I think of him so often. The Register has only little squibs that this or that contract has been signed. Somebody sent a copy of The Pilot to Sr. Alberta a while back and in it was an article re: a college girl (somewhere around Boston) who had gone down (to Fla.) to work with him and gotten herself killed "accidentally", run over by some strikebreakers, I think. It sounded so much like the kind of thing the first book talked about, in Calif. Cesar & Co. had sent a beautiful telegram to her parents.

The same _Pilot_ said that there is to be a big celebration in Boston next weekend for the 100th (150th?) Anniversary of the Society for the Propagation of the Faith, and the highlight of it is to be a Mass at St. Ignatius with Bishop (China) Walsh, among others, concelebrating. Somehow it made me feel very happy to think that such a holy veteran will be in our St. Ignatius [church we attended in Boston].

I've been re-reading his life and you can't help but think that the work and suffering he [Bishop Walsh] has given to God is enough for about 20 lifetimes - a real "other Christ" if there ever was one.

Somehow I've been on a China kick, perhaps inspired by the tiny hopes that have arisen of the Church getting some small re-opening there. Am reading the life of Bishop Galvin, co-founder of the Columban Frs - another one of God's noblemen. Those missionaries are certainly a miraculously selfless crowd. Their hardships, sicknesses, failures, etc. make you think we have no idea what penance is - and all with the most glorious faith and sense of humor. Like St. Thérese (stumbling along behind her) I am drawn more and more to see them in the center of our own vocation.

And, did you know that our little habit of putting -o on things is very Irish? Bishop Galvin's brother was always called Seano - and the Sisters (here) tell of a dear Irish lady who used to come to the Monastery. When asked how many children she had, she could never remember, so she would list them all on her fingers, ending with "...Mary and the baby-o." So you see you can't get away from your glorious heritage.☺

I will stop here so as to get this off as soon as possible. As for me, have been

*housecleaning with great gusto since
I've discovered that by opening all the
windows where I am I can accomplish
quite a bit (also this obviously insures
working in solitude!)* ☺

*I thought The Prayer for the 3rd
World by Sr. Ruth J. was most excellent.
How good is this sentence: "when it
comes to the sub-culture of the poor, help
us please, to discover the qualities which
led You to choose it above all others."*

Sr. Christine to Lorraine Stewart
A Boston friend and artist whose husband, Sid, was very ill. Sr. Christine
shares lighter aspects of convent life. Frances Nevins and Lorraine met on
retreat at the Boston Cenacle in 1955.

*Carmel
May 27, 1973*

*Many thanks for your good letter of
some time ago, and your lovely cheerful
Easter card. I think you are much better
at getting your thoughts on paper than I
am, and your letters really convey you
- which is a real gift and a joy for the
receiver.*

*I'm not sure what your situation is
right now re: Sid [Lorraine's husband],
etc. but I hope you are continuing to find
that deep inner peace whatever comes
along. This, too, is a wonderful gift
from God, isn't it - as well as the fruit
of our persevering efforts to accept and
love His will. I find, as St. Thérèse says,
that so much lies in confidence (even in
the little ups and downs of convent life,
which are mostly quite minor but can be
trying!) that God has everything in His
hands and will make "all things work
together for good." I've been reading a
book called <u>Growth in the Holy Spirit</u> by
Bishop Gerard Huyghe (glad I don't have
to pronounce it!) which I like very much.
He shows how the Holy Spirit leads each*

of us through different experiences and trials, etc. to growth in faith and hope, in the same pattern that He led Abraham, Mary and the Apostles - as he says, "For our faith grows constantly, during the whole course of our lives, under the guidance of the Holy Spirit, by ways which follow the paths traced for us in holy scripture." He has the gift of writing so simply that a child could understand it, and yet there is great depth, I think.

I've had no real experience with the charismatic renewal movement but I've read that in many cases it's had wonderful results in people's lives (more than just passing emotion) which is what counts, I guess - "By their fruits ye shall know them." I suppose that, as with most everything, there is an authentic core to the movement, something which really comes from God, and then there are various other aspects which come more from the human qualities (and maybe imperfections) of various people who are involved in it. I think what you say is the main thing - "Time will tell."

Our Duke continues to be a treasure - he is just as you said - "loyal and forgiving" and also quite comical in his distinctive ways. Jumps right up in the air when he barks, sleeps on top of his doghouse, kisses you when you spank him (did I tell you?), lies with back legs stretched out behind like a bear rug - etc., etc. Right now we are having a little trouble as it is the nesting season and he goes wild at seeing so many birds around - Thinks he has to hunt them all down so is running around barking up trees, etc. He was a house dog and I suppose his outdoor environment and all the wildlife is like a new world to him. But he keeps me going, trying to teach him the Carmelite rule of silence!

I expect to be in Retreat during the Novena of Pentecost. This is when we thank God for Duke as he is a wonderful *guard for the hermitages - lies peacefully outside, perfectly contented to think he is doing a job. (And he is - last fall just before he came, one of our teen-age bandits opened the door and was quite surprised to find me inside - so he asked me if we had any work for him!)*

I must go and houseclean a cell - we switch each year and I am in charge of this operation, getting the Srs. moved, etc. I do seem to love these humble little tasks which go so well with the inner life - and after 12 1/2 yrs. still feel I can't even thank God enough for my vocation.

I keep you very deep in my prayers and will especially during Retreat - thanking the Holy Spirit, too, for uniting us so firmly that I feel time or distance can never touch it.

Sr. Christine to Lorraine Stewart

Lorraine's husband has died. Sr. Christine's beautiful statement, "I am never remote in heart" is her comforting response to the news. She mentions her sense of isolation at holiday time. Recommends a special book by Caryll Houselander.

Carmel
December 27, 1977

Wherever you may be, I wish you a Christmas full of joy and peace. How I miss your letters - and yet I can understand how it must be difficult to write. Sometimes it seems to me I have to face the fact that my vocation has made me seem rather remote to those I love (not just you, but others too). This, too, I can understand - But please believe that I am never remote in heart - no distance, grilles, cloistered life, etc. can ever change that. Rather, it is just the opposite, though I think I am not very good at communicating it!

We have 2 new novices, very buoyant

and full of life - Sr. Paul and Sr. Thérèse.
How good it is to have young people
around! For quite a while we didn't.
The years have gone by unbelievably fast
(do you find it so?) and yet inside I don't
feel any older, and am somehow more
at home with the young ones. (Maybe
second childhood?)

Do you like Caryll Houselander? I
am reading a book of hers called The
Comforting of Christ*. There seems to*
be a kind of strong quiet light for me in
everything she writes. What a beautiful
vision and sense of the Mystical Body
she had. Sometimes, especially around
holidays, I have a sort of sense of
isolation, and then I realize it's really
an illusion because we really are one in
Him, more joined to one another than we
can ever realize - and it will last forever.
May he make us feel the joy of it this
Christmas.

Carmel
1979-1980

Sr. Christine to Annamarie Pluhar
Sr. Christine's godchild is the daughter of Anna Pluhar, a friend from
Connecticut College. Sr. Christine sent a poem by Chardin to Annamarie.
On the top of the page on which the poem was written, Sr. Christine wrote:
"I do not think you are impatient, but I like the overall message - especially
the last part".

Patient Trust in Ourselves and in the Slow Work of God
by Pierre Teilhard de Chardin, S.J.

Above all, trust in the slow work of God,
We are, quite naturally, impatient in everything to reach
the end without delay.
We should like to skip the intermediate stages.
We are impatient of being on the way to something
unknown, something new,

And yet it is the law of all progress that it is made by
  passing through some stages of instability --
And that it may take a very long time.

And so I think it is with you.
Your ideas mature gradually - let them grow, let them
  shape themselves, without undue haste.
Don't try to force them on, as though you could be today
  what time (that is to say, grace and circumstances
  acting on your own good will) will make you
  tomorrow.

Only God could say what this new spirit gradually
  forming within you will be.
Give our Lord the benefit of believing that his hand is
  leading you, and accept the anxiety of feeling yourself
  in suspense and incomplete.

In 2009, Annamarie wrote to me:

> *"Aunt Franny (as I called her most of*
> *the time) sent this to me sometime during*
> *my first year at the Episcopal Divinity*
> *School (1979-1980). The multiple push-*
> *pin holes are testimony to the many*
> *bulletin boards it has been on over the*
> *last thirty years. It has yellowed with age*
> *but the words are timeless. The last line,*
> *'...accept the anxiety of feeling yourself*
> *in suspense and incomplete' makes good*
> *what feels bad. This poem, along with the*
> *implied affirmation that Sister Christine*
> *writes at the top, 'I do not think you are*
> *impatient' is a treasure from her and has*
> *made a difference in my life."*

Sr. Christine to Joy Anderson

A warm, gentle letter following the death of Joy's father. While at Connecticut College, Frances Nevins visited Joy's parents, Reg and Polly, several times. With death coming very soon for herself, Sr. Christine's comments about a reunion in Heaven are especially poignant.

Carmel
October 25, 1980

How my heart goes out to you - a sudden death is such a jolt, as I know from experience both with my Uncle Cal and here - and can only imagine what it must be like when it is someone as dear as your dad. From this distance, I can see how in one way it was a mercy since he was spared more extreme sickness and helplessness, and more loneliness for Polly [Joy's mother] - but being in the midst of it all, and having found him yourself, is something else. How I pray that time and God's help will smooth away the sorrow as much as possible, and soon. I was touched to think of your boys grieving so much because it's such a beautiful sign of their love for him, yet I ache for them. "The Lord is close to the broken-hearted" keeps coming to my mind, and I ask Him to make it very real in all your lives. Thank God you have each other!

About the premonition, I guess it's yes and no. I had no idea what was going to happen the next day, and never dreamed Reg [Joy's father] was close to death, but I felt moved to write what I did. As for the little card, I asked myself (rather, I asked the Lord) if it would be a little too "lugubrious" to send, and got a sense that no, it would be right. So off it went. I'm glad if my letter was some help - to me it was another sign that all things do work together for good, as I had hoped and planned to write you sooner but just couldn't get the free space of time I needed, and had been feeling regretful and frustrated about it. But God has His own time-table, as He showed this time!

I feel very close to you all, and to dear Polly, too - I wonder if it will sink in eventually - perhaps not. (We have a dear Sister who I think must be somewhat the same mentally - what a mystery.) I've been remembering the happy days

-112-

*we had together, and how much I owe to
your family - you said it so well: "He
and mother were remarkable the way
they reached out to people." (And yes,
you do, too!) Besides my Mil, your family
were the ones most of all, in my younger
days, who showed me what real goodness
was, and how I appreciated it! I am truly
looking forward to a reunion of all of us
in heaven when I can tell them so myself.*

*Dear Reg. I'm sure he's closer to us
now than we can realize. I believe the
bond between parents and children never
ends, but only grows stronger, and they
love us even more now that they are with
God. What you said about a parents'
love being unconditional was beautiful,
and made me think what a wonderful
image a real father is of our Father in
heaven. Some people (including myself)
take a long time to realize what God
is like because of the lack of a strong
experience of that unconditional love in
childhood. I don't think I knew what I
was missing as far as family goes when
I was young, and I guess it was a mercy.*

*I must stop because I want you to
have this soon. My love and prayers are
there with you. I'd love a copy of Reg's
service - God bless all of your dear ones
- a verse I love from the letter of Peter
keeps coming to mind. "Cast your care
on him, for he cares for you." I do, too!*

Sr. Christine to Theresa Lagoy (Sr. Clare Joseph, O.C.D.)
Less than two weeks before she was stricken, Sr. Christine writes to her friend
who transferred to the Barre, VT Carmel in 1975. It is a companionable
letter between friends who know Carmelite life very well. Sr. Christine writes
about what she expects of friendship in Heaven.

*Carmel
November 23, 1980*

*This space of time to at least begin
a letter to you is like a feast day gift to*

-113-

me. It seems I have been waiting for it so long. At present I am helping Sr. M. with some work she does for a missionary in Peru, (she receives all his offerings and takes care of sending them to him). The financial part is quite beyond me but my job is to try to "cadge out" the letters from his Italian benefactors! This also is beyond me since I never studied Italian, but the Spirit helps, sometimes quite surprisingly. You will wonder how we got into this and I'm not really sure, but he's a unique person - has visited us twice, speaks only Italian and Spanish so Sr. Maria interprets. There's a quite unusual sort of integrity, wholeness, total focus on God (I can't find the word) about him - in fact, I think he is a saint. If I can get a hold of one of his newsletters, I'll send it sometime. He's a priest-doctor among the poorest Indians in Peru. Fr. Giovanni Salerno, O.S.A.

That was a long introduction just to explain where my writing time has gone! Actually, I'm glad for the job as it helps build community.

Mother D. [deceased Prioress] is helping in so many little ways - I ask her especially for the things I need to help make my life of solitude more liveable - more suited to continual prayer - and she answers unfailingly. She used to like to provide me with whatever she could, considering the opposition, and now she is much freer! How I thank Him for this sharing between heaven and earth, which I become more aware of as the years go by. I loved your own thought about how "every relationship, bond, covenant in our life is so precious and in some way eternal" - I think what I look forward to in heaven most of all is the great unity you used to speak of, and which has become so real to me now. It's no wonder the Lord made it the object of His last, beautiful prayer. One with God and with each other - all the depth of His presence which we find here only in solitude, combined with the fullest possible communication with each other. It takes my breath away!

It interested me that you feel the bonds with Schenectady "as real as blood ties in a family" - I have felt that it is that way but never could make the comparison with assurance because I never knew the family ties. (What an enormous lack - but God supplies in His own way.) I saw a card the other day (from Reno Carmel, I think) with a quote from T.S. Eliot on the front: "Love is most nearly itself when here and now cease to matter." Nice, don't you think?

I was so happy to hear that your near-sightedness has arrested and even improved a bit. How beautifully He provides for every need. I, too, have a physical grace to thank Him for, as that lumpy affair behind my knee has disappeared. I had asked Mother D. to see to it so I thank her, too. Surgery would have been a particular nuisance combined with my other condition, and would have made me dependent on others, so once again He answered the need and protected my life of solitude.

You probably know (?) it has been decided to give up the idea of moving and settle ourselves here. (Mother D. again, I'm sure, as everything fell into place soon after she died, and I marvel at the contentment of those who were most anxious to move.) Having a sense of stability (as much as one can have in this unstable world!) makes a big difference, though I'm sure the whole experience of living "up in the air" for some years has deepened my trust in Him, and surely that is what counts most of all.

I'm praying for your cousin Susan - what a beautiful grace to really grasp the sense of being a 'child of God' in depth. This, too, has become more real to me lately - the wonder of it, which can

be overlooked because the phrase is so
familiar. Special union of prayer during
the beautiful season of Advent - the
season of our vocation, I always think.
  In the unity and love and peace of the
Holy Spirit. Christine

Sr. Christine summarizes her ministry of friendship in a retreat note dated 6/22/1978:

> Jesus – we have given up all opportunity to help others in an outward way, and yet You have often let me speak a word of encouragement and consolation, which is the ministry I love most of all. These words come out of the depths of the life I live with You.

NOTES
9: Friendships, Part One: A Sample of Letters 1960-1980
48. See Ref. 35, . 65.

-116-

Nuns at Prayer:
Schenectady Carmel

10

Friendships, Part Two: Death of a Prioress

Unlike Christine's letters to friends, retreat notes and on-going journal entries had a less confident quality in the early days. Toward the end of her life, however, the immanence of her letters was fully present in her journals. She wrote with perfect boldness, using her phrase, about what was happening to her and around her until a few hours before her unexpected death. Most importantly, she finds words that the rest of us can understand to explain the inexplicable. She tells us what her relationship with God was and why she struggled so hard to protect the conditions that affected this relationship. As with Teresa, Sr. Christine was all about friendship with God, not fear of God. She was single-mindedly occupied with living the demands and joys of this friendship, and extending it to others as much as possible. With God, she was in a dynamic relationship, never static and sometimes deeply troubling.

Her journals for the last year and a half before she died in 1980 shine a laser beam on her soul. The journals for the period 6/1/79-12/4/80 are of such depth and quantity the reader will understand clearly what is going on between God and Sr. Christine.

Among several illustrative relationships in that time period, three stand out in importance to her as judged by the amount of detail and passion she invests in each one. In precise, transparent and very moving words she describes her experience at the bedside of a dying Prioress; her intense struggle to save the life of a man about to be electrocuted on death row; and her deep emotion and turmoil at the prospect of losing Fr. Henry Tansey, her friend and Confessor.

Almost a year after Sr. Christine died, Sister Mary of Jesus and St. Joseph, O. Carm. agreed to an interview that included references to Mother Dolorosa who served as Prioress and Mistress of Novices for both herself and Sr. Christine. Sr. Mary had been a member of the Schenectady Carmel from 9/15/1949 to 10/23/1976. Fully professed, she held offices as Sub-Prioress and Mistress of Novices, and served as Infirmarian. Leaving that Carmel she would later found a new community of Carmelites. Her comments provide some background for Sr. Christine's very moving, intimate observations about what transpired at Mother Dolorosa's bedside:

"Sr. Christine had been there all night with Mother Dolorosa when she died. And to think that Christine would be the next one to go. That was beautiful. When I was the infirmarian, I took care of Mother Dolorosa when she had a mastectomy until my Novice took over when I left. Mother Dolorosa and I were very close, too. We were close in the sense that we both could express what we thought and come to a totally different place. But, we could talk it out so there was no tension. It was sorrow, but it was truth. Even after I left, I was always close to Mother Dolorosa. Mother was about 4'6". Very tiny. I don't think Mother went beyond the 6th or 7th grade. She was trained in two different languages in Canada. She had a mind and spirit that was indomitable. And her mind was very keen. And wisdom, deep wisdom, and common sense - the bond between two feet on the ground. Mother was deeply compassionate and very quiet. She was a born leader. But for her to be Prioress was a crucifixion. She hated being in office. But she took it as the will of God and put all her love and wisdom into it. It was always very hard for her to be in Office. How would I say? In the beginning Mother would seem very strict. She certainly had her expectations. I think maybe Sr. Christine and I had a similar relationship with Mother Dolorosa. Open, totally trusting. She would tell you just what she thought. Taking care of her in the infirmary was absolutely amazing. She had cancer, so she got a book. She read up on cancer. It had metastasized to her bone. That was the beginning of the end." [49, 50]

Sr. Christine records her sense of Mother Dolorosa's dying by inches and her own response of tender love and caring. The journal entries here and elsewhere are reported verbatim as Sr. Christine wrote them.

7/18/1980 Journal Entry

Jesus - How can I ever thank You for last night's grace? I cannot doubt now that You have given me a special gift of being close to the dying. How I have longed and longed to be, like Mary, a "comforter of the afflicted" and You have let me be so several times through correspondence - but this time it was in person. Mother D's waking out of her coma when I was watching with her was like a little miracle. You gave her a lucidity, an awareness that she has not had for weeks (months) and we prayed and sang together like two children. This was the beginning of the child-like intimacy of heaven. Her response to my words and prayers confirmed beyond question the inspirations You have been giving me. Her heart needs to expand in expectation and hope and welcome. The beautiful images of heaven and the entrance into heaven from the Prayers for the Dying gave her comfort and joy, and echoed in the depths of her being - this was the right word, Your word for her now. How did I know? By listening to You, and then listening to her. To listen to the sick and dying takes such silence of the self, such loving openness of heart. You are just beginning to train me in it, but I long to learn this science more and more. Not from books, but from Your Spirit. I have never seen so clearly that we have nothing to give except what You put in our hands. Why did you let me be the one to bring her comfort last night? Because I knew my poverty and asked Your help and John Paul [I]. Many words and questions try her patience now; I "hear" that so clearly. Lord, help the Sisters, help us all, to sense her needs, to silence ourselves, so that we can hear and respond.

This is what Fr. Henry was talking about in his homily the other morning - listening to God in other people. With the sick and dying it is specially important - and specially delicate. The real person is the spiritual person - the one who thinks and prays and worries and hopes. This person's needs must be seen to before any other.

Jesus - fill her with peace and comfort and hope now til the end. The peaceful joy of expecting You.

Jesus - I will always treasure the memory of last night. Mother was her very best and sweetest, most appealing self...the self we have only glimpsed from time to time in the midst of the pressures and burdens of this life. This was her real self, her new being as a child of God. The person we will know and delight in, in heaven. O sweet familiarity of our homeland - last night we began it.

In spite of her physical weakness, she was fully alive, totally present to me and very delicately responsive to everything I said. This was a little miracle, totally unhoped for - a gift from You and John Paul [I]. I had put in his hands my desire to be a comfort and a help and asked him to arrange it all according to Your will. Being in touch with her so closely like that has intensified my prayer - given it confidence and a new urgency.

Spirit of Love - Burn sweetly in her heart til she is totally pure, totally ready for Jesus.

7/19/1980 Journal Entry

"It was for no reason but His own compassion that He saved us...renewing us with the Holy Spirit...to become heirs looking forward to inheriting eternal life." (Titus 3:5,7)

Jesus - I claim your compassion today. Have pity on this little heir who looks forward to Your coming with all her heart. Lord, finish Your work; "make new in her whatever has been damaged by earthly weakness or profaned by the deceit of the devil". "Give joy O Lord, to her soul by the sight of You". Jesus - I offer her to You incessantly on the paten of my heart. We appeal, she and I, to Your love and mercy, to Your own desire to possess Your little bride completely. Lord, how can You resist such love and longing?

"O Lord, have pity on us, for You we wait..."

"Come Lord, do not delay."

"Not because of merits, not because of patience or years of suffering but for no reason but Your own compassion."

Yes, my Jesus – with all my heart I unite myself to her. This is what You are asking me unmistakably these days, drawing my thoughts back to it if they stray – it is as if we were as one, waiting for You. I cannot share her physical pain, but the tedium, the oppressiveness, the sense that You are never coming – and so the work of faith, hoping against hope, or rather, against feeling. St. Paul speaks of "your work of faith and labor of love and steadfastness of hope in our Lord Jesus Christ." (I Thess. 1:3) These words have always puzzled me a little but now I am seeing this "work and labor" lived out before my eyes. "Pray I will be faithful to the end" she said to me over and over – what can that mean in her condition but this inner labor to keep oneself in the right dispositions through this time of severe trial. Jesus – she is not alone, for I am laboring with her, happy to give this invisible help which only the Father who sees in secret is aware of. My prayer for her is a "we" prayer, in all sincerity. "O Lord, have pity on us, for You we wait."

7/20/1980 Morning Journal Entry

Lord, this work of faith and labor of love etc. is a work of prayer – it is the climax of her Carmelite life of prayer. "Because his soul had labored, he shall see a long-lived seed." (Is. 53) I can share this labor, like Moses' helpers holding up his arms when he was weary. Wasn't this above all the way Mary shared in the work of our Redemption? Her soul, too, labored – it was a "work of faith" to hold fast to the goodness of God, His love and promises, as she stood before the Cross and watched You suffering.

I can share in Mother D's labor, too by the humble work of offering You the heat these days – not simply bearing but offering. Everything, no matter how small, with the most perfect dispositions – like the poor widow who "put all she had".

7/20/1980 Evening Journal Entry

"Love is strong as death."

Jesus – Your Spirit forges such strong family bonds that not to be present when she is dying seems a kind of violation of what is sacred. Here above all, formalism should give way to what is personal – but if this lesson has not been learned or practiced in normal circumstances, I cannot expect it to happen tonight. Jesus – put me where I can help her the most. I will offer my little aloneness that she may somehow not feel alone at this supreme moment. Your plan is perfect – I will embrace it, and "give thanks in all circumstances."

7/21/1980 Morning Journal Entry

Jesus – this death resembles Your Passion in more ways than one. Last week's extreme thirst; the sense that You do not respond to her call; ("My God, why have You forsaken me?"); disillusionment in someone who had been trusted through the years. All of these "wounds" will shine gloriously in heaven. "Those who He knew, knew He also was predestined to be conformed to the image of His Son." (Rom. 8:29) Not being able to turn was perhaps her greatest physical suffering – she spoke of it with a deep quiet desperation. Yet when I told her she was "nailed beside You" she said, "Oh, I'm glad." And she thanked You for prolonging her life so she could suffer for the 3 priests who are tempted to leave the priesthood.

Jesus – this sense of isolation and

separation is all I have to give for her, so let me offer it willingly, consciously, wholeheartedly. Who knows if she isn't experiencing the same thing, imprisoned in that little body? I do not know how it is with her, and this distresses me – but she does not know either, how long this thread of life will hold, and she is longing to be free.

Sweet Mother – did you also wonder how the Father could let Jesus suffer so intensely? Although I know all the reasons, in the end, this has to be accepted in sheer faith: "Though He slay me, yet will I trust Him." Lord, though You leave her here in this condition indefinitely, yet will I trust You, with all my heart." Receive this act of faith as my offering for her.

Lord, if I cannot be beside her in body, I will be there in spirit, and nothing can prevent me from this, nothing but my own weakness, my vagueness, and wandering thoughts.

This is a new way of imitating Mary. Her place was beside the cross steadfast in faith (faith in God's goodness) to the end. This service of mine parallels Mother D's urgent plea for prayers that she be "faithful to the end". It is my poor and humble way of being united with her.

7/21/1980 Evening Journal Entry

Jesus – our Love – do not tarry, this death is so hard, so hard, but Your grace is stronger, and she will overcome. This holiness and sweetness of soul will shine forth "like the sun" when Your moment comes, and that is what You are preparing during these trying hours. Why so much, Lord? That is Your secret, and as St. Teresa says, "it's all redemptive" – at the moment, focused on those 3 priests who are wavering.

Jesus – thank you for arranging a little conversation for me with Sr. T. today. It took away the sense of being out of touch, and gave me a deeper peace. Every way the family can be united at this point is important.

7/21/1980 Night Journal Entry

Lord, what is this sense of expectation and joy I have tonight? Are you coming? Jesus – we don't deserve it – a thousand years of suffering could not deserve it. But come, out of pure mercy, because of Your love and desire, and the desire of Your little bride for You.

"Come to meet her, Angels of God, receiving her soul, offering it in the sight of the Most High."

Lord, what solemn words are these, piercingly beautiful. We too, offer You the soul of our sister, whom we have loved imperfectly but truly – now make our love and unity complete.

7/22/1980 Morning Journal Entry

"Behold all things are now in readiness." This antiphon from Christmas Eve expresses the feeling You have given to me today. Since last evening I have the sense that the struggle is over, and a great peace....Fr. Henry was here and prayed that You would shine Your face on her today. After Communion, Your Spirit prayed His prayer of "Come" more strongly than ever before. Jesus – we await You – this silent, steady desire will conquer You at last.

7/23/1980 Morning Journal Entry

Feast of the Mother of Divine Grace

Mother D went peacefully to the Lord about 2:30 A.M. with all of us praying and singing hymns around her bed.

Sweet Mother – You kept your promise. Mother believed that You told her You would take her to heaven on your feast – only You meant not Mt. Carmel but its Octave day. This beautiful feast of Mater Gratiae [Mother of Grace]. We could make no mistake that it was You; after more than ½ an hour of praying, with no change in her condition, as soon as I said, "Mother of Divine Grace, pray for her and help her", the agony ceased immediately – she breathed a few more times and slipped away so quietly we could not tell the exact moment....

Jesus – is there anything more You could have done for us that You did not do? This death was an outward sign, a confirming seal on everything that has been passing within me (and within Mother D) for the past 2½ weeks. For those who have eyes to see, it was a vindication of her own prophetic words, and for me, inwardly, of all the lights and inspirations that have filled my prayer during these days. "Come, Lord Jesus" – how glad and grateful I am to have been used as a vessel of this prayer, this "unspeakable longing" of the Spirit.

Lord, You wove me into her final days in a way that was humbling and awesome. She had extraordinary, unexplainable confidence in my prayers, and at the end it was, in a way, at my word that You consummated the sacrifice. How could this be? Only because You had put me in tune with Your plan for her, and at certain moments You chose to use me very plainly as Your instrument.

Jesus – this experience is bringing me to a deeper conviction of the power of Your prayer in me. Do I ever believe in it enough? I must learn to be more and more perfectly Your instrument, and this alone – ready to pick up or put down whenever You wish, neither reluctant nor over-eager to be used by You.

Lord, what a strong Marian character there was to this death. Piecing it together with the Sisters, we realized that after the invocation to the Mother of Grace, which was the turning point, we had said, "Holy Mary, Mother of God, pray for us sinners now and at the hour of our death" three times, and then sung the Salve Regina – during which she breathed her last, clearly conscious to the end. Salve Regina – the Marian hymn of Carmel.

During the past week, I had often been impressed by the thought that the Salve was a beautiful prayer for the dying: "After this our exile show unto us the blessed fruit of your womb, Jesus." And this morning's Gospel (Cana) ended with "…and Jesus let His glory be seen." Once again, Lord, You did it at Your Mother's request.

7/24/1980 Morning Journal Entry (after Father Henry's Mass)

My little sister in heaven, you have not come to me as mother but as sister, and beyond that I do not even know what to call you. You are no longer Dolorosa – rather the happiness you let me glimpse is so overwhelming that my soul cannot begin to contain it – a flood of happiness, beyond my reach, yet over-shadowing me and all around me. When I said to you, "How do you stand it?", it came to me immediately that the depth of your suffering had made it possible. "Sorrow with His pick mines the heart: He is carving out deeper places for Joy to dwell in." This old saying which is true even on earth, gives me the logic, the reason-why. My sister, how can you look at poor Christine when you are so absorbed in happiness? You do not explain it, but only send another flood of this joy into my soul, to assure me that it's true. My heart cannot contain the love I have for you – this flame of love that springs from the contact of our spirits. How will I keep back these tears in public? Little one, I am supposed to be saying the Office of the Dead for you. How can I pray Miserere when your beatitude fills me to the brim?

"Rejoice in the measure that you share Christ's sufferings; when His glory is revealed, you will rejoice exultantly." (1 Pet. 4:13-14)

Lord, another of Your words has come clear to me as never before – "in the measure". Not simply because the abundance of suffering earns a great reward but because it gives us the very capacity to receive a deeper joy – this is why You always give the Cross to Your best friends. It is not only that they may keep You company on it, but much more, that they may share more closely and intimately in Your heavenly joy. Until this morning, this idea was unreal, distant, abstract. Now the visit of my little sister has placed it before the eyes of my heart. She does indeed "rejoice exultantly" – with a joy so glorious that it cannot be described". (1 Pet. 1:8)

It's true I have no standard of comparison but each of my heavenly visitors, those just released from earth, has shown me something special about themselves – a special quality of their new experience. With Mother Magdalen it was an overflowing love for us on earth; with Pope John Paul [I], the joy of his new freedom, the freedom to be child-like for the first time; with Pope John [XXIII], his universal fatherhood now brought to perfection. "Star differs from star in glory." Not only in degree, but in kind. "There is one glory of the sun, another of the moon," etc. Lord, are You saying to me by these experiences that our heaven is tailor-made to fit the uniqueness of our life on earth? The happiness of heaven will have quite a special taste for one who has been Dolorosa in so many ways in this life.

Jesus – I am worn out with the joy of today. It seems as if You have overwhelmed me, indeed all of us, with consolations in honor of our little Mother's entrance into heaven. Fr. H's Mass and homily in the AM; the Bishop's in the PM, the visit of my little sister and my vision of her happiness; the sense of her presence and responsiveness off and on all day; the peace and joy and gratitude that fills the Community and overflows at Recreation. The beautiful pattern of her death, the way You arranged every detail was like a page from the lives of the Saints of the Order, matching or surpassing anything I have read. The words of St. Teresa keep coming to my mind: "O who will give me a voice to proclaim to the ends of the earth how You are faithful to Your friends."

7/25/1980 Morning Journal Entry

Jesus – the touch of God is on this little body. She is growing more and more beautiful – this noon, in just the daylight, she looked distinctly like a young girl. I am sure that this is not imagination – I have seen this happen before, with those of our Sisters who were really close to You, but never so clearly as this. Lord, I think there was more of a holiness here than even we who lived with her knew. Holiness is a quality of heart, often hidden under ordinariness, as in Mary. Here was a soul who sought nothing but the truth – simply, relentlessly. A temperament which was by nature neither spontaneous nor joyful but of a deep warmth, whose spirit had blossomed into motherhood, generous, loving, loyal. A motherhood that was absolutely selfless, giving security, freedom and deep affirmation to those in her care.

"Veni, sponsa Christi, accipe coronam, quam tibi Dominus praeparavit in aeternam." [Come, spouse of Christ, receive the crown, which the Lord has prepared for you for all eternity".]

Lord, these words are very solemn as I watch this little one turn into a sweet young bride of Christ before my eyes. The image of what I saw today has been before me all afternoon. Aren't You trying to tell us that You mean what You say? Even outwardly, she is becoming a bride fit for the King.

My little one, what a joy it is just to kneel beside you. Your peace radiates into me and I cannot even tell you the thousand things that I could say. Our communion is silent, peaceful, contemplative – full of quiet joy.

7/26/1980 Morning Journal Entry - before Mother's funeral

Jesus – what was it that I saw in her face last night? All our human words are too flat and empty to begin to describe it. Peace – but solemn, majestic and triumphant; a peace such as I have never seen except in the faces of Mother Magdalen and Sr. Angela as they lay on the bier. Lord, is what I see objective, physical, or is it Your gift to me? I think it is there for all who have eyes to see, but one must look, with recollection, love, and openness. For me it is a clear and unmistakable sign of their heavenly happiness, and You assured me that all 3 of these sisters were in heaven. Others have looked to me quite ordinary, and for them I had no other assurance.

7/27/1980 Morning Journal Entry

Little one, our conversation in the Spirit is delightful. I ask you questions inspired by Him and you reply with an outpouring of consolation, love, and joy; promising not to leave me but to be with me at the hour of death, to help me grow in faith, etc. Truly you were "sown in weakness but raised in glory" and this transformation of your being and of our relationship is more astonishing than any fairy tale. It is the beautiful surprise that God is waiting to reveal to each one of us and for me He has opened the curtain a bit, not once but many times. "Jesus, why such goodness to Your poor one?" I will never understand it, til I am there myself. It is simply the mystery of Your choice of "the weak things of this world", those who are of no account, etc. Mother D sensed this mysterious predilection of Yours for me, she spoke of it often. She knew well my nothingness and helplessness, and saw clearly that my secret was "clinging to God all the time", as she put it years ago. She knew me better than I realized, even in those days – with that knowledge which is Your special gift to Superiors who have love and a pure intention. Lord, this too is something beautiful to thank You for. And another consolation, since her perfect knowledge of me now is simply the flowering of what began in our Novitiate, nearly 20 years ago.

7/28/1980 Evening Journal Entry

"I have fought the good fight, I have finished the race, I have kept the faith." (II Tim 4:7)

Jesus – When we sang "Holy God We Praise Thy Name" after Mother's death, it was like the burst of applause for an athlete as he crosses the finish line after a long and difficult race. The sporting imagery of St. Paul never meant anything to me before, but now it comes to me spontaneously as the only way of explaining the experience of that moment. That hymn came from us spontaneously as an acclamation, an outburst of honor and thanks and praise to You and to Your little servant, "faithful to the end", as she so longed to be.

"All there is to come now is the crown of righteousness reserved for me...." (-4:8)

Mother knew that she had absolutely no fear of Purgatory, no expectation of anything but total happiness. It is indeed a grace to have all one's Purgatory on earth. This grace Your Spirit asked for me many years ago, during 3 days I spent in Assisi, when I hardly understood what His prayer meant. "Perfect love casts out fear." It must indeed be possible then to have "perfect love on earth, as You told me Pope John [XXIII] had. (He went straight to heaven because he had perfect love – this You said to me.) And Mother must have had it too. St. Paul says the crown will be given to "all those who have longed for His appearing." There is a depth of meaning here which I never suspected before. Indeed, she longed for Your appearing, and it must have been the very sign of her readiness for the crown. You even used my own words to encourage this longing in her, and to fan its flame. Never before have I been so caught up in the deepest mystery of our human existence. The passage from this life to the next, the singing of "Holy God We Praise Thy Name", was the most charismatic moment I ever experienced.

7/29/1980 Journal Entry

Jesus – teach me to thank You. I want to send up a constant stream of thanksgiving – days and weeks of petition for Mother D should be counter-balanced by this thanksgiving for her beautiful death, for her overwhelming happiness, for all the signs and graces surrounding her departure. "Pray for us now and at the happy hour of our death" was her own version of The Hail Mary during the last days. How much did she know, by revelation or by intuition? We cannot tell but it is clear that You prepared her soul and molded her dispositions to expect and welcome You. Here was no "sudden and unprovided death" but a death lovingly awaited and planned for, like the birth of a child. And indeed, there was a startling similarity between this death and a birth. Her agony reminded me forcibly of the labor of childbirth. Our reaction at its ending was joy and exultation – joy that this everlasting child is now born into the world of heaven.

7/30/1980 Journal Entry

My little one – You do not want me to call you "Mother" now and yet, what a mother you were. It was so good to live in this atmosphere which never tried to force me into a mold, which wanted only that I be my best and truest self. From you, for the first time, I learned to appreciate what motherhood really is. You were never afraid to point out my faults – rather you knew this was a deep part of your service of love, to help me grow into the person God wanted me to be. My little sister, in your humility He gave you great light, great insight which helped reveal me to myself. This is the gift I ask of you now, in our new life together: be with Mary, the mother of my perfection. Show me how Jesus wants me to grow.

You were mother too, in the beautiful way you always provided for my real needs – the silence and solitude which you somehow knew were as vital to me as the air I breathe. And in protecting and defending me against the opinions and attitudes of others who would have taken these things away. Be then, my little advocate now when you see the dangers threatening.

Sr. Christine's description of care for her dying Prioress has two audiences; first, those of us who are present with the dying and need a reminder to listen to the sick. She says that the dying take such silence of the self, such loving openness of the heart...We need to silence ourselves so that we can hear and respond. Formalism should give way to what is personal. The second audience includes persons particularly attuned to the spiritual connectors that mediate between Heaven and Earth, God and people at the time of death and dying. Recall that Sr. Christine says that an unforgettable moment came when, at 2:30 A.M. on the sixth day, with the Sisters gathered around the bedside, she addressed the Blessed Mother: "Mother of Divine Grace, pray for her, and help her. The agony ceased immediately-she breathed a few more times and slipped away so quietly we could not tell the exact moment."

St. Teresa was no stranger to the direct involvement of God in human affairs. "Oh, who will give me a voice to proclaim to the ends of the earth how You are faithful to your friends." Once again, centuries later Sr. Christine clearly shows us how a human voice is enlisted to proclaim God's faithfulness and what messages will be made known.

NOTES

10: Friendships, Part Two: Death of a Prioress

49.   See Ref. 36.

50.   See Ref. 36.

Cemetery of the Holy Cross - Rotterdam, NY

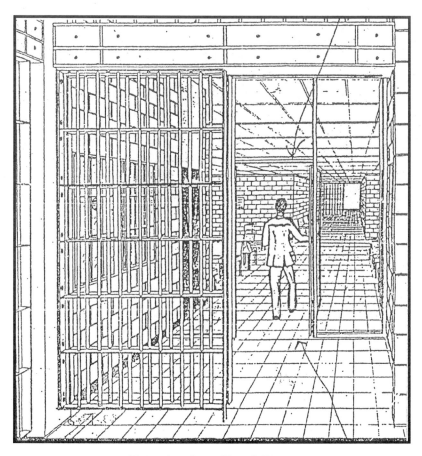

Drawing from Death Row
by Jack Potts
March 1980

11

Friendships, Part Three: Saving a Life on Death Row: The Mantle of Prayer

"The death penalty is the practice of slowly bringing a fully conscious human being face-to-face with his or her own extinction and then killing the person". [51]

Introduction: The Days Before Execution

Sr. Christine read an article in a Catholic periodical about a man scheduled to die in the electric chair. While on death row he had become a Catholic and helped other prisoners to change their life for the better. This description of Jack Potts and his crimes makes him as real to us as he became to her. The Sunday Visitor dated June 1, 1980, reported in detail the actions of two men with improbable names – Jack Potts and his victim, Michael Priest. Potts was sentenced to die on July 1, 1980 at the state prison, Reidsville, Georgia. Reidsville prison was described as "hell on earth" by its Chaplain, Father Raymond Kulwicki.

The background of his story was complex. Potts had a long history of trouble with the law. Teachers found him impossible to handle. He quit school and he and his girlfriend decided to get married. Jack was not yet 16 years old. Not long after his wife was expecting a baby.

With a wife and child to care for, Jack went to work for his contractor father. He thought that since he was on the losing end of everything already, he would "go all the way and be a criminal". He began to steal payroll checks from nearby contractors' offices which he would forge and cash.

When he was caught, Jack was sent to Alto, Georgia, a detention center for youthful offenders. The juveniles there spent most of their time discussing crimes they would commit when they got out. Jack himself decided he would never again work without a gun.

Back at home, young Potts bought not one but three pistols at a pawn shop. A few short weeks into his life of freedom, he robbed liquor stores and grocery stores. After a while, however, he went back to forgeries when police shot a black man during a robbery and reported that the jobs Jack had been responsible for were cleared up.

In 1967, Jack shot a man during a poker game and left, never finding out if he'd killed the man or not. In 1968, he was arrested again and given a stiff sentence for many counts.

Out of prison in the early spring of 1975, Jack was ready to tear things apart. His wife had finally divorced him. His father died of cancer. Jack took up with a woman named Norma Blackwell and he took up drugs. In Florida, Jack and Norma bought $9000 of cocaine. They found out by accident that the cocaine was laced with something deadly. Jack shot and killed the pusher.

Back in Georgia, Jack, Norma, a man named Snyder, and another woman began a ride made dizzy with liquor on May 8, 1975. The four, riding in Snyder's pickup, drove through the night. Jack and Snyder argued. As the tension increased, Jack reached over and shot Snyder several times in the face. Snyder did not die but Potts got out of the stopped truck, ran around and pulled Snyder out on the ground. A farmhouse was nearby and since another car was needed, Potts ran up to the house and told the Gurley family and their son-in-law, Michael Priest, that he'd had an accident and needed help and a car. Priest agreed to go with the others. Down the road, Potts ordered him to pull over and flashed a gun in the young man's face. Priest pleaded with Potts, telling him he had a wife and a baby on the way. Potts didn't listen, led him off to the side of the road and shot him through the head. That's what Potts now says he does not remember. He can't remember either Priest's face or the killing. On death row, Jack Potts has had time to think about his life and the meaning of it. He became a convert to Catholicism. Religious pictures now hang on the walls he keeps in spotless shape. He prays the Rosary and leads others in prayer. Five others on death row have become converts as well.

Potts says that one of his fellow prisoners offered to kill him. "He said he wouldn't let me die in that chair. But I told him that was just like committing suicide and I couldn't do that. I am guilty of murder. I am humbly sorry for the murder. I know how precious human life is now." [52]

Sr. Christine's Reaction to Jack's Turning His Life Around and the Threat of His Impending Execution

The journal entries describing the fate of this prisoner cover seven days. In her own words she describes what she is doing. On Tuesday, July 1, 1980 Jack Potts was scheduled to die. Between Saturday, June 28 and July 4, 1980 Sr. Christine prayed unceasingly. "Everything in me cries out against this outrage".

Saturday, June 28, 1980 Journal Entry

"Do not return evil for evil, but overcome evil with good".

"It's fantastic the number of prisoners he has brought to prayer".

Jesus – open our hearts to the potential that is hidden in these "hardened criminals". Here was a man who, apparently fully sane, murdered people in cold blood for fairly trivial reasons. Yet he has been touched and transformed by Your grace into a magnetic apostle of those around him. Make us realize that our attitude toward these men is so important, even if we never have occasion to express it outwardly.

Jesus – Are they going to snuff out this life which has become such a miracle of grace, such a monument to Your mercy? It is true we cannot directly apply the Gospel precepts in the social order, but can it be right to do the exact opposite? You have triumphed over the evil in his life, turning a murderer into a radiant witness to his new-found Catholic faith. He is a new creature, a brother, a "praise of the glory of your grace". Yet our society clings to its vindictive "justice" through capital punishment and prison conditions which are often worse than death. May the execution of our brother make us ponder well this monstrous contradiction.

Jesus – make Your eternal life so real to his experience, that it will lift him far above the horror of that day. Say to him, when

Tuesday comes, "This day thou shalt be with me in Paradise". Make this death fruitful for Your kingdom, in ways that You know best. We will not abandon him, but surround him with prayer and with love as he comes to You. If You have re-created him, given him new birth – as indeed You have – could we possibly treat him as anything but a most dear brother? Catherine of Siena held the heads of those who were being executed. I can only hold them in my heart, but I will do it with all the love and fervor that I can.

Your love affair with this soul is passionate, intense – You will not fail him when Tuesday comes. He has a "rendezvous with death" but You can make it a rendezvous with glory. By withdrawing his appeal, he has chosen death over continuing imprisonment so that, in his own words, he could die "in the state of grace when best prepared to meet You". This is not totally unlike the martyr's deliberate choice of "death rather than sin". Jesus – reward him even now by the strength and comfort of Your presence as he goes towards death by execution. You, too, were executed as a criminal. Keep him firm in faith and prayer, a steadfast witness to Your mercy to the end.

Saturday, June 28, 1980 Journal Entry

And when this grain of wheat falls into the ground, or is put there by our human "justice", let it bring forth abundant fruit. Strengthen and support the priest who has literally been his salvation and who will walk this last mile with him.

You want me also beside him, though I would gladly turn my thoughts to happier things – so I will stay here til You dismiss me. This whole Recollection Day has been his, as another one a couple of years ago was devoted to another murderer, Richard Herrin.

(I wonder if there could be interpreted

a criticism of the crucifixion or at least, an implication that while God approved the sacrifice He did not bless the means?) "Around me the just shall assemble, when You have been good to me". (Psalm) You are making sure that he has companions and helpers in this dark valley.

Jesus – when the moment comes, give him, like some of Your martyrs, such a strong experience of You that he will not feel the horror of it. "Your mercy is above all Your works." From this moment, let him meet with nothing but mercy – in the priest who ministers to him, in the Scriptures, in his inner experience and in all with whom he comes in contact. Let him be so steeped in the beauty and joy of Your mercy that he will not notice what is being done to him. If you like, I will be horrified instead. I am already horrified by the vindictiveness which takes away a life that is "having a tremendous spiritual impact on those around him". (Fr. Kulwicki)

Sunday, June 29, 1980 Journal Entry

Jesus – I confess I am appalled when I read of this man's former deeds. It is You who have inspired this extravagance of mercy and invisible friendship for him, as You always seem to do when someone's sins have been especially "scarlet". What is the secret of this seeming preference of Yours? The same secret which inspired Your words "there is more joy in Heaven over one sinner doing penance, etc.". You communicate this special joy, this preferential love and protectiveness to me without explaining it. It is enough that You simply put it in my heart.

Perhaps it's because such a one embodies the real human condition - he is what we all would be, if Your grace had not prevented us. He is the person that You died for, and furthermore, he knows it as I do not, for I have never sinned like that. So You can pour out on him the love You had (and will always have) for sinful man when You gave Your life for him. In Jack Potts You meet the naked reality of the humanity You came to save, and You are irresistibly attracted.

Jesus - The horror of this act seems almost infinite, to take life from a man in the very prime of his life, who is full of Your Holy Spirit. But he took life from others. Yes, but he was blinded by our common heritage of sin, by drugs, and by unhealthy living - he could not fully evaluate what he destroyed. "I know the value of human life now", he said not long ago. He is not now the man who did those things, but a new creation - and this new man is being put to death, deliberately, coolly. Some other human being will throw that switch, in full consciousness of what will result. Lord, what are you saying to us by permitting this sacrilege to happen? Holy, holy, holy is Your gift of life - let him who lays hands on it tremble.

Jesus - Tuesday is "the day of Christ" for him. Fulfill Your work of mercy in him now, preparing him in every way for the offering of his life, fortifying him within and without for this grueling experience. "Where sin abounded, grace abounded all the more". Bring this grace to fullness in him now, so that this death may be literally swallowed up in victory -- the victory of faith and hope and steadfast clinging to You. "My soul clings to you; your right hand holds me fast".

Lord, why is an execution so much more horrifying to me than murder, or killing in war? Because it is done dispassionately, with full awareness, in the name of law and order and the common good. Thus it is a greater perversion, a more monstrous distortion of the only real order, which is the way of life You taught us. The way of unlimited readiness to forgive, or never losing hope, never giving up on anyone. It looks straight at this individual and says: "There is nothing more to be hoped for from you". Thus it apes

God, who alone knows the final outcome of a life, the fruit to be hoped from it.

Lord, what must Mary's sense of horror and sacrilege have been on Calvary, if I can feel this way about Jack Potts? Far greater and deeper even than the wound to her mother's love.

Monday, June 30, 1980 Journal Entry

Jesus - the real horror of this act is that it is a direct countersign to the mystery of redemption. You went to unspeakable lengths to save and restore what was wretched, fallen, "worthless". We, for our part, make a final irrevocable judgment that this life is beyond redemption, better annihilated, not worth trying to save. The destruction of his natural life is sign and symbol of an attitude, and that is why it is so hard to bear. The spiritual comfort and affirmation surrounding such a death must be very strong indeed to overcome the force of the action. What is being done to this man, which shouts aloud, is that he is refuse, fit only for destruction. Everything in me cries out against this outrage.

Lord, I did not know how deeply I felt about this until You put this beloved son of Yours before my eyes. His total change of heart throws a spotlight on the monstrousness of this form of "punishment". It is a denial, acted out in the most powerful way, of the infinite value of every human life. And yet, You Yourself plunged into this very experience. Lord, I had never really thought of this before - You felt, not only their hatred and violence, but this deliberate attitude of final, total rejection: the desire for Your annihilation. "We have a law and by this law he ought to die."

Jesus - remind him now of this. You have indeed walked this very road. You have lived Your last days knowing the time and place and manner of Your death - You too were judged not worthy to go on living. Lord, how I thank You that he is not alone -- Your cross says to him in the clearest way, "I am with you". Let this vision be stronger in him today than the vision of that chair.

Lord, he can make his death a sacrifice if You give him the right dispositions -- lend him your humility, serenity, acceptance -- let him show the world that even a condemned murderer can become a reflection of You. This is "the glory of Your grace". Let it shine forth now, so that this death, too, may glorify God in its way.

Jesus, what a Brother You have made Yourself to this man. Have I ever really grasped Your mercy before? "...that you may know the length and breadth and height and depth...". He enables me to know it, when I read the depth of evil in his life, and know Your mercy has surpassed it, when I think about the depth of misery he faces now, and know You have been there to keep him company.

Jesus - lift him up now to this broad and spacious view, this vision of the Truth. Lord, "remember that I stood before You to speak good things for him" and for all his brothers on death row, who in some sense knew not what they did. His own words are a witness to that: "I am humbly sorry for the murder. I know how precious life is now".

Lord, isn't this the poignancy of our human condition -- we are all half-blind to what we do to one another, whether the harm be little or great. Only You can sort out motives, weigh responsibility, measure guilt.

"For man judges by appearances, but the Lord looks into the heart". This is true even of the worst and most deliberate crimes -- only Your eyes see clearly.

Just as I am, without one plea

But that Thy blood was shed for me

That I may live eternally -

O Lamb of God, I come, I come.

Jesus - You have put these words from an old Protestant hymn into my head tonight and I pray them over in his name. He is coming to You on the first day of the month of the Precious Blood, the day of my own Baptism. In heaven we will celebrate Your mercy together, as free and unmerited for the one as for the other. Mercy which shielded me from serious sin, and raised him up from the depths. "What have you (either one of us) that you have not received?" I have received a gift of prayer, and I would cover him with it like a mantle, til he wakes up in Your presence.

Tuesday, July 1, 1980 Journal Entry

Lord, what is happening at Reidsville? Last night the sense of horror over the execution seemed to recede, and I thought it must be because You had given him the grace of a deeper peace - but now it sounds as if You had prevented it once again. Jesus - all things are possible to You. If You will, You can give him a new start, a real and permanent reprieve, better living conditions. This intense experience we have shared with him could be a turning point, for him and for others. I do not know what You are doing, but I will go on "speaking good things for him", and You will do for him whatever is best. Lord, do not let him lose patience for an instant, if they are still keeping him in suspense. Keep him rooted and grounded in faith, growing closer to You every moment.

"As I live, says the Lord, I do not desire the death of a sinner, but rather that he turn from his wickedness and live". Lord, I too desire him to live, You know how much. Not the living death of Reidsville's death row, but a new life with healthy work, human relationships, prayer and worship. Allessandro Serenelli lived a truly human life, most of it in prison but growing always in the knowledge and love of You -- his penitent life and holy death gave great glory to God. And now there is a beautiful book about this murderer of a saint. His frightful act became a _felix_ _culpa_, and Maria Goretti was the heavenly companion of all his later years. All this took time, and he was given it. Jesus, open our minds to Your renewing, restoring will. You can work wonders in these twisted, broken lives if we do not close the door. That nightmarish door of the death chamber which is an image of the gates of hell: "Abandon hope, all you who enter here". It's true You can turn it into the gate of life, but can we presume to force Your hand like that?

Jesus - I am so glad to be beside him, it doesn't matter how dreary it is. Isn't this part of the mystery of our vocation in Carmel -- to be an invisible companion to those in special need? "To whomever I send You, You shall go". It's true that usually they do not know it, but You can make them feel the effects of it, in new strength and courage and spiritual consolation. He has not asked for my prayers, but he has cried out to You for help, "and the Lord stirred up the spirit of a young man named Daniel". This is the delicate network of mutual aid in Your Body. The more we are silent, open, listening, the more we will feel what is happening to our brothers and sisters, in Georgia, in Rome, in China. "When one member suffers, all the members suffer with it". But only if they are attuned to the life and soul of the Body, The Holy Spirit.

"The swallow had found a nest where she may lay her young -- Your altars, O Lord of Hosts, my king and my God".

Lord, what deep meaning there is in that - Your altars are the only place where I can "lay my young", offering and entrusting to You completely these spiritual children You give me, one by one. This is the perfection of my service to them, since only You know how to care for them according to their deepest needs. But I cannot simply leave them in Your care and go away. You want me there beside the altar, in deepest communion with whatever You are doing, assisting by love and longing for their good.

It does not really matter, then, that I do not know exactly what is happening to him now. I can still serve him in the Spirit, who loves and prays for him within me. "God who searches hearts knows what the Spirit desires, for He asks for the saints according to God's will". (Rom. 8)

Jesus - Jack Potts appealed his death sentence at the last minute. Wasn't this the answer to my prayer, to my horror and distress at what was being done? Tonight I saw a picture of him and his eyes haunt me. Full of humility and anguish, clear and beautiful with Your grace shining through them. Lord, there is a very deep mystery to this man's soul, to his place in Your plan, and I have somehow been drawn into it. Remember he is mine and I am sponsor for him.

Jesus - thank you for this remarkable picture. It tells me exactly what Your spirit has been telling me about him.

Lord, didn't You answer my prayer for him more fully than I dreamed of? I asked You not to let him experience the horror of the execution - this was the desire You inspired in me. But I thought it would have to be by means of a special interior grace. Instead, You prevented it altogether, at least for the time being. And now we are asking, he and I together, for a new chance at life. "Choose life." Lord, isn't this the right approach, for a man who is deeply repentant and committed to You? "I do not desire the death of a sinner but rather that he turn from his wickedness and live." So shouldn't he take every means open to him to avoid this horror of capital punishment, so shockingly opposed to Your own way of treating him? His eyes, his face are those of a man who is praying, pleading with God and his fellow men for a new chance at life, and who knows the rightness of his plea. I know it too, Lord, and I stand behind it with my whole being.

Why didn't You inspire me last week to pray for a literal stay of execution? Because this way was more peaceful, it went right to the heart of things, and allowed me to concentrate on his deepest needs. This is always Your way of acting -- to focus on the spiritual side, which is the most real.

Lord, this face is beautiful, it reveals what is within. Woe is me if I do not commit myself to persevere with all my strength in this loving, protecting prayer for him.

Jesus - your compassion for one who has been a murderer is so great because You know the agonies of guilt and contrition he experiences -- these depths that ordinary people will never know. Even this, You took into Your soul in some way, in the Garden. You know, too, the weight of human disapproval, even revulsion, that will "follow him all the days of his life", in spite of his total change of heart. Many people will not see or know the new man, because they have already closed the door to him. He will be a poor one, a man of sorrows til the day he dies -- therefore Your heart goes out to him more than others. Dare I say that? It is the testimony of my inner experience, this singular compassion, caring and protection that You have put into my own heart for him.

He is not then only a brother by Baptism, a member of the Mystical Body, but a very special member, uniquely formed by suffering.

Friday, July 4, 1980 Journal Entry

Jesus - aren't You and I together more powerful than Mr. Thurmond (U.S. Senator) - this man who wants to restore the federal death penalty "because it is a deterrent"? There is no actual proof of that, and he must know it - then how can one take human life so lightly? Because for him, the condemned criminal is not of the number of precious ones. I myself have seen this mentality in the environment where I grew up - this attitude of excluding whole groups of people from the human race. Even as a child I revolted against it, choosing these very people for my friends. This must have been You, hidden within me, for I acted only from instinct and "knew not what I did".

For You, the rejected are precisely the most precious. The 99 must wait while the lost sheep is searched for and brought lovingly home. The publicans and harlots enter the Kingdom first -- the "sinners doing penance" are the ones who give most joy to Heaven (cf. Jack Potts), the last shall be first, the poor (including the handicapped, the unendowed, the unattractive, etc.) are the most cherished -- for You they are irresistible - "Injure not the poor because they are poor...for God will plunder them." These are startlingly strong words, like "Depart from me, ye cursed" to those who simply neglected the works of mercy.

"...It is precisely the parts of the Mystical Body that seem to be the weakest, which are the indispensable ones...God has arranged

the body so that more dignity is given to the
parts that are without it, so...that each part
may be equally concerned for all the others.
If one part is hurt, all parts are hurt with it."
(I Cor 12) Lord, I have never understood the
passage about the "parts with less dignity"
until today. The poor ones are the ones who
need the greatest care, yet in a way they
are the most indispensable ones. Christians
must live this beautiful teaching all the more
intensely, now that it is threatened on every
side.

Commentary

Precisely because Jack Potts was so unlovable, God sought
him out most particularly. Sr. Christine criticized severely any
action that interferes with this action of God. To kill a human
being is to make an irrevocable judgment about the ability of the
human being to respond to the grace and mercy of God. It is a
statement to the person and to the world: there is no hope for you.
No state or representative of the state, in her judgment, should
make this statement about another living human being.

Sr. Christine used what she knew about Jack Potts in her
prayer for him and in her reasoning about his execution. She fully
recognized his wretched history and horrible crimes. "You want
me also beside him, though I would gladly turn my thoughts to
happier things - so I will stay here til You dismiss me."

The journal entries that describe a near-literal pulling of
Jack Potts back from death's door need some repetitive patience to
slow down the flow of ideas and events for a better understanding
of what happened to him and to her.

Only 13 hours before he was due to die, his sentence was
appealed. Sr. Christine did not know that fact for several days. She
does note, however, that she senses the danger had passed. She had
prayed that he not experience the horror of the execution, naming
him a brother of hers by Baptism, uniquely formed by suffering.
While Sr. Christine does not mention St. Therese of Lisieux here,
she, too, named public criminals as her "brothers". A biographer
of French saint Therese of Lisieux writes:

"What is very important is to see that while a murderer is a great sinner in Therese's eyes, she never speaks of divine vengeance, nor does she despair of his conversion. Better, she continues to call him 'our brother', and finally and above all, after she uses the term which indicates 'the table of sinners' at which she will take her place, calling them her 'brothers', there is a tiny phrase which avoids all the Pharisaisms: 'No one knows whether he is just or a sinner.' [53]

Therese, a famous Discalced Carmelite who lived in late 19th century France, humanized the perception of God by her loving ways that were far removed from a God of fear. A century later, Sr. Christine, also with great love, did things somewhat differently for Jack Potts. She extended "brotherhood" to include "the guts of life", as it were.

Lord, I, too, desire him to live, You know how much. Not the living death of Reidsville's death row, but a new life with healthy work, human relationships, prayer and worship....Jesus: And now we are asking, he and I together, for a new chance at life...So shouldn't he take every means open to him to avoid this horror of capital punishment, so shockingly opposed to Your way of treating him?...As I live, says the Lord, I do not desire the death of a sinner, but rather that he turn from his wickedness and live.

"Jesus - I am appalled when I read of this man's former deeds". In her level-headed, calm way, Sr. Christine draws a distinction between his sins and hers.

He is the person that You died for, and, furthermore, he knows it as I do not, for I have never sinned like that. In Jack Potts You meet the naked reality of the humanity You came to save, and You are irresistibly attracted. Lord, remember that I stood before You to speak good things for him and for all his brothers on death row, who in some sense knew not what they did. His own words are a witness to that:

-151-

'I am humbly sorry for the murder. I know how precious life is now.' She judged that if he lives he will be a marked man, hated and unlovable. "But,... in heaven we will celebrate Your mercy together, as free and unmerited for the one as for the other. Mercy shielded me from serious sin, and raised him up from the depths. What have you (either of us) that you have not received?" "I have received a gift of prayer, and I would cover him with it like a mantle, till he wakes up in Your presence.

The journal entries written by Sr. Christine are without pause, hesitation, or changes. Crossing out a phrase here and there never happens. She records her conversation with Jesus as it happens. How can this be?

In confronting human suffering we again can be helped by Burrows' *Fire Upon the Earth*. Analyzing St. Teresa of Avila's methods, Burrows stresses that a prerequisite to prayer is "loving God without any motive of self-interest. ....Prayer must mean forgetfulness of self, not a watching of self in order to detect how we are praying, what is happening to us, how we feel, etc. We do what best urges us to love God and our neighbor." [54] It is unimaginable that Sr. Christine would veer off into a comparison of her cell and Jack Potts' prison cell; or his life of unremitting austerity and hers; or her diminishing health and his life of severe stress and anguish. It is also totally out of range that she would have moved quickly to a political answer for him, or to a legal one, although she certainly supported his using every means available to him to ward off execution. She was, however, totally engaged in learning what Jesus' plan was and her part in carrying that plan out. ... "Let him be so steeped in the beauty and joy of Your mercy that he will not notice what is being done to him. If You like, I will be horrified instead".

7/2/1980 Journal Entry

Jesus - I am so glad to be beside him, it doesn't matter how dreary it is. Isn't this part of the mystery of our vocation in Carmel-to be an invisible companion to those in special need? "To whomever I send you, you shall go". It's true they usually don't know it, but

You can make them feel the special effects of
it, in new strength and courage and spiritual
consolation. He has not asked for my prayers,
but he has cried out to You for help."

Sr. Christine describes briefly her reaction to Jack Potts' appeal
at the last moment…"Lord, didn't You answer my prayer for him
more fully than I dreamed of? I asked You not to let him experience
the horror of the execution-this was the desire You inspired in me.
But I thought it would have to be by means of a special interior
grace. Instead, You prevented it altogether, at least for the time
being".

Christine marvels at what Jesus has done and, yet, she does
not lose her own footing. She knows she has learned the secret of
loving as He loves. She also knows that her part was invaluable to
Jesus and His plan. Praying in this intimate fashion with Jesus'
initiative, may have also reminded her of St. Augustine… "it is
only by way of love of neighbor that we can love God, and that
therefore love alone provides access to the vision of God, both in
this life and the next". [55]

After Sr. Christine's death I gained permission from
the Federal Prison System to correspond with Jack Potts. We
corresponded periodically from 1982 to shortly before his death.

In a notarized letter dated March 8, 1999, Jack Potts
expresses his continuing gratitude to Sr. Christine.

Notarized Letter From the Prisoner

Re. Sister Christine.

My name is Jack H Potts I am on death Row now for nearly 25 years. I was baptized And confirmed in 1977 on death Row by Bishop Raymond Lessard Savannah Diocese And Fr. Kulwicki who was our prison Chaplain. Since 1977 I have had the opportunity given to me to help many many other men be baptized & confirmed. It was not me who takes credit at all, it is the Jesus in me... I am but A sinner saved by the Graces of God... Saved by Our Lord Jesus death and ressurection. And helped And saved by Our Lady who helped Jesus Her son, She was at the foot of His Cross on Calvary so she knows great suffering. My pitiful bit of pain & suffering is nothing compared to what Jesus and many suffered. There is no Comparism... Sr. Christine was praying constantly for me all through these years and at the time I did not know of her holy prayers but I was reaping the benefits And thanks be to God for Sr. Christine.. My days now are filled with prayers and Sr. Christine now is Closer to me and more Available than ever before. Many many prayers have been Answered through Sr. Christine. Each day I get up at 5:am, Divine Office, Scripture, Rosary, And meditation on my Readings. And each time I pray, whether it be at Angelus or Divine Mercy

Page II

At 3:pm each day, or Evening prayer II Divine office or night prayer, Sr. Christine is close And I Ask her to pray with me And for me... I often Ask her advice and Think to myself — "Now what would Sr. Christine do in This situation or prayer request"? All Those years Sr. was praying for me have come to light, And now its been Life Row instead of death row for so many years. Little did I know that one day I would be her brother in Carmel, She, my sister in Carmel but God in His Mysterious way has a way of letting Things simply to fall in place. I began my stay on Life Row in 1974... All The men who were with me (13 in all) in 1974 are now dead, freed to society or in regular prison. There are now 121 men on Life Row. I am still working with more & more, Thanks be to God, trying to lead Them to Jesus And Mary who will lead Them To Our Father. The Father, The Son And The Holy Spirit. Our Lady Mary most Holy gently takes each man And guides him to Jesus just as 'she' did me... And Yes!! Sr. Christine helps me, now even more - for I call on her to help me daily with the Converts.

-155-

I have my morning talks with her
in prayer, morning, noon & night.
    I am now 55 years old, and
I have one brother (older) and one
Sister (older) I do not get visits
but I understand They have Their own
families and lives to live. My dear
mother went Home to the Lord This
month Feb 7, 1999 R.I.P. And I
am confidant That Sr. Christine
led her gently to Jesus, And where
Jesus is, There we find Mary...
So she is in good Hands...
As I was reading The Works of St.
John of The Cross, studying and
especially The story of a soul, I could
just see Sr. Christine a smiling...
And when I pray I ask her to
please keep praying for me, And I
Thank her for all answered prayers
even One mes I didit know about...
I so look forward to be united in
prayer with her And I am one of the
Miracles of Life, I am one of Her miracles
of Life. And I will continue to be just
That Please God. And its so wonderful
to be able to pray to her for her
help, And help me she has,.

Most recently I had asked her to help
my dear mother. And my mother had
a tumor, brain tumor so large that
it filled the entire side of her
head inside.. I had asked Sr. Christine
to pray that my mother not have pain.
to ease her pain and for many
many days before my mothers death.
The doctors told my family, "If you
want a miracle, if you are looking for
a miracle, here it is, Your mother has
this large tumor, but no pain at
all. And thats how she went to the
Lord, simply went to sleep and did
not hurt. Praise be Jesus Christ.
So yes!! Again I had asked a
special prayer and Sr. Christine
provided... How good and holy my
Sister in Carmel has been. and still
is.. as I write.

In Jesus Mary & Josephs
Love,

SWORN TO AND SUBSCRIBED
BEFORE ME THIS 15 TH DAY
OF July 19 99

Notary Public, DeKalb County, Georgia.
My Commission Expires June 6, 2000.

Jack H Potts
8 March 1999
G.D.P. D·30329
Jackson, Georgia
30233

Jack Potts remained on Death Row under the threat of a final death sentence. Interestingly, he became a Third Order Carmelite before his death of liver cancer on December 11, 2006. Jack also credits Sr. Christine's prayerful intercession for sparing his mother the pain expected to accompany her death from a brain tumor.

Catholic publications spread Jack's story far and wide. His conversion was particularly well known in Ireland, both north and south. Until his death, hatred still lingered against him. The internet reported: "I, for one, am glad he's dead"; "justice was carried out without the help of the court system. He won't bother anyone else". Sr. Christine predicted that many people will not see or know the new man because they have already closed the door to him. "He will be a man of sorrows till the day he dies".

While not directly related to Sr. Christine/Jack Potts material, it is relevant to note that the work on behalf of death row inmates by Sister Helen Prejean, C.S.J. began in 1981 through the correspondence she maintained with a convicted murderer, Elmo Patrick Sonnier. An autobiographical account of her work with Sonnier served as the basis for the film, Dead Man Walking. She has become a leading American advocate for the abolition of the death penalty.

NOTES

11. Friendships, Part Three: Saving a Life on Death Row:
The Mantle of Prayer

51. D. Bruck, The New Republic, December 12, 1983.

52. Chester Goolrick and Barry King's article in The Atlantic Constitution reprinted in The Sunday Visitor, June 1, 1980 under title "Jack Potts Waiting for a Time to Die", p. 6.

53. Jean Francois Six. *Light of the Night, The Last Eighteen Months in the Life of Therese of Lisieux* (Notre Dame, Indiana: University of Notre Dame Press), p. 187.

54. See Ref. 34, pp. 68, 69.

55. Bernard McGinn, S.J. *The Foundation of Mysticism* (NY: Crossroad Publishing Company, 1992), p. 87.

Archbishop John F. Donoghue
of Atlanta with Jack A. Potts, 1998.
Potts was a death row inmate.
He credited Sr. Christine with saving him
from the electric chair.

Some members of Carmelite Community
at Schenectady, 1968. Left to Rt: Mother Magdalene (d.1973);
Srs. Baptista; John; Alberta; Christine (Frances Nevins);
and Clare Joseph

Mother Mary John of the Cross,
O.C.D.Prioress at time of
Sr. Christine's death

Theresa Lagoy (Sr. Clare Joseph, O.C.D.) transferred from Schenectady Carmel to Barre, VT Carmel February 1, 1975. Later moved to solitary life in Northern Maine. Good friend of Sr. Christine at Schenectady Carmel.

12

Sincere Love in the Monastery [56]: Temperament and Community Life

> Jesus - a conversation in which there
> is no human link of sympathy and
> friendship is like eating a meal which
> neither nourishes or satisfies.

This statement is a signal that the emotional temperature of the community is too low. Beginning in the late spring of 1980 and continuing until the September Retreat, Christine's writings reflect preoccupation with the state of affairs. She tries to understand what she could do to help by amending her own behavior. Throughout, her temperament and characteristic way of wanting to bring peace is evident.

5/22/1980 Journal Entry

> What has been amiss in my attitude? I have concentrated all my energies on accepting and offering this situation to You as it is, without recognizing that You might also want to change it - for the sake of the community, for the sake of Your own glory and the more perfect living of Your new commandment. We must always seek to 'make it according to the pattern' - the pattern of the N.T. Church of perfect Christian living - even while we willingly bear with difficult relationships, imperfect attitudes, etc. as a way of fulfilling the vocation to sacrifice. Jesus - only Your Spirit can keep this in perfect balance for me.

6/12/1980 Journal Entry

> "Mother of Unity, teach us constantly the ways that lead us to unity".
> This is a perfect prayer for community life. So often these ways are hidden from us: we do not understand how to really meet each other - but you are the Mother of each one, knowing perfectly our uniqueness, what we

need to give and receive - and you are ready and eager to share this knowledge with us. Delicacy, sensitivity, openness, love - these you can teach us and so form us to the unity that Jesus desires so much.

9/15/1980 Retreat Notes

"Say only the good things men need to hear; things that will really help them." (Ephesians?)

Jesus - I think what You are asking of me from now on is that all my conversations should somehow be love - building up others in some way, (even if only to genuinely amuse them.) But no idle comments just because a subject is interesting - no remarks that only amuse me - no giving information when it's not truly helpful, etc. This will restrain me from talking simply as an outlet, and allow the Spirit to take over my words much more completely. Lord, help me for without You I can do nothing - least of all this difficult restraint of the tongue which goes so much against my nature. But I sense it is lifting me to a higher level, and will perhaps help me get control of my expression, which is even more involuntary.

9/23/1980 Retreat Notes

We are living in an atmosphere where, for various reasons, the capacity to trust one another's "sincere love" has been wounded, and it has affected us all. Healing this will be a slow process, but we must work at it steadily and patiently. You do not ask us to succeed, but only to keep trying.

Lord, help me to eat the dry, tasteless bread of this community life in "kindness, humility, meekness and patience" till the end. It is nourishing in the deepest sense because it is "the will of Him who sent me."

Jesus - give me the patience to bear with

this situation, which suddenly seems to weigh very heavily. It distresses me to see others diminishing, at least in an outward way. Help me to find ways of radiating Your warmth and affirmation to them although the opportunities seem so few. This is the substance of real community, and we must communicate it to one another as much as possible under the circumstances.

When my impulse toward real Christian community is thwarted outwardly I must be careful to keep it alive and burning brightly in my heart. Everything centers in the heart - again and again in the Gospel You spoke about attitudes of the heart as most important. Sometimes I think the whole Gospel is summed up in purity of the heart.

Jesus - my one desire is to live in my present situation, "holy and blameless in Your sight in love." Give me the deep understanding which will make me excuse everything - give me constant, generous, unconquered love.

And yet, if we fail to live in this way, Your providence still harmonizes us and works out our very faults into the pattern. We can be content with our actual situation however imperfect it may be. You will reap the harvest that You desire, even in this weedy field.

If only we could realize that You leave us incomplete on purpose, so that what is lacking can be filled up by our brothers and sisters, because this mutual dependence is so pleasing to You. This knowledge keeps us in humanity and openness to one another. It is the foundation of real community and where it is lacking, community is formalistic - which is no community at all. (Romans 12:3-5)

9/25/1980 Retreat Notes

Lord, sometimes I am amazed and distressed at other peoples' lack of love and trust for those around them. Is this a tiny hint of what You experienced? This feeling is not "rational," it does not come from reflection, but from having an inner sense of what things should be like. Once we really know God and the beauty and sacredness of His children, we are appalled when others do not see it. But it is "normal" (sadly so) for them to be cold and indifferent, they do not have the inner vision of the truth, this "Family instinct of love" that the Spirit gives. Who understands why some seem to be imprisoned in this spiritual frigidity? It is good to experience this amazement and distress over them, since it lets us share Your own experience of the world a little.

Drawing on his experience as a Trappist, Michael Casey explains: "for most people the solution lies in accepting that no social setting can ever be more than an approximate framework in fulfilling one's destiny. ...Each person has finally to walk their own path and at their own pace restraining their impatience when the going is good, not losing their nerve when things start to go wrong".[57]

Sr. Christine, however, was not like most people according to confessors and spiritual directors who knew her. Indeed, it is likely that she was having experiences that might be described as overloading the circuits with communications not in any way under her control. [58]

This mixture of need for solitude and silence as well as human contact sets off a range of responses in a community of friends. For everyone involved, a sustained life of contemplation is impossible without a certain ordering of life, an acceptance of discipline and a willingness to be changed. "Nobody survives within a fixed institutional setting without some difficulty or friction. But to be creative within such a context brings with it a degree of isolation, misunderstanding and frustration which requires proportionate effort and single-mindedness to overcome." [59]

Ten years earlier, Sr. Christine was questioning Carmel itself. This criticism was deeply personal because she was increasingly certain why she must have solitude and silence. She reasoned this way:

6/6/1970 Retreat Notes

> In the early days of the Reform, everything
> was permeated with the ideal. Now we cling to
> the forms - even with a kind of complacency,
> but the conviction of the ideal is not there. The
> primitive ideal is what gave life and soul to
> the Reform, and it could do so again, in a new
> form of contemplative life. My vocation is the
> worship of God - that is why I have such need
> of a sanctuary. My true and only sanctuary is
> solitude and silence.

Sr. Christine never sought any office in the community.
Sr. Alberta O.C.D. told me that Christine could have been Prioress
or Mistress of Novices if her health had been better. Christine's
writing, however, explains her view:

6/13/1972 Retreat Notes

> I would be a witness to - an embodiment
> of - the Carmelite ideal pure and simple -
> prayer, work, and sacrifice - to live this in
> as pure (unadulterated) a way as possible.
> To give to others as Our Lady did - not in
> any official capacity or place of authority, but
> simply as a member of the community - as
> sister and friend.

The issues about solitude and silence were central to the
struggle about the hermitage and the proposed Rules changes.
When the proposed changes were turned back, the issues became
more localized in Schenectady Carmel. [See Chapter 7.]

In 1976 I sent to Christine a description of the Discalced
Carmelite Monastery, Port Tobacco, MD. The monastery consists
of a small number of hermitages. Her response reports some change
in her need to look afield for more solitude.

> ..."*Your description of the Port Tobacco
> setup makes me feel rather wistful - actually
> I think my best hope at the moment is
> trying to work with the present small group
> more and more, as I do realize that, all*

things considered, (and especially the Communities I know about) they have a rather high degree of acceptance of my needs and peculiarities - ...

I sense more and more that the greatest need of the traditional Carmels is to develop a real sense of community - (in each community, I mean) without losing the general atmosphere of solitude which is no small task. The liberal, outgoing Carmels have been working on community with considerable loss to the solitude and silence element I think. In the past the latter was largely maintained by each Sr. having a relationship only with the Prioress - but this approach has got to go. We are now in the throes of this I believe - and hopefully if it succeeds, there will be greater understanding and acceptance of personal vocations and individual needs. I do love my community and know that in spite of (or maybe even paradoxically because of) my marginality, I am deeply a part of it and looked upon as such. Perhaps this has been increasing lately - it's hard to know as one can't see the woods for the trees. [With good humor, Christine noted in the post script]: "I have become the Official Community Peeler (potatoes and vegetables). I can even bring them to recreation, if not too messy!" [60]

10/6/1977 Retreat Notes

Jesus - it seems to me that in a way my situation is a test case as to whether a community is something built on personal love and friendship or on regular observance. Help me to strengthen the human and Christian bonds with each one, as You give the opportunity. The ideal would be to be understood and loved in my uniqueness - help me to offer this to others as much as I can.

St. Teresa favored small groups rather than the large convents of her time. Schenectady Carmel followed this small-group model, never exceeding 21 or 22 Sisters. Teresa's ideal was a community of friends. For Sr. Christine that ideal was well suited. Pre-Carmel, while Frances Nevins studied alone, she enjoyed being with a small group of friends discussing a point, or travelling with them. She had an affectionate disposition and was very thoughtful of the comfort of those she loved and demonstrated it by acts of kindness and interest. Before she went to the Sisters of the Good Shepherd and to Carmel, she joked about her sanguine temperament and how her impulsive, warm qualities would fare.

One of the themes in both journal entries and retreat notes throughout Christine's last years in Carmel was her strong distaste for formalism in community. Clearly reflecting her temperament, her natural inclination was toward reaching out to others and making them feel more comfortable.

Answering a description of original songs sung at a friend's birthday celebration, Sr. Christine described how the Carmelites celebrate:

> *"We write songs for one another when we celebrate a feast day or Profession. Sample: when one of our Novices received the habit (Cindy was her former name) I put words to 3 Blind Mice, thusly: Brand new nun; see how she glows; Did you ever see such a welcome sight, our Cindy dressed as a Carmelite, May Jesus fill her with love and light, our brand new nun. --- which we sang as a round. Mostly they are longer, with more and better content, but that will give you an idea".*

6/25/1977 Retreat Notes

> Jesus – what matters is to be able to bless others with love, to make them feel it as much as possible. Let this be the substance of my community life.

Bad Health and Unremitting Austerity

After studying what was different about persons with very rare spiritual gifts, Burrows concludes that this condition of specialness, or "Light On" is forced on the person. The experiences of God tend to result in a physical weakening - the pressure on the person is very intense for it is not a natural way of experiencing God. [61] If her conclusion is correct, then certain probabilities inevitably follow. Health will be poor. Community life will be lonely. And questions about one's vocation and the meaning of communications received will perplex the receiver. "The point is if the Carmelite life is to do its work it will be inherently perilous in a good many ways". [62]

In 1972 Christine had been in Carmel 12 years. The days of high energy were over. She was often severely dizzy. Hospital tests diagnosed "vasomotor instability" and prescribed a high protein diet and hard manual work to keep her circulatory system going. She tried to walk quickly for the same purpose. But, she could barely stand, or sit upright, without everything swirling. To complicate matters, it is likely the thought occurred to her and others that this dreadfulness was "all in her head" as the ridiculing phrase goes.

6/18/1972 Retreat Notes

> I live in a state of more or less constant physical discomfort and strain, and very frequent humiliation which calls for an attitude of more or less continual self-oblation - which is just what I wanted and what I asked for - but it seems to me I respond to it so badly ... I am so often filled with annoyance when someone deprives me of something I seem to need - and if I am not annoyed, so often I seem to be just barely enduring things and dragging myself along, rather than offering everything in a wholehearted and fervent way - if I could gather my forces and prepare for the attack, but so often I seem to be besieged from every side and don't have the strength to cope with anything as I ought - what is the remedy,

Lord? - Is it perhaps that somehow I have never fully accepted the smothering aspects of this ailment, because it deprives me of the consciousness of You?

Seven years later, without any sentimentality or bargaining Sr. Christine talks with Jesus about her health and its place in her life. Christine puts her own quotes around a description of this ailment that is so much a part of her everyday life in Carmel. With a kind of serious playfulness, she tells us about the hardships and what she understands them to mean in refashioning her temperament.

9/1/1979 Retreat Notes

This paradoxical "illness" that requires of me a greater austerity than those who are well -- living in cold places, always sitting on the floor, constant hard work to keep circulation going, etc. - Lord I think this is Your little joke, for You knew I was lazy and comfort-loving, and would not have patience or ingenuity to "mortify myself". Or, rather, this, too, is Your precious gift, for it has taken care of this need without my having to pay attention to it, so that all my attention could be for You.

A year later, Christine took being 50 in good spirits, despite everything. She was surprised to have lived that long, since three of her immediate family had died earlier including her father, who died at 42.

9/18/1980 Retreat Notes

Jesus - Being 50 had been for me like coming upon a bright new horizon, because of the two precious 'birthday gifts' You have given me: this discovery about thanksgiving, and its central place in my life - plus the awareness that my lack of self confidence in Your love is healed. I am beginning life fresh, with new strength and joy and serenity in our union. Lord, how can I thank You for this beautiful surprise?

V. 10-11 "This will...prepare you for the Day of Christ, when you will reach the perfect goodness which Jesus Christ produces in us for the glory and praise of God."

This echoes V. 6, where Paul states his faith that God will complete His work in them for the Day of Christ. Lord, for us this is the day of our death, the day of the "Blessed Exchange", as Mother Seton calls it - and we too have this longing and hope to be perfectly ready when You come. Up to now, I have not been looking at life with this overview, this sense of a course to be completed, that Paul has - but now You are beginning to show me this completion and perfection as my goal. Lord, how different are human ideas of perfection from Yours. People talk about 'striving' for it, but the N.T. tells us to let You produce it in us, over the whole course of our lives. "He who has begun a good work in you will carry it on until it is finished." "We are His workmanship created in Christ Jesus... " (Ephesians).

Jesus - this is how I want it to be. I would rather be half finished under Your hand, than a 'perfect' creation of my own.

NOTES

12: Sincere Love in the Monastery [56]: Temperament and Community Life

56. Elizabeth of the Trinity, O.C.D. "We must be sacrificed souls, that is, sincere in our love". A favorite quotation of Sr. Christine's. Elizabeth's letters were a source of inspiration before Christine entered Carmel and afterwards.

57. Trappist Michael Casey's essay, "Within a Tradition of Prayer", in *The Legacy of Thomas Merton* ed. by Brother Patrick Hart (Kalamazoo, MI: Cistercian Publications, 1986) pp. 25-47.

58. Rowan Williams, *Teresa of Avila* Outstanding Christian Thinkers Series, ed. by Brian Davis, O.P. (Harrisburg, PA: Morehouse Press, 1991), p. 55.

59. See Ref. 57, pp. 26, 28.

60. Letter written by Sr. Christine to the author, 9/26/1977.

61. See Ref. 34, p. 98.

62. See Ref. 58, p. 87.

"She was the holiest person I ever knew".
Jesuit theologian, Charles Reardon, S.J.

13
After the Eastern-rite Liturgy

As a special observance, the Schenectady Carmel invited clergy from the Eastern-rite Church to celebrate their Liturgy in the Monastery Chapel.

Despite terrible health (she was within one month of her death) Sr. Christine's response to the Eastern-rite Liturgy is an excellent example of her singleness of purpose, "keeping her compass set" as Burrows says, without narrowness, or exclusion of new paths to the Spirit.

11/14/1980 Journal Entry

> Jesus - this intense homesickness for the Eastern Liturgy is like nothing so much as being in love. The Jerus. Bible says that <u>Song</u> 5: 10-14 is a description of the Temple - "My Beloved is fresh and ruddy, to be known among ten thousand, ..." His conversation is sweetness itself, : etc. This does not seem to me farfetched, for God lives among men most intensely in His own house, in the worship we offer Him there - He is "enthroned on the praises of Israel." (Ps. 22) If this is ever true, it is true in this unique, wholly inspired form of worship that our Eastern brothers have preserved as a precious treasure. The perfect harmony of priest and deacon, cantors and choir, words and music is itself an image of the harmony of heaven. Here all is unity, beauty, intensity of prayer, ecstasy of joy and praise. An ancient form of worship, but without any formalism - a form that the Spirit fills with exuberance, spontaneity, and childlike delight. "Now that we have prayed to the Saints again and again" it says toward the end. Yes, again and again like children full of the joy and wonder of life, who do not want to stop their play. It is the wonder of Life itself that fills us, the Life that never ends, and we want to clasp it to our hearts forever - "I held him, and I would not let him go."

"We cannot explain it, but here God dwells among men." This is what the two envoys from Russia said, centuries ago, when they first attended this Liturgy in Constantinople. It is the same God who became incarnate in the Lord Jesus - the Beloved Himself, who dwells here. So these thoughts are founded on truth - It is not foolish to have fallen in love with an act of worship, for this is simply God and His heavenly city, manifesting themselves to our earthly perception for a moment. "Whither has your beloved gone, that we may seek him for you?" I do not know when he will return, and this is my sadness - but I will offer this "homesickness" that all may be one, East and West, opening their treasures to one another in mutual love and appreciation, thankfulness and praise.

Jesus - the attitude of most of the community towards this bit of heaven on earth is perhaps the same as most of the Western Church: non-appreciation, unresponsiveness, sometimes even distaste. This parochialism is painful to me, and hard to understand - somehow they must be wakened and sensitized to the spiritual beauty and riches that are there, but how?

Sweet Mother, how this sword of our division must pierce your heart - to see your Eastern and Western children so blind and insensitive to each other. I have lamented the extremes of prejudice and ignorance I have heard of among the Orthodox, and these things will not be healed unless there are those who are willing to pay the price. These little sorrows of the heart which I experience in my small world can help, and I must meet them with a pure heart which is willing to let go of all personal satisfaction for the sake of this great cause of unity. Mother of Unity, pray for us - Pray for me, that I may be <u>sincere</u> in following this ideal and not only writing about it. "We must be sacrificed souls - that is, sincere in our love." (Sr. Eliz. of the Trinity.)

Lord, what is this mysterious love affair of mine? It is because I have a longing for the outward forms which express the passion for God and His Kingdom that I carry within me - Here I have found them, and it seems we were "made for each other." But if I am kept back from experiencing this by those around me who do not want it, then this must be made to serve the cause of unity to the utmost.

11/15/1980 Journal Entry

Jesus - I will dare to say it - this Liturgy seems to me more deeply <u>Christian</u> than any I have experienced. Full of the boldness and confidence and "joy unspeakable" of being a child of God and an intercessor before the throne - full of the <u>awareness</u> of the Kingdom already present. "Blessed is the Kingdom of the Father and the Son and the Holy Spirit, now and always and forever and ever." This is the opening, the Keynote, and here we remain throughout. Has our Latin Rite ever reached the <u>sureness,</u> the total authenticity of these prayers? In the past it was too sin-centered, and the new Liturgy has not yet found its voice - the purity and depth and holiness of true Christian prayer. "The Liturgy is the primary and indispensable source of the true Christian spirit", said Pius X, and if we could truly enter into the Liturgy of our Eastern Brothers we would drink deeply of this spirit and be nourished, to our good. This does not come from copying their outward forms, borrowing elements from here and there - but from humbly opening ourselves to the total experience their Liturgy offers us. Jesus - if this is not to be, in my little world, then spread my desire far and wide. Perhaps I do not need it, since I am already your spoiled child, and you need my sacrifice much more.

In recent years we Westerners have been trying to express the freedom and simplicity of a child of God, the family likeness of the Kingdom - and have often lost the sense of the Holy, in the process. The East has succeeded in combining both, and thus expresses the fullness of the Christian's relationship to God. "Our Father," Our Abba - but also "Hallowed be your Name." Jesus - this union of opposites (seeming opposites) is a precious gift of your Spirit - He alone can introduce us into the presence of the awesome God, with the heart of a child.

11/16/1980 Journal Entry

Jesus - This Liturgy is a pure response to Life. It takes its stand, not on your power and mercy, Your willingness to forgive, but first of all on your love and goodness. The prayers habitually end with - "...for You are good, and You love mankind, and we send up glory to You, Fr., Son and H. Spirit, now and always and forever and ever. Amen." This is why it answers the need of my heart to praise You as You are. Our Liturgy, our preachers (at least in the past) commonly used the expression, "Almighty God." "The good God", as the French say, is much better - but the Eastern Rite habitually says, "O Lord and Lover of mankind," and this is best of all. "The ways of God are unchanging: they are one continuous act of love. Not as if love flowed from God: Love is God and God is Love." - Prologue, Byzantine Prayer Book.

The whole Liturgy is consistent in expressing this vision - It is the Biblical Revelation pure and simple, the same vision of

God that Father H. presents in his preaching. It celebrates, from beginning to end, the mutual love of God and man, the wonder of it, and the joy.

"Arise, O Jerusalem, and stand on high... and behold our children gathered together... by the word of the Holy One, rejoicing in the remembrance of God". Baruch 5:5 This quotation is placed opposite the title page, and it perfectly expresses the theme. When we enter into this Liturgy with recollection and openness, it makes us "rejoice in the remembrance of God" like nothing else. Lord, isn't this what you had in mind? "Do this in <u>remembrance</u> of me." Not simply to honor me, or even just to thank me, but to <u>rejoice</u> in me." Your desire is that "your own joy may be in us, and our joy may be complete."

This is the testimony of St. John the Beloved, and this Liturgy seems full of his loving, contemplative spirit, his passion for unity, his sense of the Kingdom present, and eternity already begun.

If we are truly <u>reconciled</u> with God (as indeed we are) the worship of Him should be pure joy. Joy for what He has done for us, all that He has given us; joy in the expectation of the "good things to come."

Lord, you <u>must</u> be worshipped in this way - it is the only fitting response. "Joy is the most infallible sign of the presence of God" - (Leon Bloy); "Nothing glorifies God like joy." Not a worldly, secular kind of joy, such as often taints the modern liturgies, but joy of the Holy Spirit, which is dear and familiar, but sacred all the same. The Jews longing for the Temple - "how could we sing the songs of the Lord in a foreign land?" ... "My soul longs and yearns for the courts of the lord," etc. Up to now, these verses have meant for me the temple of solitude, where I find Your inner presence most of all. But through this Byzantine Liturgy You have let me experience some of this "longing for the temple" such as the Jews had. In heaven we will indeed have a temple, with the inner and outer presence united as one: the temple of Your Body, of Your very self, where we will love forever and ever.

Jesus - This love and devotion for the Eastern tradition will be all the more pure since I have no means of possessing or enjoying it. Can't this love and longing help to make the two of us one? ... "They long for you and pray for you, because of the surpassing grace in this tradition - "The Lord is in this place, and I knew it not." Division is the devil's work, and here he has done it well, sowing seeds of misunderstanding, hostility and distrust. We have failed to appreciate your presence among them - doesn't reparation, reconciliation, healing begin here, with a new birth of appreciation and love? Christian unity begins in prayer, says J.P. II, and he stresses it over and over. This love and longing is a strong prayer of the Spirit, and to carry it within me and foster it is a work of reunion. It is the part assigned to me, and I must fulfill it with total fidelity, grateful to be given a share in the work. So the answer is not to try to forget it because the absence of it in my life is painful - but rather to let this appreciation deepen and grow, as an unspoken prayer for the great unity yet to come. "If I forget you, O Jerusalem, let my right hand wither".

Author's note: Eastern-rite [Oriental] Church - The term used to describe the Catholic Churches which developed in Eastern Europe, Asia, and Africa. The Eastern-rite churches have their own distinctive liturgial and organizational systems. Each is considered equal to the Latin rite within the Church. The Official Catholic Directory, 2010, p. A-8.

14

Experiencing God: The Heart of the Matter*

The critical task for me was to make an informed choice among the many writings that captured Christine's unique mystical experience. Reliable guidance came by closely following descriptions of infused contemplation and mystical union explained in well-regarded texts by Ruth Burrows O.C.D.; Rowan Williams, Archbishop of Canterbury; and Fr. Paul-Marie De La Croix O.C.D. Sr. Christine mentions in several places that Fr. Paul-Marie's article "always defined my vocation for me better than anything else". Burrows and Williams were published after Sr. Christine's death.

Significantly, the selection of journal entries and retreat notes was made by me primarily from the last 18 months of Christine's life. This arbitrary limitation of time inevitably meant that some important entries were excluded. Another effect may have been to focus on her at the top of the ladder, or, as she says, "standing on the tiptoes of my faith." Even with these caveats, there is sufficient evidence that Sr. Christine was given remarkable gifts that are, ultimately, indescribable.

If there were no other writings available than the following three entries, we would still know the most important facts about Sr. Christine: her experience of God was rare and direct; heroic virtue characterized her life as a Carmelite nun; and she was faithful to the end.

8/26/1980 – 9/6/1980 Retreat Notes:

> My need for the simplicity of this little
> hermitage corresponds to my need of "wide-
> open" spaces, my love for being in mid-ocean
> – all of these lift me above the entanglements
> of earth and everything which could obscure
> my vision of You. But I could not live the way

*Author's note: "...the mystic intuition is not conceived as in opposition to the temporal life, but rather at its heart". [Nevins commentary on Cardinal Nicholas of Cusa . Nevins was 21 years of age when she did this original work.]

I do, without dependence on the larger house and the Community. My way of life is simple, solitary, poor and hard-working, without the anxieties and distractions that would come from having to provide for myself. This is yet another cause for Thanksgiving: the wisdom and tenderness of Your care for me.

For years, I could not see my path ascending, but this year You have given me this precious vision of what You have accomplished in me. St. Teresa says that the gift is one grace, the knowledge of it another, and the ability to express it is a third. All these have come to me from Your Spirit, each in its time. My thanksgiving must try to be as habitual and constant as Your gifts to me. But for that, I need this precious gift of discernment, so as to "know the gifts" I have from God.

"Let everything you do have the word of God for accompaniment." (Rule of Carmel)

Lord, this meant nothing at all to me until recently – but now everything, everything I "do" in my inner life, everything I think, is indeed accompanied by some word of Scripture which Your Spirit brings to my mind. This gift blossomed in me without my knowing how. It is a precious, habitual confirmation of His inner teaching. As He forms the thoughts in my mind, He reminds me that St. Paul or St. John, etc. said the same, and helps me find the passage if I do not know it by heart. We search for the translation which fits best with the thought He gave me, or sometimes go to the Greek, where the agreement is closest of all. This has become so habitual that I hardly realized what I was doing – today He is helping me to lovingly examine this gift, so as to be more thankful.

11/1980 Journal Entry:

> "A thousand years are but a day to You."
> You see me already "all finished," with each
> stage of my life making its indispensable
> contribution to the eternal person You are
> creating. You lose no time, and waste no
> moments, even though we may seem to be at
> a standstill for many years. Lord, I rejoice, I
> glory in being your handiwork. I never sought
> to wriggle out of Your hand – this is all I can
> say for myself, and this too is Your gift.

12/2/1980 Journal Entry:

> Jesus, I want to bring before You all my
> physical disabilities and discomforts that
> hinder prayer, to make You absolute Lord
> of all these, and above all of my response to
> them. "Your constitution is your penance."
> This is the word of direction that was said to
> me many years ago when I was seeking some
> kind of voluntary mortification, and it is true
> now more than ever. Jesus, only You can
> show me when I really need relief in order to
> fulfill my vocation to prayer more perfectly,
> and when I am simply giving in. And perhaps
> some of these hindrances which lessen my
> centered-ness, my perfect recollection, are
> things You want to heal, rather than penances
> that please You. "All things serve You," but
> you alone know what service You want them
> to perform. "Whether I live or whether I die,
> may Christ be glorified in my body." Whether
> I am experiencing one kind of discomfort
> after another, or have enough well-being to
> forget the body, as I long to do – may you
> be glorified, served, praised at every moment.
> [Sr. Christine was stricken on 12/4/1980]

These few examples of journal entries and retreat notes are
similar in originality, clarity, and succinctness to those written by
Sr. Christine during the entire 20 years she was in Carmel. For the

last 18 months, she gave her writing to Father Tansey two weeks prior to their meeting for Confession. He made a little line at the edge of the page noting a point for attention, and returned the pages prior to their appointed time. Sr. Alberta, the extern Sister, would see that the pages went back-and-forth.

Other than searching for the truer translation of a scriptural text, there is no evidence that she spent time rummaging for the right word or phrase. If she self-edited at all, she must have done so before putting pen to paper. There are few words, or even punctuation marks, that she changed. Christine's explanation of the purpose of her writing may explain this lack of the need for editing.

9/22/1980 Retreat Notes:

> Writing is a way of focusing receptivity
> on the action of the Spirit. It forms itself into
> a thought, is put down, and then I am empty
> again and ready for the next.

Elsewhere, she explains that she could not do otherwise than write about what is happening to her.

3/7/1980 Journal Entry:

(Christine writes at some length about false teachings about the Church and the priesthood, the devaluation of celibacy. Then she comments about her writing):

> Lord, who am I to write these things –
> a poor nun who does not have to face these
> struggles? I think it is my love that gives
> me the right – this enormous love for the
> priesthood which You have put in me and
> which has lived in me for so many years now.
> And, as if to further encourage me, You made
> me understand at my Visit today that I would
> not be faithful to You if I did not write down
> what You inspire.

The Language Problem

The journal entry for 3/7/1980 appears to be an example of Sr. Christine's experience of God. Is she referring to God Who visited today? And to God Who made her understand that she would not be faithful if she did not write down what God inspires?

However these words are understood, they are communications that are unfamiliar and disturbing. When other words are used that explain the relationship with God in intimate terms – spouse, bride, brother – the reader may become even more uneasy. But, remarkably, the language and the landscape is not all that unfamiliar to generations of Carmelites. It has been true for centuries, and is true today, that "a direct and intimate experience with God is the basis for Carmelite spirituality." [63]

Mystical, even amorous, language that mystics use need not put anyone off, or lead to misunderstanding what the mystic is attempting to communicate. Father Jean-Francois Six, controversial biographer of St. Therese frames the issue this way: "Literature, including erotic literature, can help us to grasp what goes on in the depths of the mystical life, in the hearts of lovers like Therese....One might think that there is something to fear in this Fire which is going to take you away, fear of being too totally taken and seized by it; on the contrary, the mystic, like the one who is possessed with physical love, no longer has any fear." [64]

To this day, the biblical Song of Songs continues to create discomfort with its explicit, provocative language. St. Teresa, St. Bernard of Clairvaux, St. Therese, and Sr. Christine, however, understood the Song in the traditional sense of Christ and the individual soul, and, moreover, each used the text of the Song "in a free and easy way – in a sense, the text becomes a trampoline to propel one into deeper reaches of love". [65]

Song of Songs:
Sr. Christine Marie of the Holy Spirit, O.C.D.

9/26/1979 Retreat Notes

The Song of Songs. Lord, this book is opening its mystery to me now so simply, as never before. These images are unsurpassed in expressing the union of the soul with God.

They nourish a humble sense of the wonder and dignity of being His spouse – this great reality which overshadows everything else. As always, You lead me to just what I need.

"The King has brought me into his rooms" – that is where I am, and it is indeed He that has brought me here, bringing about this union without my even understanding what was happening. "In his longed-for shade I am seated" – his constant nearness and protection which are increased so much in this state – the unshakable stability of this union, which I have experienced for nearly 18 years. I could write a commentary on almost every line.

"You are wholly beautiful, my love, and without a blemish." I think we can dare apply this not only to Mary but in a way to every soul in this union, since the will clings to Him so unshakably in spite of external imperfections. There is, indeed, integrity in this most interior part of our being, which lives in His presence – He chose us to be "holy and unspotted in His sight in love." (Eph. 1)

2:11 "The rains are over and gone, the flowers appear on the earth" – The joy of living always with You, no matter what we are experiencing outwardly. 2:16 "He pastures his flock among the lilies" – The mysterious fruitfulness You have given to purity of heart.

Lord, this poem is too beautiful to take apart like this, but I have seen how it corresponds in many ways to my experience and reflects it back to me in a way that is very holy and sacred.

9/27/1979 Retreat Notes

Jesus – what bride would spend her time in anxious preoccupation about displeasing the one she loves? This is a foolish, Jansenistic attitude. Rather, let me simply and joyfully seek only how to please Him more – to possess Him more, like the bride in the Song.

I do not think that anyone who had experienced this inner relationship could think this book is a description of human love alone – it fits too perfectly the other, and there is an element of depth and mystery that belongs only to God.

"Catch us the little foxes" – very often it is the shepherds who will catch them for us. They have eyes to see these imperfections and faulty attitudes that mar our pure and joyful communion with Him.

"I will rise and go through the City" (3:2) – It is good to seek Him in and through the Church, no matter how close our personal relationship may be. "…scarcely had I passed them (the watchmen) than I found him whom my heart loves." The watchmen help us in ways both open and secret – after we have been to the Sacrament and received direction. He comes to us more fully and with greater perfection.

Why does she always say "him whom my heart loves"? Because this expression fits best this kind of love which has the Spirit as its source – "My soul magnifies the Lord" – it is almost passive, something I perceive happening in the deepest part of myself.

3:4 "…nor would I let him go till I had brought him into my mother's house…" This great longing to bring him into the whole Church, the whole human race. For me this has a special meaning – my poor mother symbolizes the terrible need of those who do not know God.

Why does she bring him into her mother's house – does she think, "I ought to"? No, she wants to, she has to. Her deepest I is the Holy Spirit – that is why she can speak so surely and unself-consciously. Mary is the perfect Bride – we do not think of her as being like this in her relationship with God.

This book shows what she will be to Him, and what He will do for her if she responds to the full. 'He has brought me into his banquet hall," "in his longed-for shade I am seated," etc. This is the bride in <u>this</u> world – "My dove hiding in the cleft of the rock" – "a garden enclosed, a sealed fountain." Her beauty shines for Him, but is veiled.

5:3 "I have taken off my tunic, I have washed my feet," etc. – This sluggish response is part of human nature even when it is not positively unfaithful. He disappears because He wants a perfect response. She will be purified by her anxious search, and the sufferings she meets with (5:6, 7)

4:8 "Come from Lebanon, my promised bride, come on your way.... From...the haunts of lions, the mountains of leopards." This is the way she has to come – our human life is full of sufferings, dangers, sometimes even horrors. But He encourages her – she is "on her way" to the marriage, to the everlasting union.

5:10ff All this imagery shows the impossibility of expressing God's beauty – There is "coalescence of the senses" all through this poem. Much about "fragrance," etc.

6:1-2 "Where did your Beloved go...? ...He went down to his garden," etc. He disappears from our surface experience to take up his dwelling in the deepest part of our being. It is now that we can say "I am my Beloved's and my Beloved is mine" – unshakably, forever. And we experience Him in an incomparably deeper way.

6:11, 12 "I went down...to see if the vines were budding...Before I knew...my desire had hurled me on the chariots of my people, as their prince." This is a magnificent image of God's desire to be with His people, leading to Incarnation. No doubt, the sacred writer did not think of this, but I think God did.

7:1 Maid of Shulam – "she who has peace" – This is indeed the name of the bride in the Biblical sense – telling what she is within.

"Return, return" – that is all that the bride-soul needs to do after attending to the things of the world – turn her eyes within, and she finds Him. He draws and calls her back, over and over. Full of peace, she is also full of life and joy: "dancing." (7:1)

7:4 "Wine flowing straight to my Beloved," etc. This is contemplative prayer – how could it possibly be better expressed? Also, all the allusions to sleep – "I sleep, but my heart watches," etc.

7:10 "His desire is for me" – This unspeakable fact. This poem unveils God's love, the nature of His love, as nothing else does.

Bernard, Teresa, Therese, and Christine understood the most important fact: "God is not the same as anything else". [66] Holding tight to that statement makes reading and understanding the mystics' words human and lovely.

Questions / Definitions / Preparation

Before addressing the questions that follow, Burrows constructs a sturdy floor on which to stand.

"Let us remind ourselves over and over again that holiness has to do with very ordinary things: truthfulness, courtesy, kindness, gentleness, consideration for others, contentment with our lot, honesty and courage in the face of life, reliability, dutifulness. Intent, as we think, on the higher reaches of spirituality, we can overlook the warp and woof of holiness." [67]

Burrows lays out the key questions and the definitions:

What is not mystical, infused contemplation.
What it is.
What does it mean to say that Jesus and His Father come to dwell in believers?
What goes on? [68]

When St. Teresa and St. John of the Cross speak of "contemplation," it is always "infused contemplation" to which they refer. They know no other. For St. Teresa, contemplation is a state that "we cannot bring about by ourselves. In it the soul feels passive". Infused contemplation depends on God alone. [69]

Infused Contemplation and the Mystical State: What It Is Not

Burrows explains the meaning of infused contemplation and the mystical state by first explaining what they are not:

"The term 'mystical' is by no means confined to Christianity. The word suggests awareness of mysteries, an experience of transcendence, exaltation, a vision through and beyond what immediately strikes the senses, a passing glimpse of the unseen world....It is this range of experience commonly dubbed 'mystical' that we need to look at, for, by and large, it is precisely this that is confused with the truly mystical, the breakthrough into this world of the divine.
It is not so that the mystical life will inevitably manifest itself in an increase of the psychic powers. Feeling of being out of the body, looking down on itself; knowledge of things to come; scents that seem to come from no natural source is part of the vast range of experience, often awesome and mysterious, that belongs to, is part of our material being. There are many people who have well-developed psychic awareness. What they have is a natural endowment.

It is possible to have most lofty 'spiritual experiences,'
and yet be a mere embryo when it comes to capacity
for God." [70]

Infused Contemplation and the Mystical State: What It Is

Firmly putting aside psychic phenomena, Burrows explains
mystical, infused contemplation. She begins with Jesus:

"Jesus Himself gives us the criterion. It is loving
'as I have loved you,' keeping his commandments as
he keeps his Father's, it is living as he did in total
surrender, is impossible to human effort, a divine
gift is needed, an infusion of divine energy, the
Spirit of Jesus himself, the Promise of the Father.
This is precisely what we mean by mystical, infused
contemplation.

It is pure gift, something we can never achieve
for ourselves...however much we may practice
meditation, however much we do violence to
ourselves, and however many tears we may shed,
we cannot produce this water in those ways. It is
something entirely new. It is a direct encounter with
God. It purifies and transforms.

It calls for generous preparation. We must practice
penance, prayer, mortification, obedience and all
the other good works we know of. There is nothing
esoteric involved, no magical practices, nothing that
lies outside our own everyday life experience.

This has nothing to do with psychic awareness,
it happens in day-to-day life. It involves constant
watchfulness for the call of God so as to answer with
an immediate 'yes'." [71]

Burrows gives a "head's-up," a warning really, against using
suffering to make the case for proof of advancing in virtue.

"There can be an enormous amount of useless
suffering that we really induce because we feel it to be
authenticating, a sign that we are making progress,
are specially close to God, a 'chosen soul' and so
forth. We are wrong to attach such significance to

suffering. All that matters any time, any where, is a strong, resolute cleaving to God, a determination to do His will, cost what it may." [72]

Mystical Union: The Perfect Marriage

In *Fire Upon the Earth*, Burrows traces what happens to a person moving towards union with God using St. Teresa's metaphor of seven mansions. In the fifth mansion, for example:

"It does not mean that one never fails but it does mean that the compass is always set, the will stretched toward God without any slackening. It is not a mansion in the sense that it is a place where we are, it is a dynamic moment of decision, an invitation offered and accepted, understanding that this acceptance is beyond our power and is a direct effect of God's contact."

"Once someone has really signed the contract, or shot her rocket, something very momentous has happened in God's world. This person is going to have a profound influence on God's world and draw many along with her." [73]

Using her clarifying phrase "light on" for this kind of person, she adds: "The 'light on' just because she 'sees' undergoes suffering such as the rest of us cannot know." [74]

"This unutterable work of God, let us call it a wooing, takes place in deepest darkness and secrecy. Figuratively, immense distances are traversed and, chronologically, also, we can expect the journey to take a long time, consisting as it does of a total self-emptying, a dying to everything that is not God. It involves a tremendous growth and maturation far outstripping any natural maturation." [75]

The last state, the seventh mansion in Teresa's metaphor, is this vision of Jesus. Burrows frankly admits that any description using human words is a struggle for meaning. As usual with her, she rules out certain notions about this vision:

> "The last state is transforming union. He living in us and we in Him, the perfection of marriage....We must not think for a moment that transformation into Jesus robs a person of individuality, that from henceforth they have no emotions, no preferences, no interests. Transformation into Jesus means we become fully human.
>
> "The mystical marriage is not a state of psychic bliss, not a comprehensible fulfillment. It is utterly remote from such paltriness; it has nothing to do with self-states. It is to be with Jesus a total 'for-Godness' which means being totally for others; it is an ecstasy of devotedness with no concern for self. And, most important, that the direct action of God in the human being is totally secret. It can be known only by its effects and even those are not easily assessed by 'flesh and blood'." [76]

Sr. Christine's Unique Experience

Burrows insists that very few people know of these things by lived experience. Even the words, plain as they are, require a "reach" to translate into some kind of comparable idea or emotion. Sr. Christine, as one of these very few, never loses her feeling of awe; at the same time, her writing accurately describes the step-by-step profound change that has occurred in her very being.

Sr. Christine meets St. Teresa's expectations in many, perhaps all, of these writings because Christine acknowledges the gifts she has received and includes enough information for us to grasp what was going on. The reality of God's action is apparent.

In chronological order, the following small portion of entries makes the case for the infused mystical contemplation and mystical union that Sr. Christine experienced.

9/26/1979 Retreat Notes

> "My sister, my bride" – This unspeakable relationship with God cannot be expressed in just one image, and is unique for every soul.

I am sister to Jesus, bride of the Spirit – in our communication it is always the same. For (most?) others, the Lord Jesus is the Spouse – but They want it this way with me. This uniqueness is maybe the most precious thing of all – no one else can be for Them exactly what I have been chosen to be.

2/19/1980 Journal Entry

"We too are weak in Him…"

Jesus – what consolation in these words of Scripture. All my weakness is in You, for You, in order to share in Your work. Physical weakness, mental weakness, the weakness of being without influence or external means of helping others, the weakness of my position in the community, being almost without a voice. Yet the more faithful I am to this path You have traced out for me, the more You act.

The Carmelite vocation itself is a call to this weakness, this being reduced to nothing. Its hope, its ideal, its apostolate is: "to live with Him by God's power in us." The Word became flesh in order to be wholly ours, and to make us wholly His." These beautiful words of Fr. Paul-Marie express the marriage theme of Scripture – "I am my Beloved's and my Beloved is mine." This is the best way of expressing the Incarnation – no other way brings out the kind of love God has for us, for all humanity. It is always, at least potentially, the love of a bridegroom.

3/20/1980 Journal Entry

So all of this calls me to a deeper recognition of my helplessness and dependence on You – and reminds me once again that You chose me in order to have someone in whom You could do all. I am the Holy Spirit's Carmelite – as He said to me at the time of my first Profession – created by Him out of nothing. This is a continuous creation – when He calls me to take a new step, it means He wants to carry me there Himself. "The Lord your God carried you all along your journey." For protection, but also for progress.

3/24/1980 Journal Entry

Truly being with another means sharing his deepest dispositions – with You it is Your love and desire to win us by Your suffering – Your immense zeal for God and for us. This is deeper in You than pain and sorrow and disappointment, and You need someone to keep You company at this deepest level. You showed this to me very clearly years ago and each year in Passiontide You renew the insight. "I saw in one of those wordless lights which fulfill and even surpass every desire..." I read this the other day in the writings of a French contemplative and it seems to express what I mean when I said above, "You showed me clearly." One of those pure inpourings of vision and knowledge which come only at special times – not often – but which color and define my thought and prayer for the rest of my life. Your Spirit is always faithful to these "revelations", renewing them again & again in a more ordinary way. When I "see" You at these special times, You are always the way You want to be for me. You are different in some way for each soul. I do not find You quite like the person I read about in books, but with a unique "personality" perfectly suited to my need, and I am sure it is like this for everyone who is close to You. And so it is true in a way that each one You love is Your "one and only" since Your relationship with each is absolutely unique. Infinite Love alone can be Bridegroom to a multitude of souls without watering down the meaning.

3/27/1980 Journal Entry

There comes a point where there is no division, separation or disharmony between the Spirit and our own deepest spirit. This is a really spiritual marriage and He is for the hour everything that the bridegroom is for the bride, and more...loving and taking delight in her – guiding & protecting, providing for every interior need with absolute and eternal fidelity. My beloved – You purified & prepared me for this "marriage" without my knowing what was happening and then You revealed to me in an experience of the most unspeakable joy that it had taken place – the inner celebration, the overflowing happiness of this new state going on for weeks and weeks and in a quieter way, ever after. I could never have dreamed that You were a person with the same desires and sentiments, the same tender love as a human bridegroom – You, who had not even a human form like the Lord, Jesus. To be spouse of the Holy Spirit is not a pious expression but an unspeakable inner reality. "Who is sufficient to understand these things?" I can only testify to what I have seen and known and experienced unmistakably over & over for nearly twenty years.

7/8/1980 Journal Entry

"I will espouse you to Me forever." Lord, the expression is very exact. It was You Who did it all, without my even knowing what was happening – all the purification and enlightenment that was needed as preparation, and then the mysterious interior act itself.. when Your Spirit said to me unmistakably that He was the "Spouse of my soul forever". I did not understand the deep meaning of this expression – (anymore than Bernadette understood when Mary said, "I am the Immaculate Conception") – but little by little He revealed to me what had happened, and all of it fitted perfectly with what I read later on in mystical theology about the spiritual marriage. At the time I knew only that something new and unspeakably wonderful had happened between us in the depths of my being, and I had been lifted to a new level of peace and happiness never experienced before.

"Forever," says the Lord in Hosea. This was the very word He said to me, and the theology books in their dry language explain that "this union is inamissable". Lord, how could You give us a gift like that? Simply out of love, as part of our heaven-ahead-of-time. "Divine union knows only one change," says Archbishop Martinez, "constant progress while life lasts". Jesus - help me to appreciate Your unspeakable gift. "He who is mighty has done great things for me".

NOTES

14: Experiencing God: The Heart of the Matter

63. Paul De La Croix, O.C.D., *Some Schools of Catholic Spirituality: Carmelite Spirituality,* ed. Jean Gautier, trans. by Katheryn Sullivan, R.C.S.J., (Paris: Descles Company, 1959), p. 114.
64. See Ref. 53, p. 139.

65. Roland E. Murphy, O.Carm. "The Song of Songs and St. Therese" in *Experiencing St. Therese Today* ed. John Sullivan, O.C.D. (Washington, DC: Institute of Carmelite Studies, 1991) , p. 90.
66. Rowan Williams, *Wound of Knowledge* (Cambridge: Cowley Publications, 1990), p. 166.
67. See Ref. 34, p. 19.
68. See Ref. 34, p. 50.
69. See Ref. 63, p. 172.

70. See Ref. 34, pp. 46, 47.
71. See Ref. 34, pp. 42, 43, 86, 88.4
72. See Ref. 34, p. 97.
73. See Ref. 34, pp. 83-85.
74. See Ref. 34, p. 88.
75. See Ref. 34, p. 91.
76. See Ref. 34, pp. 117-118.

◆ **PART III** ◆

――――――

Conclusion

Schenectady Carmel grate or grille
used at times of confession
and visits by priests and family

15

Loaned to Each Other[77]: Sr. Christine and Fr. Tansey

Before moving to explore the facets of the relationship between Sr. Christine and her confessor, it is useful to consider St. Teresa's ideas about this relationship central to monastic life. Rowan Williams summarizes:

> "Teresa discusses at considerable and candid length the relations between her sisters and their confessors, once again acknowledging possible risks, but encouraging proper intimacy and friendship. The sister must exercise discernment: confessors may be silly or sinful and if you discover one to be such, find someone else, as tactfully as you can. A bad confessor indulges your failings, even encourages them, and if there is inflexibility in the community about changing confessors, many will find themselves at odds with their conscience. The superior should not allow a situation to develop where sisters are afraid to be honest, 'a situation in which if the prioress gets along well with the confessor no one dares to speak to him about her or her about him'....Teresa pleads for liberty to discuss matters of conscience with as many qualified people as possible....In support of this plea, Teresa points out the sheer diversity of the needs of souls ('one confessor perhaps will not know them all')....We can be assured that God will see to it that there will be someone who will love us properly, desiring the best for our souls." [78]

Fr. Tansey: Chosen as Confessor

Sr. Christine eventually chose Fr. Tansey as her regular confessor, but only after attending the Masses he celebrated at the monastery and going to him occasionally for confession. She also attended the talks about Vatican II he gave to the sisters.

Even so, when it came to a choice of confessor, she was cautious because she knew her charism was not easily understood. At some point after they began their confession schedule, Fr. Tansey fell out of favor with the Prioress about an unrelated matter. Sr. Christine chose to retain him as her confessor. [79]

In 1977 Sr. Christine was 47 and Fr. Tansey, 56. He had been a Mill Hill Missionary priest for almost 30 years; she, a Discalced Carmelite nun for 17 years. While different in primary purpose, the religious order to which each belonged linked contemplation and apostolic work so the life of each was readily understood by the other as to hardly need explanation.

For 17 years, Sr. Christine had been a Carmelite in the Schenectady Carmel. He, on the other hand, had been a missionary in Africa and maintained Church and family ties in Ireland. In the Albany Diocese, he carried a variety of priestly assignments, including chaplaincies to large Catholic organizations. Well educated, his first assignment after seminary was to take a B.A. degree at Dublin University. At age 38, Fr. Tansey was named Rector of Freshford College.

In 1979, Fr. Tansey wrote a brief essay about his path to the priesthood. The essay became part of a commemorative publication celebrating the founding of Our Lady of Keadue Parish. His "Irishness" shines through the text:

> "There is no place on earth that has deeper memories for me than the Church of Our Lady of Keadue. It was there, early in January 1922, that I was baptized. I was eighth and last child of my Stonepark family. It was there in Keadue Church that I made my first confession, received first Holy Communion, served Mass and was confirmed by Bishop MacNamee. It was there that I returned on July 14, 1948 to offer my first Mass. As I was getting ready at home on that morning, I was conscious that other priests of Keadue had lived in the same house and had used the same bedroom as I was standing in, while, over many years before, they served the people of Keadue and Kilronan and lived in the Tansey home at Stonepark.
>
> The Church in Keadue was the focal point of my boyhood days. I passed there many times a day journeying to and from school and doing errands. Often I would drop in to make a visit. If it was late afternoon, I would expect to see Mrs. Beirne and the Misses McGinn in their usual places and always absorbed in prayer. Their example helped me immensely.
>
> Of our parish priest, Canon Pat Meehan, I have very

fond memories. I knew him when he was old – and I mean old – from his 84th to his 96th year. I was one of his little team, comprised of Tony McGinn, James Finnerman and myself. I can still see him vividly – 'The Canon' arriving in the sacristy, an ice-cold place with a cold stone floor, in the cold of winter. The Canon's hands were also ice cold as he searched through the cabinet for the vestments. He had no light except that of a candle. While offering Mass, he had a wax candle on each side of the tabernacle and a third candle to light up the missal.

Sometimes things didn't go according to plan as between the Canon and us servers. At these times, he resorted to a fine vocabulary but one mostly confined to farm animals not noted for intelligence. But we never took these words to heart and I mention them only to give you a better flavor of this man whose hair was snowy white – and not without cause.

Indeed, in spite of all our little misadventures, our dear Canon was the Sagart Aroon [beloved priest] of my boyhood days. We were very proud of him and would stand up for him anytime, anywhere." [80]

Terms of the "Contract"

From the beginning of their "contract", it was evident to Sr. Christine that Fr. Tansey brought three authentic attributes she valued highly:

1. Committed priesthood
2. Social vision
3. "Irishness"

Like St. Therese, Sr. Christine entered Carmel to pray for priests. She describes priesthood as an "unspeakable grace". And from his homilies at Mass, she knew Fr. Tansey's concern for the predicaments of real people with their special needs. She agreed completely with St. Teresa of Avila: "the more advanced souls are in contemplative prayer, the more they are concerned with the needs of others". [81] Re: the "Irishness" – perhaps that quality she so admired in Fr. Reardon and saw in Fr. Tansey linked her once again with Grandfather Nevins to whom so much was owed.

Sr. Christine brought to the "contract" a different combination of attributes:

1. Rare experiences with Divine Love
2. Well-stocked mind[82]
3. Gift for friendship

Sr. Christine had been both helped and hindered by confessors. She mentions to a friend that a well-grounded confessor could help her "plunge into scripture" but, there was this life-long shyness with strangers to reckon with:

> "I am as shy as ever with people I don't know and can't seem to find the right word (or even know what I think) until several hrs. or days later. I truly am at a great loss in on-the-spot conversation. If any clarity comes it is only after pondering. I do much better putting it on paper." [83]

Carmelite literature provides examples of good work by confessors; the match with the penitent, however, remains highly individual. A youthful St. Therese illustrates an excellent, albeit very brief, intervention by a confessor who changed her life:

> "I had hardly entered the confessional than I felt my soul expand. After speaking only a few words, I was understood in a marvelous and even intuitive way and my soul was like a book in which this priest read better than I did myself. He launched me full sail on the waves of trust and love which so strongly attracted me, but upon which I did not dare advance".[84]

St. Therese was, of course, in the very early stages of her unique journey [1873-1897]. Sr. Christine, on the other hand, had 15 years' experience with Divine Intimacy. Yet Sr. Christine and St. Therese both know instinctively when they find a confessor who understands them in their attempts to describe the indescribable. Sr. Christine also knows, despite her shyness, that her sanguine temperament responds well to human support and genuine friendship.

The "Contract" Enfolds

6/21/1977 Retreat Notes (before confession)

> Jesus – that I might be able to bring out
> in him [Fr. Tansey] what is best and most
> spiritual by my communications – only Your
> divine wisdom can draw from me what will
> do this.

6/21/1977 Retreat Notes

> Jesus – on Tuesday You created a
> relationship of dependence and submission
> that I had not intended. Is this a lesson for
> me, that in some things he is to be my guide?
> I can now lay all my graces before him – and
> he has not violated anything You have asked
> of me, but only blessedly confirmed it. This
> would be relying on Your gifts of discernment
> in another – another manifestation of the
> Body of Christ. How blessed it is to deposit
> both the graces and the human weaknesses
> into another's keeping – to see me as God
> sees me. We will help each other to holiness
> – our great goal.
> Jesus – my heart overflows with gratitude
> for graces given to souls through his ministry;
> for understanding, guidance and support; for
> the rest and relief of depositing Your graces
> in someone else's heart – for this reverent,
> tender, chaste, and apostolic union You are
> building between us. This retreat began in
> loneliness and ended with the deep, quiet
> friendliness of a new brother on earth. How
> can I thank you?

The best priests are fully recognizable human beings.[85] Early
on, Sr. Christine credits Fr. Tansey with qualities implied in that
statement – a "priestly priest"; intelligence; prudence; empathy;
sense of humor; and a good listener. For her part, she had no fear
of friendship with such a person. Her very positive experience with
Fr. Reardon over 20 years supported her judgment.

Jesus – all power is given to You. Of course, You can give him [Fr. Tansey] this gift. If You want him to have it – the gift of freedom and openness in friendship – the gift of unaffected love. If this will mean greater Christian perfection and a closer resemblance to Your heart, then I desire it for him. The unambivalent and loving acceptance of the sacred beauty of another person. This takes purity and strength and assurance of rightness – all gifts which Your Spirit can give. "Human love as found in friendship is suggestively similar to Divine Love." Jesus – how true this is of Your love as I have experienced it. This is why friendship is somehow the perfection of Christian life and the key to everything.

Sr. Clare Joseph observed that Fr. Tansey helped so many people. "He was an incredible grace to Christine. As a very good teacher, he opened the world of scripture to her. And he brought out both sides of her personality (introvert and extrovert). With his ministry, he focused her prayer on people with immediate needs". [86]

A Powerful Healing

The deeply moving experience of "Healing" as part of the Sacrament of Reconciliation cemented the relationship between Fr. Tansey and Sr. Christine. After that, their love and friendship flourished until the end.

9/28/1978 Journal Entry

Jesus – I had no real experience of this family attitude from parents, and this wounds and blinds our spirits unavoidably. Why? Because we are formed and marked indelibly by the first experiences of life. But I am a new creation, learning to be at ease in my divine Family circle – learning all my life long.

We are "children of adoption," and adopted children always need time to adjust.

"We have come to know and to believe in the love God has for us" (I Jn 4:16). For me, perhaps it should read, "We have known and come to believe" – and it is a cry of victory. I have seen and known this love again and again in my experience – and yet for so long I was kept back from believing firmly and fully by this distressing inner paralysis of heart. But now Your healing touch has reached to those inner depths which were so totally beyond my control, and my faith in Your love grew strong and sure. How has this been done? By all the means through which You touch my soul – Sacraments, Scripture, direction, the silent work of the Spirit in prayer. This is a mighty healing that only heaven can see, but I will give thanks with the one who has helped so powerfully to bring it about.

"Off the Record"

There is, of course, no "off the record" to this relationship – no secret trinkets and trifles. "The mature lovers of God can't be so anxious to avoid imperfect friendship that we deny our natural need for human support. Otherwise, we shall never learn pure love: genuine spiritual friendship builds on ordinary foundations, but learns at last to see the loved friend in the light of what God wants for him or her". [87]

St. Teresa knew that pure love was a different goal, a different level of relationship altogether. Closer to our own time, Chesterton coolly dismissed the petty smirking that sometimes greeted his telling about love between Francis and Clare. "Modern romanticism knows that romantic love is a reality, but it does not know that Divine Love is a reality." [88]

Lord, what is this mysterious influence of one soul on another? Sr. Elizabeth of the Trinity said to her Prioress at the end of her life, "I bear your mark." I bear Fr. Henry's mark – more than that, I have been so formed by him in recent years that I cannot tell where what is his in me begins and what was mine leaves off. Lord, I think You have been enjoying Yourself, working in my life – For a long time – 15 years or so – You were so jealous of my formation that I learned almost nothing from anyone but You. Then You completely reversed Yourself, and began to speak to me continually through the voice of another, without lessening our intimacy and my constant communication with You. It seems to me that this is as it should be – the human instrument should never be someone who stands between us, but someone who stands beside us, connecting, encouraging, strengthening my union with You – "the friend of the Bridegroom."

I Will Just Leave Them With You

The surest test for authenticity of experiences with God is whether or not there is growth in generosity. Once again, Burrows is a sure guide:

"True generosity is always alert, always 'there.' It doesn't drift through life, sticking to patterned behavior and missing these living encounters in my neighbor, in the duty of the moment, in this little humiliation, in this physical pain, in this disappointment, in this pleasure and joy....It is a determination to disregard self, to accept life as it is, to be wholly at the service of others, faithful to our obligations great and small no matter how tedious, unromantic, unrewarding;...." [89]

Looking back, Sr. Christine's pattern of growth in generosity is traceable. She experienced both "the giving up" and "the being deprived of." In the latter, she never had a happy, stable family. In the former, she gave up a marriage that had barely begun. The prospects for a brilliant academic career were put aside. And it is not for nothing that the Bible makes quite a test out of requiring the young man to give up his fortune and follow Jesus.

From time immemorial, giving up money and possessions is an emotional, complicated challenge. For some children, their mother's Cadillac and chauffeur, prize peacocks on the lawn, and the best toys are sources of pride. For Frances, money and what it bought was associated with unhappy events when she was shunted aside and left in the care of servants. She developed an antagonistic relationship with money and, sometimes, with people who had money. Eventually, she matured into a posture of stewardship, giving regularly to former caregivers, to programs for abandoned children, and to the Dominican Sisters caring for the terminally ill.

In 1965, she made her Profession of Solemn Vows. She relinquished complete control of her fortune; she never regretted it or referred to the matter.

Entering a religious community is, in itself, an act of generosity. Her work for the Sisters of the Good Shepherd was done with whole-hearted spirit; and, during her early years in Carmel, Sr. Christine had a broad vista that included the poor, refugees, the sick, and petitioners who came to the Monastery. "I would be sister to the whole world."

Out of her concern for the poor came a very strong conviction about Cesar Chavez and his life-long, non-violent struggle for social justice for farm workers. "Cesar, burning with a patient fire" was a favored quote in her letters. She admired his integrity, his solid Catholic spirituality, and the righteousness of his cause. He suffered and fasted for the laborers in the farm fields. She sought to unite her discomforts with them and for them.

6/10/1970 Retreat Notes

> Cesar: "a totally non-violent struggle against injustice." If I am to be in union with them, I cannot harbor the least annoyance [and] welcome occasions rather than seek to be free of them.

From the beginning, Carmelite prayer has had an apostolic side and overflows with missionary fervor on people whom Carmelites both know and will never know. Writing letters has always been seen as one way to extend the friendship of God, albeit to a relative few. [90]

On July 8, 1980, Sister Kateri Maureen Koverman, S.C. came to the monastery to thank Sr. Christine and the Sisters for praying for her refugees in Central America and Asia. Sister Kateri is known internationally for her care of families and soldiers, all of whom she considers victims of war. She did not expect to visit Sr. Christine.

> *"The chance to be in her presence for the first time carried with it an anticipation on the one hand. On the other, my introverted self was melting inside thinking what would I say in the very limited time we would be given.*
> *In fact, when the curtain was pulled back and I was face-to-face, Sister Christine's welcoming manner put me at ease. She was equally as comfortable talking about a convicted death row inmate for whom she prayed daily or asking me questions about my third world experience in war-torn countries".* [91]

11/5/1980 Journal Entry

> Lord, why can't I too be a purificatorial vessel, simply holding in my heart all those who need to be cleansed and enlightened and brought close to You? Sometimes there are no human means to help them, but this means is never lacking. Fr. T. said to me last week about these 2 hard marriage cases, "I will just leave them with you." What shall I do with children left on my doorstep? Just hold them in my heart, under the healing rays of Your merciful love.

Coming very close now to the end of their lives, Sr. Christine and Fr. Tansey know how to work together for their Friend, God. They are spiritually and emotionally legible to one another. The roles are clear. Divine Love is a reality.

15: Loaded to Each Other[77]: Sr. Christine and Fr. Tansey

77. Pablo Neruda. Phrase attributed to this well-regarded Chilean writer.

78. See Ref. 58, p. 84.

79. Conversation with Fr. Henry Tansey M.H.M. by the author, December 19, 1980.

80. Essay written by Fr. Henry Tansey for inclusion in commemorative booklet of his home parish, Keadue, Ireland, and given to author by Eugene Tansey, Fr. Henry's brother, at Keadue, Ireland, May 18, 1999.

81. See Ref. 63, p. 143.

82. See Ref. 35, p. 112. A felicitous phrase.

83. Letter written by Sr. Christine to her friend, Lorraine (Mrs. Sydney) Stewart, August 19, 1977.

84. See Ref. 53, p. 24.

85. M. Ruane, Washington Post, June 14, 2000.

86. Conversation with Sr. Clare Joseph O.C.D. (Theresa Lagoy) by author, October 24, 1981.

87. See Ref. 58, pp. 81-82.

88. G. K. Chesterton, *Francis of Assisi* (NY: Image Books, 1924), p. 102.

89. See Ref. 34, p. 32.

90. See Ref. 63, p. 120.

91. Letter written by Sr. Kateri Maureen Koverman, S.C. to author, July 9, 1999.

16

A Terrible Agony

12/2/1980 Journal Entry

[Fr. Tansey reluctantly told Sr. Christine he is missioned to California for a fund raising assignment beginning next month.]

After Confession:

"Your plan is perfect, born of perfect love".

Jesus – if this is truly Your perfect plan for my brother's life, then I want nothing else. I cannot even ask You to "let this cup pass from me" as I had started to do, for I do not want my own will but only Yours. Indeed, I have no will, only a heart that is silent and clings to You while this blow takes its full effect.

"Jesus offered up a strong cry and tears...and he was heard because of his reverence."

Lord, we too offer this reverence which You taught us – this bowing to the Father's will however hard, unthinkable, upside-down it may seem. And, we know that it is precious in Your sight – precious like the sacrifice of Abraham, which made the Father exclaim, "I swear to you that because you have done this thing...I will multiply your descendants as the stars in the sky. etc."

"Whoever does the will of my Father in heaven is brother and sister and mother to me." Lord, if this is so, then it is these moments of submission to the really hard things that cement the new family most of all. Your will binds us together, wherever we may be – it is the only real bond of the new family, which is not "born of blood or of the will of the flesh or of the will of man, but of God."

Jesus, it would ease my heart to write this morning but I do not want to write much till I can sort out the precious from the ordinary – the word which is truly Yours from the human reactions which are passing through my soul. "It is good to wait in silence for the mercy of the Lord." (Lamentations)

How much I could say, how many thoughts and words of Scripture pass in and out, along with the waves of sorrow which I will not harden my heart against. You have taught me over and over to open it wide to love and sorrow, which in this world are inseparable as I have known for many years.

"May this Communion teach us to love heaven." These words from the Advent Masses have struck me in a special way this year. You are bent on teaching me to love heaven, Lord, and rightly so for it is Your best gift and the one which will never be taken away: "I will see you again, and your heart shall rejoice, and your joy no one shall take from you." But You are not separate from this brother of mine in whom I have seen and known and loved You, and so You will not mind if I borrow Your own words to fit our present situation.

Lord, is it right, is it sensitive and loving to pour out my own sorrow in front of him like this, when he already has sorrow upon sorrow in this affair? "What do you mean by crying and breaking my heart?" said St. Paul to the Ephesians. I only know it is useless and foolish and impossible to try to hide it. But I will also pour out my peace and joy and pride at his willingness to do this thing which on the surface seems so senseless and turns his own life upside down. "I have no greater joy than to see my children (my Father, my brother, those I love) walking in the truth." Listening, following Your word through whatever authentic channel it may come. This joy can indeed coexist with tears – and God will wipe away the tears, as He has promised, but "they who do the will of God remain forever in the joy that no one shall take from them."

Lord, only You can show him how to respond to this word which has come, and if You have asked for silent acceptance, then I unite myself to that response. I will it, I love it, and affirm it. "We know not what we should pray for as we ought." No, I do not know, and I will not make a prayer of my own desire – I only know all hearts are in Your hands, to turn them as You will and I must leave them there. This is above all a time for silence, waiting, listening – forgiving to the fullest. A time for gathering up, not fragments but this heavy chunk and holding it fast, unless and until You come to take it away. "You see the trouble and sorrow; You note it, You take it in hand." (Ps. 10)

Fund-raising is hardly a job my brother would have chosen. Lord, what can I give him in these days? I long to forget my own sorrow and let all of its value flow into his life. Jesus, this one thing I ask You, and I know You will hear me. All things are possible to You. If this is not for Your greater glory, then act to prevent it. You will hear this prayer because it is pure, free of any vestige of self-seeking, and focuses totally on Your will. It is another way of saying, "Your Kingdom come, Your will be done." In him, in us, in the Church of Albany and the Church of Hollywood, in Mill Hill, and its missions, Your will be done.

"Father, we adore You, lay our lives before You" – What did Mary do during her Advent trial but be silent, wait, lay her life before You – hers, Joseph's and Your own. It is Your life in the Church that is at stake most of all – the use of the gifts You have given to this chosen servant of yours – and You will watch over this.

"Let us commend ourselves and one another and our whole life to Christ, our God."

"To You, O, Lord." (Byzantine Liturgy)

Yes, to You, O Lord, and to Mary and Joseph during this beautiful season which is so specially theirs. Who better than they can understand all the spiritual and human dimensions of this situation? And we have a double claim on their help, since they are the patrons of our religious families. Sweet mother, dear father, "here we are, we now come to you" absolutely sure that you will take care of us for our best good, and for the good of our souls.

"Father, if it be possible, let this cup pass from him. Nevertheless, not our will but Yours be done." This prayer, too, is pure and it relieves my heart to say it. And if it is not possible, Lord, then send an angel to strengthen him; send Your own Holy Spirit to pour in continual peace and consolation and strength. *Consolator optime, dulce refrigerium, in labore requies, inflet solatium.* [Thou best of Comforters, sweet refreshment, may you rest in your work, may solace breathe forth within you.]

Lord, I am content tonight because it seems to me that in the last 2 pages I have found the way to pray, and now I will simply offer You these prayers continually until I hear some further word.

This is indeed a crossroads in his life (and also in my own) and it is important to surround it with a prayer that is as nearly constant as possible. The next two days are days of total solitude and silence. Thank You, Jesus, for You watch over every detail.

For those who do the will of God, there is joy at the heart of sorrow which even now, no one can take away – the bittersweet, nourishing joy of sharing your earthly meal: "My food is to do the will of him who sent me." All those who share the same dispositions are together at this banquet – this is "the fellowship of His sufferings" and it is perhaps the deepest fellowship of all. Have I ever seen so clearly the depth of my love for this brother of mine? Suffering brings enlightenment, says St. John of the Cross, "If you want great light, plunge into the thicket of the cross." Whatever the outcome of this affair, it is bringing us closer to you and closer to each other – giving us greater purity, strength, and "power in Jerusalem." Jesus – what more could we ask for? You never make a mistake, and this time is no exception. <u>You will not let this thing happen</u> if it is not an irreplaceable stage on our road to holiness, as it has been for so many apostolic souls in the past.

Giovanni [John XXIII], Gianpaolo [John Paul I] – my precious friends in heaven, pray with us now. You too at different times experienced the very same trial which hangs over his head: the thwarting of your desire to give yourself totally to the work of the Shepherd. When you saw it was God's will, you "did not open your mouth" and it made you Saints in very truth with an apostolic radiation that reached to the ends of the earth. This kind of submission, when done from the pure motive of obedience to God's will, is an unfailing road to holiness. I know that he is listening, listening, listening, and if it is not Your will, he will hear it – what then, could disturb my peace?

"He that is holy, let him be sanctified still." Love that is pure, a gift from the beginning, let it be purer yet. Wasn't this what happened to Mary on her earthly pilgrimage? A deeper, purer love for You, the further You went from her externally. Lord, I do not know how he sees it, but to me it is unthinkable that this relationship could end, or even lessen in vitality. Isn't it something like growing older? The children of God do not really grow older – instead, they come close to perfect childhood. And those whom You have united for Your glory in such a unique way do not grow apart, but simply come closer to the fulfillment of Your perfect plan. "ut unum sint, sicut nos." [that they may be one, as we] Lord, this is Your desire for Your whole creation, but You do not often find souls who are ready, willing, and able to mirror God in this way. "The image of God is chiefly in the communion of persons." (John Paul II) I believe it; You have shown it to me clearly and unmistakably in prayer, through the years. This is Your heart's desire, and You will bring it to pass, if we are poor, and small, and open and place no obstacle.

Reading from today's midday Prayer
"one moment, yet a little while, and I will shake the heavens and the earth, the sea and the dry land."

That is what is happening, Lord. You are sharing our lives in every dimension – his above all.

"Greater will be the future glory of this house than the former."

We believe it: this house of God which we are will be holier and purer, more beautiful and useful to men than ever before.

"And in this place I will give peace, says the Lord of hosts!"

Indeed, You are true to Your promise. "Peace I leave with you" peace today and always, peace that cannot be shaken as long as we cling to You. We are "a nation You keep in peace, in peace for its trust in You." (Isaiah ?) Trust is the secret of peace – "Oh, for the peace of a perfect trust." Mother M used to quote from somewhere, and today I know the wisdom of this little verse better than ever. Praise to You, Lord Jesus Christ, King of endless glory, praise to you! Amen. Alleluia.

Amen. Alleluia.

These are the last words written by Sr. Christine hours before she was stricken.

Sr. Christine's last journal entry
December 4, 1980
Amen. Alleluia.

Schenectady Carmel Hermitage
where Sr. Christine was stricken

17

Dying in a Sacred Space

"On the morning of December 5th, Sister Christine did not
answer the signal for rising. It was discovered that her bed
had not been touched and a light was burning in an outdoor hermitage. To our shock and dismay, we found her on
the floor of the hermitage, comatose and icy cold. The initial diagnosis was hypothermia (her body temperature was
80°),…" [92]

Sr. Christine was taken by ambulance to St. Clare's Hospital,
Schenectady. Later that morning, Mother Mary John, Prioress called
to tell me what had happened. Toward evening of the same day, I
took a flight from Washington, D.C. to Albany, NY. I went directly
from the airport to the hospital. Sr. Christine, in the Intensive Care
Unit, was unresponsive. To me, she looked astoundingly young lying there in the hospital bed, eyes closed, following surgery for brain
hemorrhage.

Howard Hubbard, Bishop of Albany, visited Sr. Christine as
did Sister Ruth Ann Fox, Sister of Mercy. Painfully, Fr. Tansey was
turned away because visiting hours were over.

At the Monastery the next day, Mother Mary John filled in
some of the details of the previous 24 hours. It seems that December
4th and 5th were special Days of Recollection requiring total solitude and silence of all Sisters. Even on "regular" days, Sr. Christine
was seen very little because she was not able to eat in the Refectory or
pray in Chapel. She did come to Recreation for 20 minutes each evening. On Days of Recollection, however, this gathering was omitted.

Early on the morning of the 5th, after discovering that her
room was empty and a light was on in the outside hermitage, two
Sisters went to the hermitage. They found: the door locked from the
inside; light on; window open; snow blowing in; heater disconnect-
ed. Sister Christine was barefoot. It looked as if she had been leaning
against the wall and slid down the wall to the floor. Her "tuck" [piece
of headdress] was pushed down over her eyes and her habit carefully
straightened. Her arm was slowly motioning.

Mother John made it clear to the paramedics and again to
the emergency room staff that there had been no assault. The attending physician agreed. The best witness was the monastery dog,

a well-trained German Shepherd named Kukla. He and Sr. Christine were good friends, and he barked furiously when the ambulance drove away. Mother John reasoned that he would have made plenty of noise if his friend had been attacked.

The cement block hermitage was attached to the garage, not to the main Monastery building. In ordinary circumstances, it would be used for storage of lawn equipment, tires, and such. About 300 feet from the back door of the Monastery kitchen, it was small – 6' by 8' – with one door and one window. It was wired for electricity but had no modern conveniences or phone. Sisters did not have cell phones. The door was routinely locked from the inside because of break-ins at the Monastery. Hence, the necessity for Kukla to be at the ready.

For the Sisters, it was a distressing time. They came to know that one of their own, only a stone's throw from the main building, in all possibility nearly froze to death, unable to call out to them or do anything to help herself. And they, in turn, could do nothing to help because they were unaware of what was happening. Even if death was caused by hemorrhage, the circumstances remained the same because the outcome was the same. "What ifs" are unsatisfactory, disturbing even.

"Although her health was poor, the coming of the Angel of death was swift and unexpected." As Prioress, Mother Mary John took note of health issues affecting the Sisters and arranged for care when needed. Sr. Christine had a great need for cold air and very strong coffee. Those things plus hard physical work were attempts at keeping her circulation going. Recently, she had had a lump on her leg (Baker's Cyst) for which the doctor recommended surgery. Christine asked Mother Dolorosa's intervention. In six weeks, the cyst was reduced greatly and no surgery was needed. Mother John also mentioned "a throat obstruction" or problem. There was no diagnosis at the time that Sr. Christine was stricken. Taken together, there is ample reason to conclude that her health was, indeed, poor. Genetic factors were also against her living a long life; several in her immediate family, including her father, died before the age of 50.

Fr. Tansey's Priestly Wisdom

There is another way, a totally different approach, to understanding the circumstances of Sr. Christine's death. This approach requires a turning away from forensics or medical consequences. It requires a theological explanation. Father Tansey gave all the explanation that was really necessary when I asked him: "How do you think Christine would have handled what happened?" "She would have handled that magnificently," he said. He added that she wrote more about death after Dolorosa died. So, there we have it. She died in the hermitage, her sacred space with its silence and solitude. It is not irony that she was stricken there. And she left a written record that is as clear as the Gospels about her preparation for death. Fr. Tansey, of course, read this record before every Confession. It is no wonder he answered my question with calm and perfect certainty. And, it is likely that she prepared him for his own death, which was almost upon him.

9/28/1980 Journal Entry

> Love bridges the gap between heaven and earth. My loved ones come to me simply out of love, to show me that love is untouched by death but only expands to perfect freedom on the other side of the veil.

> Triumphant love. "Love never ends…these three remain: faith, hope and love and the greatest of these is love." Love is eternal, it is the very heart and essence of eternal life. All else will fall away: virtues, gifts, charisms – these are only temporary to meet a passing need. This is why we must "want love more than anything else" – it is the very substance of our "indestructible life" with You and one another. "We know that we have passed from death to life, because we love the brothers."

9/4/1980 Retreat Notes

> "…as forward we travel from light unto light." [Breviary hymn]
> "I have come that they may have life, and have it more abundantly."

> Lord, the only heaven I want is an everlasting abundance of the life we have together

here. It is impossible to desire a heaven that is wholly different from anything we know… My highest experiences are heaven with my eyes shut.

In my retreat 7 years ago, You showed me that when You call us to heaven, it's because You want to manifest the fullness of Your love which we cannot stand here. And You poured this love into me to the very limit of my capacity – a little more and the vessel would have broken.

"How shall I stand it (heaven) if I can hardly stand it here?" I wrote – and when Mother D. came to me a few weeks ago, I wondered how she could stand the intensity of happiness I saw in her.

9/4/1980 Retreat Notes

"By His grace He shall impart
Eternal sunshine to the heart"
(Breviary hymn for Easter)

"Their" hearts shall live forever and ever (Psalm 22)

It is indeed not my soul but my heart that wants to live forever. This heart that loves and rejoices, and embraces the children within it. The heart that hears Your voice ("I will speak to her heart") and longs to hear it more and more. This makes heaven closer to our experience and more human. "Man shall come to a deep heart." This is the purpose of our earthly life – to deepen the heart, so as to contain the eternal love of God and neighbor that You want to pour into it.

10/3/1980 Journal Entry

"I was in the Spirit on the Lord's day…(Rev. 1)

Jesus – To be "in the Spirit" is to be where there is no separation between this world and the other. Fr. Paul-Marie says: "The Holy Spirit is our Fatherland," and when I am deeply immersed in Him, it is "natural" that I should sometimes have converse with my loved ones who are in Him fully and forever. He is a "fountain springing up to eternal life." (Jn. 4) We take these words of Yours as a promise of heaven, as indeed they are – but He sometimes "springs up" even now, carrying me into their presence – putting me face to face in darkness with them. "My highest experiences are heaven with my eyes shut," I wrote not long ago, and I think this is the best way to say it. I know and feel and experience and drink in the heavenly presences and their love that enfolds me. I, or rather the Spirit within me, speaks to them whatever He wants me to say, and it is a prayer drawn from the depths of my being. But it is all "with my eyes shut," like my highest communication with You. "Now I know in part, then I shall understand fully, even as I have been fully understood." (I Cor 13:12). The presences which overshadow and surround me have this full understanding: They see into the depths of my heart. My intuition of this is clear and strong in every such experience. What a joy to be known so fully and completely and still to be loved with "a love strong as death." "Many waters cannot quench it," and surely no human weaknesses, no surface trivialities, can quench this love of one eternal child of God for another. Paul speaks of "…the love which you have for all the saints, because of the hope laid up for you in heaven." (Col 1:4, 5) I have puzzled and pondered over this in the past, not seeing the connection – but now I see that this Christian love is based on our new being, our new and eternal birth into God's family. "By His great mercy we have been born anew to a living hope"; (I Pt. 1:3) all of us together. 'Born not of perishable but of imperishable seed." (1:23)

Lord, all of this truth is enfolded in my direct, immediate experience of these visits from heaven, but only Your Scriptures can confirm and explain what these intuitions reveal to me. "Search the Scriptures." When I do search, in order to understand and verify what has happened to me, the experiences become rooted in my soul and bear their full fruit. Otherwise, they tend to escape into unreality, as they did for so many years. "If you know the gift of God...." Lord, I can only fully know it (understand Your graces to me) by means of Your Scripture, interpreting my personal "revelation" by the great and objective Revelation You have made to us all. "No one comprehends the thoughts of God except the Spirit of God...." We only grasp them by "comparing spiritual things with spiritual." (I Cor 2: 11, 13) How I thank you for leading me at last to these green pastures, where I find myself so at home.

Communion of Saints

It was necessary to use Ruth Burrows' guidance in understanding the language and meaning of Sr. Christine's experiences of God, particularly infused mystical contemplation. Similarly, Sr. Christine's writings about, and communication with, her friends in heaven need guidance. "This is prose fired by intensities of love and commitment far beyond the ordinary". [93]

Elizabeth Johnson, C.S.J. is Distinguished Professor of Theology at Fordham University. Her studies of the communion of saints build on a long tradition in scholasticism that the dead, silenced by death, have fallen not into nothingness, but into the embrace of God. Our solidarity with those who have died consists not only in common history, origin, and goals, but in the same Spirit who flows through and enlivens all. If we ask where these persons are to be found, the only possible answer, since they do not belong to the empirical world around us, is that they abide in God. Johnson interprets the communion of saints not only as a company of friends whose memory stirs our action in loving care and the struggle for justice but also as a company of friends whose destiny shines as a beacon of hope.

Johnson and Jesuit theologian Karl Rahner agree that "the nearer one comes to God, the more real one becomes". Johnson develops the axiom this way: "there are grounds for hope that as death breaks apart the historical existence of the whole person, the mystery of that person's human identity grows even more authentic through profound presence to God". [94] The connection, therefore, between Sr. Christine's mystical union or mystical marriage and her intuitive claim to closeness with specific persons with God in heaven is plausible.

9/4/1980 Retreat Notes

> Lord, this focus on heaven is new in my life. Mother D's death and my 50th birthday coming together have at last made me realize that is why Christian family life is a beautiful school for heaven.

> It is the "hearts" of the heavenly ones that come to me that I see, more than anything else, their enormous love and responsiveness to our human needs, their compassion for even small sorrows. When Mother M. came, You said to me: "Perfect union of hearts forever" (hers and mine). You have come to Mt. Sion, to the city of the Living God, to the spirits (hearts) of just men made perfect...." Lord, this change of word makes an enormous difference, in getting used to thinking of heaven as our home.

10/2/1980 Journal Entry

> *Feast of the Guardian Angels "They are all ministering spirits, sent to care for those on the way to salvation." (Antiphon)*

> My little Sister (Dolorosa) – this was a visit of pure consolation. You came at noontime, because in the morning I had said to you a Cana prayer – just presenting to you my need and desire for reassurance that you still loved me, even after seeing all my faults and imper-

fections "from above." A visit of pure love – all I could say to you was, "I love you so much" – and I was filled with an enormous desire for perfection such as only the Spirit can give. You made me understand that you love me, not because I am good or bad, but in the way God loves – and that you will help me to perfection not as a stern teacher or monitoress, but as a Mother. I had almost forgotten what it was like to have a Mother who wanted to help me grow, out of love, and who took joy in fulfilling my needs, as you used to do. Without ceasing to be my Sister, you have agreed to be also my Mother in order to make me more pleasing to Jesus, and I am full of joy and wonder.

My little one – what a continuity there is between earth and heaven! You had asked me, 6 days before you died, if there was anything you could ask Jesus for me and I said, "Ask Him to make me a saint – (in order to give Him pleasure.) Now you are continuing this precious alliance with the same eagerness to help. Who would believe these wonders, hidden in our little Carmel? But I could never doubt they are real.

11/1/1980 Journal Entry

All Saints Day

"The Jerusalem above, who is our mother." (Galatians)

Jesus – however much I pondered this phrase before, I could not understand it, and yet today it seems so simple. It is the whole Church of heaven, the entire "assembly of the saints" who is our mother, by their union of love and intercession and caring for us who are still "on the way up to Jerusalem." Your Bride, the perfected Church, cannot be unfruitful; she who was once a barren woman, and poor (Ps. 113), now dwells in a house (Your own) as the "joyful mother of children".

Mother D. is a member of this Bride. She has a share in this heavenly motherhood. She "possesses the one love," in union with all the rest. This must be why I have repeatedly had the impression of her as one with Mary, joined to her in the exercise of the same motherhood over my soul.

"We are the children of saints," said Tobias, and if this is not very applicable in the natural order, still it is absolutely true in the family of heaven. What a lot of loving parents I have there! Mother M. and Mother D., Bino – J.P.I.- (Albino!) – and Pope John, Archbishop Martinez, etc. etc. "Jerusalem, city of God, you will rejoice in your children, for they shall all be blessed and gathered together with the Lord, alleluia." (Ant. 1st Vespers) Lord, I long to see my real family, "whom yet unseen I love".

NOTES

17: Dying in a Sacred Space

92.   See Ref. 1.

93.   See Ref. 58, p. 162.

94.   Elizabeth Johnson, C.S.J., *Friends of God and Prophets:*

       A Feminist Theological Reading of the Communion of Saints (NY: Continuum, 2005), pp. 212, 213, 214, 215.

Thursday   1283

Prayer

Lord Jesus Christ,
you have given your followers
an example of gentleness and humility,
a task that is easy, a burden that is light.
Accept the prayers and work of this day,
and give us the rest that will strengthen us
to render more faithful service to you
who live and reign for ever and ever.

Conclusion and antiphon of the Blessed Virgin Mary, as on 1288.

THURSDAY

All as in the Ordinary, 672, except the following:

PSALMODY

Ant.   In you, my God, my body will rest in hope.

Psalm 16
God is my portion, my inheritance

*The Father raised up Jesus from the dead and broke the
bonds of death* (Acts 2:24).

Preserve me, God, I take refuge in you.
I say to the Lord: "You are my God.
My happiness lies in you alone."

He has put into my heart a marvellous love
for the faithful ones who dwell in his land.
Those who choose other gods increase their sorrows.
Never will I offer their offerings of blood.
Never will I take their name upon my lips.

O Lord, it is you who are my portion and cup;
it is you yourself who are my prize.
The lot marked out for me is my delight:
welcome indeed the heritage that falls to me!

- The Divine Office - opened to page prayed by Sr. Christine the day she was stricken, Thursday, December 4, 1980.

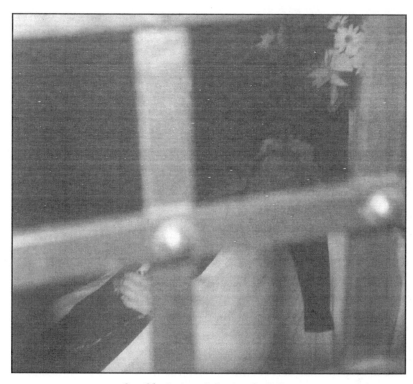

Sr. Christine Marie, O.C.D.
at Carmel Chapel grate prior to Funeral Mass
December 19, 1980.

18

A Funeral Like No Other

"Heaven is being with all those you love at the same time." [95]

"Sister Christine never regained consciousness and Our Lord came for her on Tuesday, December 16, 1980 at 9:30 P.M. She had just passed the twentieth anniversary of her entrance into Carmel.

The funeral was on Friday, December 19 and after the liturgy, Sister Christine was laid to rest in the Monastery Crypt." [96]

A monastery is one of the most dramatic places. A funeral is an occasion when drama is sanctioned and visible. For Roman Catholics, there is the centrality of liturgy with centuries of tradition and authority. Added is the authority of the Bishop, priests and the Carmelite Sisters.

At this funeral, Sr. Christine was a remarkable presence. Her gift for friendship was evident, and her ability to make others "stretch" played out in the luncheon conversation and the inevitable small talk. The topics were more thoughtful and the comments more focused on the meaning of it all. Family and friends were precisely the "stuff" of interweaving she treasured: former husband, Paul; Sr. Mary Michael and Sr. Agnes, both Sisters of the Good Shepherd; Fr. Tansey and Fr. Reardon; cousin Diana Lyman and her husband, Ted; Sr. RuthAnn Fox, Sister of Mercy; Anna Pluhar (Connecticut College); Joan Mullaney; Sr. Alberta, Carmelite; Sr. Mary of Good Counsel whose sister had worked for Sr. Christine's father; Mildred Lemmerman, on staff at the Monastery; Tom Newman, from the New Skete Orthodox Church community and on and on. The chapel was filled with people who knew Sr. Christine or knew her Carmelite Sisters. It was a wonderfully joyous affair.

Before calling hours on Thursday, Dec. 18, Sr. Alberta O.C.D. and I delivered a Carmelite habit to Gleason Funeral Home. When the body was returned to the Monastery, it was placed on a bier next to the grate that separates the nuns' chapel and the main altar. The curtain that covers the grate was drawn open, making Sr. Christine visible to those coming forward from the main part of the church. Paul, for example, approached and knelt by the grate. Over the main altar is written: Love is Repaid by Love Alone.

Liturgy

The liturgy of Christian Burial was celebrated at noon, December 19, by Howard J. Hubbard, Bishop of Albany. Twelve priests concelebrated the Mass.

<u>Liturgy of the Word</u>

First Reading: Sr. Mary Michael Kennedy, R.G.S.
                                  Mistress of Novices, Sisters
                                  of the Good Shepherd

Second Reading: Sr. Alberta, O.C.D.,
                                  Schenectady Carmel, Friend of
                                  Sr. Christine's

Gospel: Fr. Henry Tansey, M.H.M.

First Reading: Isaiah 43:2-4
    I have called you by your name, you are mine. You are precious in My eyes...and I love you. I am Yahweh, Your God, the Holy One of Israel, your savior.

Second Reading: John 4:7-12
    Dear people, let us love one another since love comes from God and everyone who loves is begotten by God and knows God.

Gospel Reading: John 11:17-27
    I am the Resurrection and the life. Those who believe in Me even though they die, shall live...

Homily: Fr. Charles Reardon, S.J.

<u>Communion</u>

Communion was received under both species (bread and wine). Among those receiving were Paul Cawein, Episcopalian, and Diana and Ted Lyman, South Congregationalists.

At the end of Mass, Bishop Hubbard came to the head of the coffin and spoke a few words to the congregation. He compared John the Baptist and his misunderstood vocation with Sr. Christine's vocation. He noted how the monastic way of life is frequently misunderstood by those of us in the faith.

Procession to the Crypt

The procession proceeded out the monastery chapel, across the driveway, and into a lower level of the monastery. The Carmelite Sisters stood near the entrance to the vault. The Bishop and priests were already standing in the vault along the walls. The others in the procession filed in, in front of the priests and behind the Bishop. The steel coffin was placed in the top tier of spaces. Bishop Hubbard led the litany of the dead. The hymn, "Salve Regina," was sung in Latin. Everyone returned to the first floor of the monastery where a luncheon was served by the Carmelite Guild members. [97]

Father Tansey Speaks

After the funeral, I was told that Father Tansey wanted to see me before I left the monastery. He was waiting in a small room near the chapel, reading the Office. We had not met before. Our visit lasted 20 minutes or so, ending with the hope to meet again before he left for California – and a surprise. He handed an envelope to me containing papers he identified as Christine's last writings. He sat quietly while I read them. When I became tearful, he urged me "to take them along". I promised to return them although he never asked that. For me, this simple, straightforward act of kindness spoke volumes about his holiness.

I met with Fr. Tansey at the Mill Hill House on January 14, 1981. He urged me to keep Sr. Christine's papers and promised to do a tape about her after he got settled in California. The letter he wrote to me in the meantime tells a lot about his generosity and kindness:

Mill Hill Fathers
Albany NY 12203
Dec. 29, 1980

Dear Joan,

Thank you for your letter and copies of Christine's writings. You did wisely to keep the originals.

I'm happy that we were able to meet. God's plans are very mysterious. If I were doing it, I would arrange a meeting beforehand when everybody was alive and well!! I'm sure Christine is smilin' as she hears me think and write like that.

I'll be looking forward to seeing you when you come this way. The only weekend that I will be here is Jan. 10th, 11th. The other weekends I work in Flint, Michigan. Midweek I am always here.

My phone is 518-456-6798. It is in my room, so nobody answers if I am not here, so never any need to speak person-to-person. Best time to find me is 11:00 P.M. till 8:00 A.M.

On Holy Family Sunday, December 28 I was back at Carmel, Schenectady. I was celebrant of a Mass honoring families in the Marriage Encounter. The Sisters sang the Mass and afterwards, all those attending went downstairs for coffee.

It was a little sad for me. It was because the annual family Mass of M.E. was scheduled there, that I told Christine, since I was honored at the Mass. Never before did Marriage Encounter have that Mass there!
However, God's plan is always best. He had a big hand in everything and I'm grateful and also can say Alleluia.

God bless you in 1981

Sincerely,
Henry Tansey

The Evangelist reported:

"The power of one Christian life was attested to last Friday [Jan. 25, 1981] when 1,400 men and women came to the Cathedral of the Immaculate Conception for the funeral Mass of Rev. Henry Tansey, M.H.M....

The Mass seemed to be a last farewell party for the priest, who had been scheduled to leave the day after the accident for a new assignment in California. Most of those at the funeral had been present at one of the many farewell parties given for Father Tansey by groups he had served during his 16 years in the Diocese.

At the end of the Mass, Bishop Howard J. Hubbard recalled a recent visit with Father Tansey who seemed reluctant to leave the diocese he had come to love." [98]

Fr. Reardon Writes

Father Reardon was always called 'Pere Charles" by Sr. Christine. His homily at the funeral Mass included an explanation of the commitment inherent in Baptism and the completion of that commitment in Sr. Christine's life and death. He followed with a more personal story about a Jesuit saint, John Francis Regis, a great favorite of Sr. Christine's. Reardon visited Frances Nevins at the Motherhouse of the Sisters of the Good Shepherd in Peekskill, NY. It was clear she had a contemplative vocation. He foresaw the many obstacles that could prevent this and she said that John Francis Regis would work it out. Reardon went back to the Jesuit House in Fairfield, Connecticut. The next morning, he was assigned to say Mass – at the altar of John Francis Regis. He told the story in his dry, low-key, Vermonter way, but it was clear that the moment was still vivid in his memory as an example of faith and trust.

Both Henry Tansey and Charles Reardon were pastoral men, seeking to reach out and console whomever they could, even though they themselves were feeling the loss. Fr. Reardon wrote a letter to me one month to the day of the funeral. His writing reveals both his concern and his sadness.

Jesuit Community
Boston College
Chestnut Hill, MA 02167
January 19, 1981

Dear Joan,

....Reflecting on the services I could not help but be amazed at the number of people Sister drew together in her last hours. There were the relatives, Paul, the various nuns she had met in her wanderings, you, myself, Anna – so many who had met her during life, and had drawn some abiding relationship. She had kept them alive by her beautiful letters. They were like small masterpieces which she composed so perfectly. (in that cold atmosphere; her hands must have been chilled as she wrote). We always used to laugh at the funny little guy she would draw between the lines. With his curved mouth he was a good sign of her own spirit – always cheerful. In my visits at the grille we never covered all the planned topics; but I always left her with a cheerful note. Seeing the inside of the chilly monastery, I thought that she must have found her warmth from the Spirit. Nothing else could have given it to her. Again, I used to be amazed at the wisdom she could advance about the world's affairs. No matter what topics I brought up (Church, priests, vocations, the Pope) she had very wise observations. The Church and its interests were very dear to her; and avidly she read what the Pope had said and did. John Paul I had a special spot for her; I think his simplicity appealed to her. After his death she often had intercessions to him; and always received an answer.

....Some days, I can't realize that she will not be at the convent, were I to visit there later. As Lorraine (Stewart) remarked, it is hard to be convinced that she is no longer in our midst. When I visit my cousins at Schenectady, I plan to visit the chapel and feel her presence there. She will always be there in body and spirit; there she found what she had always sought, time with God.

In closing, I send along prayers for your work. And thanks and admiration for all your charity toward one who was dear to you. Pray for the clergy, especially the ones getting old.

Ever Sincerely,
Charlie Reardon, S.J.

This letter was, by far, the longest I had ever received from him. Perhaps, like his friend, Frances, he "talked" best on paper.

Fr. Reardon died on June 28, 1991, at age 84. He was 73 when Sr. Christine died.

William J. Leonard, S.J., homilist at Charles Reardon's funeral, told this story:

"Charlie was a Vermonter, born and bred. He talked in the pungent, tangy style we think of as characteristic of that farming country – Calvin Coolidge's style. I read somewhere about the New Yorker who was driving through Vermont and stopped to chat with a farmer along the road. After some time he inquired: Have you lived here all your life?" And the farmer replied: "Not yet." That was Charlie's style – arresting, almost startling, but getting to the heart of the matter with the greatest possible economy of words."

NOTES

18: A Funeral Like No Other

95. Statement made by Sr. Christine to her beloved Godchild, Annamarie Pluhar, when Annamarie visited "Frannie" on 8/18/1977. Annamarie is a daughter of Anna Pluhar who was instrumental in linking Frances Nevins with the Jesuits at Boston College. Anna attended Sr. Christine's funeral.

96. See Ref. 1.

97. Letter written by Sr. RuthAnn Fox, R.S.M. to author dated 12/22/1980, including observations and audio recordings of funeral.

98. See Ref. 40.

99. Letter written by William J. Leonard S.J. to author, December 2, 1983.

Epilogue

"For years I could not see my path ascending
but this year You have given me this precious
vision of what You have accomplished in me.
St. Teresa says that the gift is one grace, the
knowledge of it another, and the ability to express it is a third. All these have come to me
from Your spirit, each in its time."
[Retreat Notes 9/5/1980]

Frances Nevins writes an English of great beauty, with both delicacy and power; most importantly, she has wonderful things to say. It is perfectly clear that she is original, not derivative and that she does not speak "by hearsay," to use Job's phrase. I think, rather, we should cherish and make known the writings of those whose eyes have seen it, to use Job's phrase again, and whose words can bring it into being for others.

Jean Francois Six, a priest and historian in France, produced two French works on St. Therese. In effect, he has spent fifteen years working on her story. In the end he had this to write, perhaps the most simple summary and to the point: "At the end of these two works, of this long tramp of fifteen years with Therese, the feeling that I am walking beside an original, indefinable personality is even stronger... 'But, then who is Therese?' the surprised and perplexed reader will ask. 'Come and see,' he/she will be told. Do you want the author to give you a key? It is the story of love, there is then no key, the door stands open. The door to death and to life, as always in a love story." [100]

After nearly 30 years spent studying the life and writings of Frances Nevins, the conclusions Six draws about St. Therese resonate deeply with me. I know now the most important facts about Frances Nevins: her experience of God was rare and direct; heroic virtue char-acterized her life as a Carmelite nun; and she was faithful to the end.

"I am the Holy Spirit's Carmelite. He is my
life, my peace, my strength, my joy, my all."

In every age there are those who embody the action of the Spirit, drawing us forward.

Amen. Alleluia.

NOTES

Epilogue

100.   See Ref. 53.

◆ **PHOTOGRAPHS** ◆

"Frannie" at
New London, CT
Summer 1932

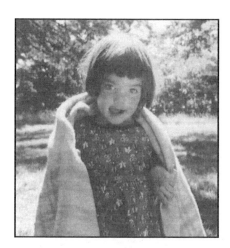

Frances Drake Nevins
at age three, 1933
East Longmeadow, MA

Frances and Ethel "Mil" Miller
Governess 1934
East Longmeadow, MA

Diana Waters Lyman and Nancy Waters Russell
first cousins of Frances Nevins, Longmeadow, MA - 2012

WILLIAM NEVINS, RETIRED PRINTING EXECUTIVE, DIES

10/18/40.

Former President of Springfield Printing and Binding Company Was Ardent Golfer—Native of Boston

William H. Nevins, 79, of 150 Pearl street, former president of the Springfield Printing and Binding company, died at his home yesterday after a long illness.

He retired about 10 or 12 years ago after heading the concern for nearly half a century, but even in retirement retained an active interest in company affairs.

Born at Boston, Mr Nevins attended the St Albans (Vt.) academy and came to this city when a young man. He was the son of the late Jerome and Mary (McCusker) Nevins.

An ardent golfer, he was a prominent member of the Springfield and Longmeadow Country clubs for many years, and it was his custom to make annual golfing trips to the famous Pinehurst (N. C.) course with other local businessmen. He also was a member of the old Nyasset club.

Mr Nevins started his business career with the Printing and Binding company as a young man. He rose to the presidency within a few years and had guided the company's destinies ever since.

He leaves a daughter, Mrs Leslie J. Ford of East Leigh, Eng., and two sons, Jerome B. Nevins of this city and Roger W. Nevins of California.

The body can be seen at the home after 4 this afternoon. The funeral will be held at the home tomorrow morning at 9.15, followed by solemn requiem high mass at 10 at St Michael's cathedral. Burial will be in St Michael's cemetery.

William Nevins
Grandfather of
Frances Nevins.

He made certain Frances
was baptized in the
Catholic Faith.

Frannie with her father - Jerome Nevins
at New London, CT 1939

Deaths *June 15 1942*

Jerome B. Nevins
Dies at Age of 42

Jerome B. Nevins, president of the
Springfield Printing and Binding
Company, died Monday at his home,
150 Pearl Street. He was 42 years
old.

Mr. Nevins was born in this city
May 10, 1900, was educated in the
public schools here and attended
Berkshire Academy and Yale University.

He had been an official of the
binding company for many years and
became president on the death of his
father in 1940.

He leaves his mother, Mrs. Arthur
H. Shaw of Hobe Sound, Fla., a
daughter, Frances; a sister, Mrs. Leslie J. Ford of Eastleigh, Hants, Eng.,
and a brother, Maj. Roger Nevins, in
California.

The funeral will take place from
the home Wednesday at 9.15 a. m. followed by requiem high mass in St.
Michael's Cathedral at 10. Burial will
be in St. Michael's Cemetery.

Jerome B. Nevins
Frances' father, at age 20
- 1920 -

Jan 7, 1967

Mrs. Charles Tenney

Mrs. Frances (Waters) Tenney of East St., East Granby, Conn., formerly of Longmeadow, died Saturday in her home. She was the widow of Charles M. Tenney. She was born in Rochester, N. Y., daughter of Goodman and Frances (Drake) Waters. She lived 18 years in East Granby. She leaves a daughter, Sister Christine Marie, Holy Spirit of Carmelite Nuns, Schenectady, N. Y.; two nieces, Miss Nancy G. Waters and Miss Dina G. Waters, and a nephew, Calvin D. Waters, all of Longmeadow. The funeral and burial will be private. There are no calling hours. Nicholson funeral home, Suffield, is in charge. Contributions may be made to West Hartford Branch of American Cancer Society.

Frances Waters Nevins Tenney
mother of Frances Nevins
with "Andy". Mother died of
bone cancer at age 67.

Home of Frances Nevins
East Granby, Connecticut 1947 to 1960

Graduation picture, 1947
Masters School
Dobbs Ferry, NY
(Boarding High School)

FRANCES DRAKE NEVINS

38 Longview Drive
Longmeadow. Massachusetts

Fran

The very spark of society.

Frances Drake Nevins
Student at
Connecticut College
for Women.

Anna Pluhar
Frances Nevins was "Senior Sister"
to Anna Pluhar at Connecticut College
1950-1951.

Annamarie Pluhar
Daughter of Anna Pluhar
is the Godchild of
Frances Nevins.

Frances on board ship to Europe in 1950.

Senior Year at
Connecticut College
for Women
-1951-

SOCIAL

Phi Beta Kappa

Phi Beta Kappa
notice in
Springfield, MA
newspaper
in spring of
1951

MISS FRANCES D. NEVINS

Miss Frances D. Nevins, daughter of Mrs. Charles M. Tenney of East Granby, Conn., and the late Jerome B. Nevins, has been elected to Phi Beta Kappa at Connecticut College, President Rosemary Park has announced. Miss Nevins, a senior at the college, was also accorded the distinction of membership in the Winthrop Scholars and the Connecticut College Honor Society. She was the only student so honored this year. She is a history major and last year won the college's essay prize in the democracy forum. Miss Nevins is a native of this city. Her grandparents were the late Mr. and Mrs. H. Goodman Waters and the late Mr. and Mrs. William H. Nevins.

FRANCES NEVINS

"Frannie" . . . amazing combination of mind and matter . . . the well-shaped Winthrop scholar . . . intriguing almond blue eyes . . . "Talk louder, I have my ear-plugs in" . . . automatic coffee dispenser . . . down to earth only in her dislike of shoes . . . morning paralysis and evening walks . . . friendly, impulsive . . . modern intellect brought to bear on the Middle Ages.

Connecticut College for Women Yearbook
1951 - Senior Picture

Engagement & Wedding
announcement in
Springfield, MA newspaper 1953

FRANCES D. NEVINS TO WED MR. CAWEIN

Nuptials Listed On Feb. 6 In Hamilton, O.

Mr. and Mrs. Charles Milliken Tenney of East Granby, Conn., announce the engagement and approaching marriage of Mrs. Tenney's daughter, Miss Frances Drake Nevins, to Paul Emile Cawein of Hamilton, O. The wedding will take place Saturday afternoon, Feb. 6, at 4.30, in the Church of the Good Shepherd, Athens, O. A reception will be held in University Center immediately following.

Miss Nevins is daughter of the late Jerome Bradley Nevins of this city, granddaughter of the late Mr. and Mrs. H. Goodman Waters and of the late William H. Nevins, all of this city. Her paternal grandmother was the late Mrs. Arthur H. Shaw of Buzzards Bay and Hobe Sound, Fla.

Miss Nevins is now associated with the Episcopal Church in Athens, O. She was graduated in 1947 from Master's School, Dobbs Ferry, N. Y., and in 1951 from Connecticut College for Women, New London, Conn., where, in her junior year, she elected a member of Phi Beta Kappa.

Mr. Cawein is a graduate of Ohio University, class of 1953, and will enter Eastern Theological Seminary, Cambridge, in the fall. He is the son of Mr. and Mrs. Emile L. Cawein of Hamilton.

* * *

Wedding Portrait
Feb. 6,1954

Mr. & Mrs. Paul Cawein at Frances' mother's home
-1954-

Duhig Home at 1140 Boylston St ~ Chestnut Hill, MA

After Frances Nevins' annulment, she moved into a
Boston College house, owned by a Catholic family.
-1955-

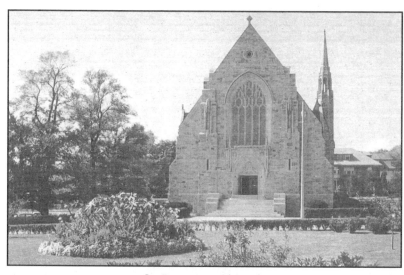

St. Ignatius Church
Commonwealth Ave., Chestnut Hill, MA

Jesuit Parish Church
where Frances Nevins attended Mass
prior to entering Carmel. 1954 - 1960

Frances Nevins' apartment
opposite St. Ignatius Church
Chestnut Hill, MA 1957 - 1959

Frances Nevins, Joan Ward Mullaney and two unidentified passengers aboard ship to shrines of Europe - 1957.

Frances Nevins, at Our Lady of the
Cenacle Retreat House, Brighton, MA

First Communion
June 11, 1955

Fr. Charles Reardon, S.J.

Confessor and Spiritual Director
1955-1960

Frances with friend Lynn Fraleigh
September 8, 1959

Postulant Dress
Sisters of the Good Shepherd.

Miss Frances Nevins,
Cenacle Convent
Mount Kisco,
N. Y.

J. M. † J. T.

MONASTERY OF DISCALCED CARMELITES
428 DUANE AVENUE
SCHENECTADY 4, NEW YORK

Pax Christi!

November 14, 1960

Dear Frances,

We just received the final permission needed from Our Superior to admit you among the Choir Sisters. To-day being the feast of "All the Saints of Carmel" we hasten to send you the good news.

Reverend Mother has set the date for November 21 st feast of Our Lady' Presentation. Can you make it for then? Only seven more days left! Its quite a short notice but no doubt you were prepared for a quick notice at any time.

Welcome to Carmel, dear Frances. It is nice to think that all the Saints of Carmel are sharing in your happiness and are anxious to present another little soul to Our Blessed Mother on her feast day.

Enclosed you will find a list of articles to

-251-

bring. It isn't necessary to buy anything
that isn't specified on the list.

May God bless you and give you
all the graces necessary for the big step
you are about to take.

We shall keep you in our prayers.

Yours humbly in Our Lord,
For Reverend Mother Prioress.

✝

My dear child,

We just received your permission
today, feast of "All Saints of Carmel"; so it looks
as though your new family in Heaven are taking you
into their keeping. May God be praised!

Frances, I forgot to tell you, when you
were here, that $200.⁰⁰ Novitiate expense money is re-
quired, besides the dowry stipulated by Canon Law.

Mother Mistress would like you to come
on the 21st. I hope you can be ready on such short
notice. A warm welcome awaits you, our dear Frances.

Yours humbly in Our Lord,
Mother M. Magdalen of the Holy Ghost, D.C.

Letters of Acceptance by
Carmelite Monastery, Schenectady, NY
November 14, 1960

If you have to buy a Bible — buy
the *New Catholic* Edition of the
Holy Bible.

A small crucifix, 3" or 4" long.
Daily Missal in Latin and English
Following of Christ by Thomas à Kempis
6 cotton underwear — Might need
    gowns — towels — wash cloths.
6 pr. of brown cotton stockings.
2 " " low heel shoes.
1 pr. of rubbers and overshoes.
3 cotton and 3 flannelette sheets
3 woolen blankets
A shawl, (if you have one)
Darning cotton, brown & white
Any sewing articles you may have
Small scissors
Large pr. of shears.
An alarm clock.
Tooth brushes, tooth paste
Pocket pen knife

List of items crossed out
by Frances Nevins as she
readied herself for Carmel

Reception into the
Carmelite Community
October 7, 1961

Sr. Christine Marie
of the Holy Spirit
Profession Day
October 8, 1962

FR. CHARLES REARDON, S.J.
Confessor and spiritual
director prior to Carmel
1955-1960
Funeral homilist 1980

ALBERT BOURKE, O.C.D.
Definitor General
supported Sr. Christine's
admission to Carmel 1960

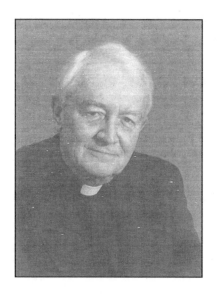

OWEN BENNETT, O.F.M.
Confessor 1965-1974
Final vows homilist 1965

HENRY TANSEY, M.H.M.
Regular confessor
1977-1980
Funeral Mass concelebrant
1980

SCHENECTADY GAZETTE,

THURSDAY, DECEMBER 18, 1980

Service for Sister Marie Tomorrow

A mass of Christian burial for Sister Christine Marie (Frances Nevins), 50, of the Carmelite Monastery at 428 Duane Ave., will be celebrated at noon tomorrow at the monastery by Bishop Howard Hubbard of the Albany Diocese.

Sister Christine Marie died Tuesday in Ellis Hospital after a short illness.

Born in Springfield, Mass., she was a member of the Carmelite Monastery for 20 years.

Survivors include an aunt, Mrs. L. J. Ford of England.

Calling hours will be from 1 to 9 p.m. today at the monastery. Gleason Funeral Home is in charge of arrangements.

Obituary Notice
Schenectady, NY paper

Obituary Notice
Springfield, MA paper

SPRINGFIELD, MA

THE MORNING UNION, SATURDAY, DECEMBER 20, 1980

Sister Christine Marie, Carmelite nun 20 years

The funeral of Sister Christine Marie, 50, of the Monastery of Discalced Carmelites, who died Tuesday in Schenectady, N.Y., was Friday in the monastery.

In secular life, Frances Drake Nevins, she was born in Springfield

She was a graduate of The Masters School, Connecticut College for Women and held a master's degree in history from Harvard University.

She entered the Carmelite monastery in 1960.

Interment was in the the monastery crypt.

-257-

Howard J. Hubbard, D.D.
Bishop of Albany, NY
Celebrated Sr. Christine's
Funeral Liturgy,
12/19/1980

12/19/1980
Funeral procession
to burial crypt at
Carmel Monastery.
In center:
Paul Cawein and
Joan Mullaney

Family and friends
after funeral Mass
l to r Sr. Alberta, O.C.D.,
Edwin and Dina Waters
Lyman (cousins)and
Paul Cawein.

Sisters attending the funeral Mass: Far right:
Sr. Mary Michael Kennedy, R.G.S. was Frances
Nevins' Mistress of Novices in Sisters of the Good
Shepherd. 9/1959 to 5/1960. Far Left: Sr. Agnes Ertel,
R.G.S. friend of Postulant, Frances Nevins

Route 20 accident kills priest in Guilderland

K.W. 1/28/81

GUILDERLAND — A Catholic priest, active in Charismatic Renewal and other church movements, was killed when he swerved the car he was driving to avoid another car backing onto Route 20.

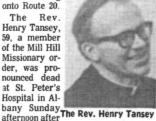

The Rev. Henry Tansey, 59, a member of the Mill Hill Missionary order, was pronounced dead at St. Peter's Hospital in Albany Sunday afternoon after receiving extensive internal injuries in the accident, state police said.

The Rev. Henry Tansey

Two other drivers involved in the accident were treated and released at Albany Medical Center Hospital, police said, and another man was given a traffic ticket charging him with unsafe backing.

Police said Tansey was driving east on Route 20 just east of Camp Terrace at about 3 p.m. Sunday when he swerved to avoid a car driven by John Zakutny of Marjorie Drive, Guilderland, that was backing onto the highway.

The priest's car went into the westbound driving lane, where it struck a car driven by Susan Reinemann, 19, of Schoolhouse Road, Guilderland, police said.

The Reinemann car was struck in the rear by another car driven by M.J. Smith of Guilderland, police said.

Reinemann and Smith were treated and released from the hospital, and Zakutny was given the traffic ticket.

Tansey, a leader in the Charismatic Renewal in the Albany Roman Catholic Catholic Diocese for the last 17 years, was born in Ireland and was the chaplain of the area chapter of the Ancient Order of Hibernians. He was active in the Worldwide Marriage Encounter movement and chaplain to the diocese's Mothers of Priests chapter.

The priest was recently reassigned by his religious order to missionary work in Hollywood, Calif., where he was scheduled to move soon.

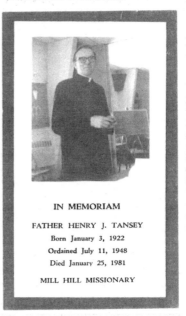

IN MEMORIAM

FATHER HENRY J. TANSEY

Born January 3, 1922

Ordained July 11, 1948

Died January 25, 1981

MILL HILL MISSIONARY

Fr. Tansey's fatal accident occurred the day before he was to leave for California. 1/25/81.

-260-

◆ CHRONOLOGY ◆

CHRONOLOGY

Frances Drake Nevins

Sister Christine Marie of the Holy Spirit, O.C.D.

Carmelite Monastery
428 Duane Ave.
Schenectady, New York 12304

b. August 17, 1930
Entered Carmel December 8, 1960

d. December 16, 1980

Education: The Masters School (Dobbs)
Connecticut College for Women
Radcliffe/Harvard

Introduction: This working document follows closely the time-line of the obituary about Frances Nevins (Sr. Christine Marie of the Holy Spirit O.C.D.) prepared by the Schenectady Carmel. Sr. Christine's journal entries, retreat notes, and letters form the basis of this chronology. Additional facts are drawn from official documents, interviews, and written statements from those who knew her.

Key Points: Frances Nevins is a modern example of faith.

Her life and writings bring forth the love of the Holy Spirit in our lives. Her writings are approachable and useful to many.

Her main goal was to pray for priests and the priesthood. Mill Hill Father Henry Tansey was a significant person in achieving this goal.

5/10/1900	Jerome Bradley Nevins, father of Frances Nevins, born in Springfield, MA. Religion: Catholic.
	Education: Berkshire Academy; Yale University
	Position: President of family printing and binding company. (Springfield, MA).
7/6/1907	Frances Waters, mother of Frances Nevins, born in Rochester, N.Y. Religion: Episcopalian.
11/3/1926	Jerome Nevins and Frances Waters married in rectory of St. Patrick's Cathedral, New York City, by the Rev. F.A. Fadden. Witnesses: William H. Nevins and Frances J.D. Waters.
8/17/1930	Frances Nevins born in Springfield, Massachusetts.
7/1/1931	Frances Nevins baptized in St. Michael's Cathedral, Springfield, MA .
	Sponsors: William Nevins (grandfather) and Barbara (Nevins) Thomson (aunt). Address at time of baptism: 986 Longmeadow St., Longmeadow, MA.
10/18/1940	Paternal grandfather, William H. Nevins dies at age 79. Godfather of Frances Nevins (FN for remainder of document).
6/15/1942	Jerome Bradley Nevins, father of FN, dies at age 42 at the family home, 150 Pearl St., Longmeadow, MA.
1943	FN confirmed in St. Andrews Episcopal Church, Longmeadow, MA.
1944-1945	FN attends Classical High School, Springfield, MA.
1945-1947	FN attends the Masters School, Dobbs Ferry, NY. Graduates June 1947.

7/23/1947- 9/4/1947	After Dobbs graduation, FN visits with her mother and step-father at their ranch near Reno, NV.
9/1947	FN enters Connecticut College for Women, New London, CT.
1948-1949	FN student activity: Honor Court Justice, Junior Year at Connecticut College.
1949-1950	FN: Secretary of Connecticut College chapter of National Student Association; Student Faculty.
July/August 1950	FN travels to Europe: Paris, Heidelberg - traveling through Germany and Italy with Helen McNab (Bunn) and Joy Anderson (Nicholson).
1950-1951	FN named Winthrop Scholar – top academic honor at Connecticut College.
5/2/1951	FN gives Chapel Talk at Connecticut College as part of senior year activity.
1951	FN elected to Phi Beta Kappa Society.
4/30/1951	FN applies to Radcliffe/Harvard College of Arts and Sciences Graduate School.
5/15/1951	At Connecticut College FN completes senior honors thesis entitled: *The Relation Between Christianity and Philosophy in St. Augustine and Nicholas Cusanus.* Most of honors work read in Latin, senior year. For honors work, FN wins the prize (shared with another student) for "Understanding and Originality of Thought in the Study of History."

6/13/1951	FN graduates from Connecticut College. Ranked 1st in class of 175. Major: History; Minor: English. FN's reason given for choosing major and minor: "Because I felt it was the one in which I would come in contact with the basic elements in the Western Tradition."
6/15/1951	FN bridesmaid for Helen McNab who marries William Bunn, MD, in Presbyterian Church, Youngstown, OH.
9/23/1951	At Radcliffe/Harvard, FN begins full-time graduate study for Master of Arts in History with special field, Renaissance and Medieval. (from application statement, Radcliffe/Harvard, 4/30/51 courtesy of the Registrar) [see chapter 2].
6/18/1952	Master of Arts in History granted to FN by Radcliffe/Harvard. "All the teaching at the Graduate School was carried out by Harvard professors…"
9/1952 to 1/1954	Athens, Ohio. Episcopal Church work/counseling college students. Summer, 1953, attended classes at Union Theological Seminary, New York City.
2/6/1954	FN marries Paul E. Cawein (PC for remainder of document) in Episcopal ceremony in Athens, Ohio.
July/August 1954	Significant trip to England and Europe with following key events: miscarriage onboard ship (FN approx. three months pregnant); FN and PC visit churches, shrines and most particularly the Shrine of St. Francis of Assisi in Assisi, Italy, which set in motion her earnest search for the meaning of the Catholic Church in her life [see chapter 3].

Late 1954– early 1955	FN seeks instruction and is referred to Rev. Charles J. Reardon, S.J. (Boston College Theology Dept.) for three months of instruction in the Catholic faith before she makes a decision about continuing her marriage to PC.
Spring 1955	Impasse between PC and FN.
	Paul sincerely believes he has been validly married. FN has set her conscience on a Catholic marriage. [see Chapter 3]
6/7/1955	Decree of Nullity granted by Archdiocese of Boston Marriage Tribunal.
6/11/1955	FN receives First Holy Communion in the Chapel of the Convent of Our Lady of the Cenacle, 200 Lake St., Brighton, MA from the Rev. Charles J. Reardon, S.J..
6/11/1955	FN enrolled in the Scapular of our Lady of Mount Carmel in the Chapel at the Convent of Our Lady of the Cenacle by the Rev. Charles J. Reardon, S.J..
9/1/1955	FN takes up residence with a Catholic family, William and Katherine Duhig, 1140 Boylston St., Chestnut Hill, MA [see chapter 4].
9/25/1955	Frances D. Mary Theresa Nevins receives the Sacrament of Confirmation at the Cathedral of the Holy Cross, Boston, MA.
9/19/1956	FN accepts a teaching post at the House of the Good Shepherd, Boston, MA. She teaches six (6) classes per day, primarily Engl
6/9/1957– 8/30/1957	FN and Joan Ward Mullaney (JWM for remainder of document) take a trip to England to visit Mrs. Barbara Nevins Thomson Ford, Godmother and aunt of FN, at Tree Tops, Crampmoor Lane, Romsey, Hants,

England. They also visit: Lisieux; Paray Le Monial; Lourdes; Lyon; Venice; Padua; Rome; San Giovanni Rotundo and Assisi.

Sept. 1957– June 1958	FN continues to teach at the House of the Good Shepherd. She continues under spiritual direction with Charles J. Reardon, S.J. [see chapter 3].
3/18/1958	Miss Ethel (Mil) Miller dies. Buried at Duxbury, VT [see chapter 1].
3/25/1958	FN writes a letter to Charles Reardon, S.J., describing her method of prayer and her approach to decision making. Fr. Reardon says: "This is a very revealing letter about her spiritual attitude towards God and His direction of her life. She manifests a deep trust of God's direction in her life". [see chapter 5].
5/23/1958	Massachusetts Probate Court, Norfolk County, grants a Civil divorce to FN from PC that becomes final on this date.
9/8/1959	FN enters the Sisters of the Good Shepherd, Peekskill, New York as a Postulant.
9/27/1959	Health problems emerge soon after entering Sisters of the Good Shepherd [see chapter 4].
3/27/1960	Meeting is held by the Sisters of the Good Shepherd Council allowing Postulants to express their desire to continue. FN does not attend.
5/15/1960	FN leaves the Sisters of Good Shepherd.
5/15/1960	FN goes to the Cenacle Retreat House, Mount Kisco, New York while she applies to Carmelite monasteries.

10/1/1960	FN meets with Fr. Albert Bourke, O.C.D., Definitor General of the Carmelites [see chapter 5].
10/1/1960	FN is interviewed at Schenectady, NY Carmel by Reverend Mother Prioress, Mother Dolorosa, O.C.D. and Mistress of Novices, Sr. Magdalen, D.C.
10/1/1960	As part of admission procedure, FN is interviewed by psychiatrist Dr. Jame Qualtere, Ellis Hospital, Schenectady, New York.
11/14/1960	FN is accepted by Schenectady Carmel [see chapter 5].
12/8/1960	FN enters Schenectady Carmel.
10/7/1961	Frances receives the Carmelite habit and the name Sister Christine Marie of the Holy Spirit.
10/8/1962	Sr. Christine Marie of the Holy Spirit takes First Vows as a Carmelite [see chapter 6].
10/8/1965	Sr. Christine Marie of the Holy Spirit takes Solemn Vows.
10/9/1965	Veiling Ceremony as part of Final Profession. Ceremony held at Chapel, Schenectady Carmel at 9:30 AM.
1/7/1967	Frances Waters Nevins Tenney dies of bone cancer. She is buried in a cemetery near the family home in East Granby, Connecticut.
Summer 1970	Sr. Christine is hospitalized at St. Clare's Hospital, Schenectady, NY, with a diagnosis of severe protein deficiency and vaso-motor instability.

6/8/1972	Sr. Christine reports continuing poor health. "I live in a state of more or less constant physical discomfort and strain and very frequent humiliation." [Retreat Note] [See Chapter 8]
1972-1974	The struggle for more solitude, more solitary prayer and a Hermitage leads to thoughts of fostering change where she is, or, possibly going elsewhere [see chapter 7].
6/12/1974	Sr. Christine and Sr. Clare Joseph, O.C.D., another professed Sister, draw up a proposed Rule for increasing eremitical possibilities in the Order. It is submitted to the head of the Carmelite Order in Rome.
9/18/1974	The Hermitage request is denied.
2/1/1975	Sr. Clare Joseph, O.C.D. transfers to Barre, VT Carmel.
6/2/1975	Sr. Christine is alert to new possibilities where she is: "The will of God flows over me and carries me along like a wave of the ocean - ... I simply find my whole inner being and attitudes changed, strengthened, and oriented toward the new thing that is to come. All this happens gradually, almost imperceptibly at times." [Retreat Note].
6/18/1977	Sr. Christine's health continues to deteriorate: "Immaculate Heart of Mary. Jesus – another misery. Over sensitivity to my conspicuousness and the inconvenience and embarrassment I give to others by my illness." [Retreat Note].
6/19/1977	Loneliness marks her vocation and reveals her temperament: "Jesus – if this loneliness is to be the constant mark of my redemptive vocation, then with all my heart, I will offer it to You day by day." [Retreat Note].

6/20/1977	"Jesus – to live in, with, and by the Spirit, with all the austere and delicate discipline this entails – this is my vocation. How can these wonders be fully real to me, with no one to tell them to?" [Retreat Note].
6/21/1977	Fr. Henry Tansey, Mill Hill Missionary, is chosen by Sr. Christine as Confessor and Spiritual Director [see chapter 14].
10/13/1977	Sr. Christine acknowledges her extraordinary spiritual gifts. "Day after day, O Lord of my life, shall I stand before Thee face to Face?" (Tagore) "Jesus – this is the meaning of it all – this is my unspeakable vocation." [Retreat Note].
7/22/1979	Sr. Christine comments extensively on a biography of St. Therese, *The Hidden Face* by Ida Gorres. *"Eleven years ago when I was in the hospital a priest lent it to me – I plunged into the middle and liked it immensely but had to give it back. We do have it now, praise God, - I have begun the first chapter, 'The Question' and find it just superb."* (Sr. Christine's letter to JWM, 7/22/1979).
9/21/1979	In a Retreat Note, Sr. Christine connects sudden death with her family pattern and the way she seeks to deal with it. "Lord, if You are going to take my life suddenly (as happens in my family) make me ready to give it on an instant, even though my desire is to live longer so as to bear more fruit in Your vineyard."

12/12/1979	Prioress Mary John assigns Sr. Christine to instruct the novices about the Marian ideal and its place in the Carmelite way of life [see chapter 8].
. 6/1/1980	"I have been blessed with the gift of friendship." [Journal Entry]
6/28/1980 – 7/4/1980	Like St. Therese, Sr. Christine pleads with prayer and care for the life of a man sentenced to death. [see chapter 10].
7/11/1980	In a meeting with the Sisters, Sr. Christine states clearly what she believes her vocation within a vocation to be, and its meaning for her.

"To me, this is the great secret: to have an intention, a single purpose for life which is so important that it gives us the fire and the energy to confront every cross, little or great, that You send us. Perhaps in a way Your asking me to pray for fervent priests has been the greatest grace in my life – the most sanctifying for me, because it impels me to do everything with maximum love and eagerness."
[Journal Entry]

7/23/1980	On this date, known in the Church calendar as the Feast Day of the Mother of Grace, Sr. Christine was powerfully involved in helping her former Prioress. [see chapter 9].
11/13/1980	Sr. Christine was much engaged by the Eastern-rite liturgy offered in the monastery Chapel, and wrote at some length about the compelling experience. [see chapter 13].
12/2/1980	Fr. Henry Tansey tells Sr. Christine that he will be leaving in January 1981, for a longterm fundraising assignment in California.
12/2 – 12/4/1980	Sr. Christine writes about her anguish and her submission to this news about this crossroad in her life, and in his.

12/4/1980	(Comment, JWM) With the advantage of hindsight, the final journal entries and retreat notes include aspects of a life-review by Sr. Christine. Here is the thunderous crescendo of the final days and hours when she seems to stand face-to-Face with God.
12/4/1980	Sr. Christine is stricken in the hermitage. She is taken first to St. Clare's Hospital, then Ellis Hospital for surgery on a blood clot in the brain. She never regains consciousness.
12/10/1980	Howard J. Hubbard, Bishop of Albany, visits Sr. Christine Marie of the Holy Spirit at Ellis Hospital, Critical Care Unit.
12/15/1980	Fr. Henry Tansey is unable to enter the Critical Care Unit to adminster the Sacrament of the Sick because visiting time had ended.
12/16/1980	Sr. Christine dies at 9:30 PM at Ellis Hospital, Schenectady, NY. Sr. Alberta, O.C.D., extern Sister, Carmelite Monastery, and Joan Mullaney were at the bedside in the Critical Care Unit.
12/19/1980	Funeral liturgy celebrated by Howard J. Hubbard, Bishop of Albany. Homilist: Charles J. Reardon, S.J. Twelve priests, including Fr. Henry Tansey, are in the sanctuary.
12/19/1980	Sr. Christine is buried in the crypt of the Schenectady Carmel.
12/19/1980	Fr. Tansey gives JWM the set of journal entries that Sr. Christine had written between the time he broke the news of his leaving and she was stricken.
1/14/1981	Mother Mary John OCD, Prioress of Schenectady Carmel gives JWM Sr. Christine's retreat notes, journal entries and Office Book set to the afternoon of 12/4/1980 as Sr. Christine had left it.
1/14/1981	Fr. Henry Tansey an JWM meet at Mill Hill Fathers' headquarters to exchange memories about Sr. Christine.

1/21/1981	Fr. Henry Tansey is killed in a car accident the day before he is to leave for California.
1/25/1981	Fr. Henry Tansey's funeral Liturgy was celebrated by Bishop Howard Hubbard and attended by 1400 people. He was buried in Ireland. [see chapter 16]

◆ APPENDIX ◆

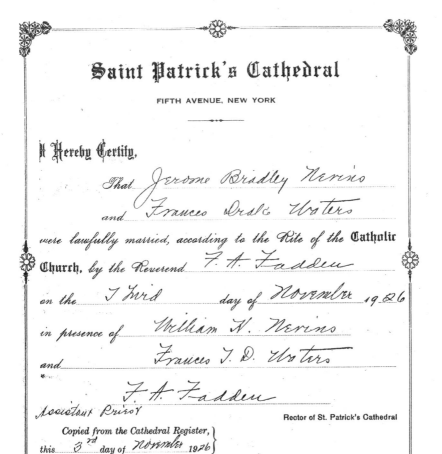

Saint Patrick's Cathedral

FIFTH AVENUE, NEW YORK

I Hereby Certify,

That *Jerome Bradley Nevins*

and *Frances Drake Waters*

were lawfully married, according to the Rite of the Catholic
Church, by the Reverend *F. A. Fadden*

on the *Third* day of *November* 19 26

in presence of *William H. Nevins*

and *Frances T. D. Waters*

F. A. Fadden

Assistant Prior

Rector of St. Patrick's Cathedral

Copied from the Cathedral Register,
this *3rd* day of *November* 19 26

Certificate of Baptism

Saint Michael's Cathedral
Springfield, Massachusetts 01103

This is to Certify

That Frances Drake Nevins

Child of Jerome Nevins

and Francis Waters *was*

Baptized

on the 1st *day of* July 1931

According to the Rite of the Roman Catholic Church

by the Reverend George S.L. Connor

the Sponsors being William Nevins

and Barbara Thomson

as appears from the Baptismal Register of this Church.

Dated December 3, 1993

Karl Huller

Rector of the Cathedral

THIRTY-THIRD
COMMENCEMENT OF
CONNECTICUT COLLEGE

COMMENCEMENT EXERCISES

SUNDAY, JUNE THE TENTH
NINTEEN HUNDRED AND FIFTY-ONE
AT THREE-THIRTY O'CLOCK

The author is indebted to Harriet Bassett MacGregor '51
for the Commencement Program

COMMENCEMENT HONORS

PHI BETA KAPPA

Elizabeth Babbott
Lois Banks
Beverley Benenson
Joan A. DeMino

Phyllis J. Hoffman
Olga Krupen Paula
L. Meltzer •Frances
D. Nevins

Patricia Roth

•Elected in Junior Year

WINTHROP SCHOLAR

Frances D. Nevins

DEPARTMENTAL HONORS

History: PriadUa Aι Meρ
Frances D. Nevins

ANNUAL HONORS
CLASS OF 1951

Lois Banks Joan
Blackburn Carol L.
Burnell Joan A.
DeMino Carolyn
B. Finn Joan M.
Gesner A. Vaughan
Groner

Arien Hausknecht
Phyllis J. Hoffmann
June Jaffe Jane R.
Lent Frances D.
Nevins Mary Stuart
Parker Patricia
Roth

Louise N. Stevens

CLASS OF 1952

Patricia   G.   Ahearn
Natalie   B.   Comen
Monique C. Maisonpierre

CLASS OF 1953

Hildegarde K. Drexl
Elaine T. Fridlund
Jean C. Gallup Loel
A. Kaiser

FRESHMAN HONORS

Jean H. Briggs Janet
R. Fenn Carol J.
Gardner Constance
Guarnaccia

Clarissa M. King
Diana E. MacNeille
Elaine B. Paul
Elaine H. Sherman

-278-

CLASS OF NINETEEN HUNDRED AND FIFTY-ONE

Judith Hope Adaskin Sheila
Ellen Albert Marilyn Ann
Alfieri Lois Marshall Allen
Joan Andrew Ann Sherwood
Andrews Joann Jane
Appleyard Renate
Aschaffenburg Susan Helene
Askin Elizabeth Babbott Iris
Louise Bain Harriet Louise
Bassett Alice Haines Bates
Nancy Jane Bath Annabel
Beam Mary Elizabeth Beck
*Reverlcy Bencnson Susan
Phillips Bergstrom Mary
Ann Best Chloe Hatch
Bissell Joan Elizabeth
Blackburn Nancy Kathleen
Bohman Nancy Lee Bolle
Natalie Bowcn Olivia
Dunham   Brock Susan
Beverly Brownstein
Wilhelmina Bertha Brugger
Sari Buclmer Sara Roswell
Buck Carol Lucille Burnell
Virginia Callaghan Roldah
Northup Cameron Mary
Burch Cardie Charlotte
Dewitt Chappie Doreen
Chen-Yin Chu Nancy
Louise Clapp Judith
Clippinger Marilyn Irene
Cobbledick Betsey Anne
Colgan Dorothy Ruth
Cramer Ann Hathaway
Daniels Margery Jane
Davison Joanne Louise
Dings Virginia Lee Eason
Marjorie Helen Erickson
Pamela Pratt Farnsworth
Elaine Fensterwald Carolyn
B. Finn Peggy Gene Frank
Janet Elliott Freeman Betty
May Gardner Phebe Ann
George Joan Merrell Gesner
Beryl Johanna Gigle

Claire Beatrice Goldschmidt
Marilyn Goldthwait
Elizabeth Eggleston Griffin
Anne Vaughan Groner Mona
Elaine Gustafson Carol Ann
Halk Martha Harris Arien
Hausknecht Louise Mitchell
Hill
*Eleanore Anne Holtermann
Elizabeth Ann Hotz June
Jaffe Mary Jane Jobson
Helen Louise Johnson
Vivian Mae Johnson Ann
Johnson Jones Joy Merchant
Karn Nancy Fanny Kaufman
Constance Alberta Kelley
Jane Elizabeth Keltic Alice
Ruth Kinberg
*Nancy Klein Dorothy Joyce
Knippel Norma Yvonne
Kochenour Jane Roth Lent
Rhoda Joan Levy Nancy Ann
Libby Barbara Seelbach
Lindblad Rosemary
Elizabeth Luke Lauralee
Anne Lutz Inez Rose Marg
Phyllis Barclay McCarthy
Ann Zachry McCreery Mary
Hughes Merkle Prudence
Elizabeth Merritt Priscilla
Anne Meyer Anne Kelley
Minar
^Barbara Molinsky Martha
Metcalf Morse Nancy
Margaret Moss Jane
Gertrude Muir Barbara
Kathleen Nash Jane Neely
Margaret Park Katharine
Falkener Parker Mary Stuart
Parker Helen Gabrielle
Pavlovich Mary Randolph
Pennywitt Emily Wilkinson
Perrins
*Barbara Jean Phelps
Cecelia Alexandra Popiolek
Elizabeth McSweeney Powell
Zita Mary Purnell Barbara
Eleanor Ridgeway

Maria Josephine Rinella

Phyllis Tilda Robins
"Janice Sargoy Rosenberg
Naomi Hannah Salit

;
Vera Clara Santaniello
Elizabeth Ann Sauersopf Janice
Anne Schaumann Donna
Christine Schmidt Lois M.
Sessions Katherine Ann
Sheehan Mary Jo Pelkey
Shepard Justine Shepherd Ann
Hope Steckler Louise Stevens
Janet Lee Strickland Mary
Martha Suckling Anita Marie
Tholfsen Barbara Adele
Thompson Lcda   Brainin
Treskunoff Joan Truscott
Constance Tucker Eleanor
Louise Tultle **Sarah J.
Wheeler Underwood Nancy
Hoyl Vail Betsy Elaine
Wasserman Carol Fiances
Wedum Diana Van Rensselaer
Weeks Marjorie Ludlow Weeks
Marilyn Elizabeth Whittum
Anne Wiebenson Elizabeth
Barbara Wicgand Joanne
Frances Willard Ronica
Lambe Williams Frances Helen
Wilson Nancy Thayer
Wirtemburg Janet Young

Honors

Lois Ann Banks
Joan Antonia DeMino
Phyllis Jean Hoffmann
Olga Krupen
Paula Lois Meltzer
Patricia Roth
Marianne Edwards Stirnson

High Honors

Frances Drake Nevins

*As of February 1951   **As of Class of 1950   of September 1950

A.C. (Div.) 8

COMMONWEALTH OF MASSACHUSETTS.

NORFOLK, ss.   PROBATE COURT

    I, Mary M. Nixon, Assistant   , Register of Probate Court

for said County of Norfolk, hereby certify, that at a Probate Court held in and for said County, on

the   twenty-second day of   November   in the year of our Lord one thousand

nine hundred   and fifty-seven,

a divorce from the Bond of Matrimony — Nisi — was decreed by the Court, between ....

Frances N. Cawein .... of ..Brookline..... in the County of ...Norfolk,

libellant, and .Paul Cawein..................... of Lenox............. in the County of

Berkshire,............ libellee, in favor of said libellant, for the cause which is fully set forth in the

decree on file in said Court. Said decree of divorce to become absolute after the expiration of six

months, unless the Court shall have for sufficient cause, on application of any party interested, other-

wise ordered. And it is further decreed that the said libellant be and she
hereby is allowed to resume her maiden name, to wit:-
Frances D. Nevins.

   And on the ....twenty-third day of   May.............., 19 58 , the said six months having

expired, and the Court not having otherwise ordered, said decree became absolute.

IN WITNESS WHEREOF, I have hereunto set my hand and

affixed the seal of said Court, this ......twenty-sixth............ day

of ....May................. in the year of our Lord óne thousand nine

hundred....and fifty-eight.....

.... Assistant , Register.

GENERAL LAWS, CH. 208, SEC. 21. "Decrees of divorce shall in the first instance be decrees nisi, and shall become absolute after the expiration of six months from the entry thereof, unless the Court within said period, for sufficient cause, upon application of any party interested, otherwise orders. After the entry of a decree nisi, the libel shall not be dismissed or discontinued on motion of either party except upon such terms, if any, as the Court may order after notice to the other party and a hearing, unless there has been filed with the Court a memorandum signed by both parties wherein they agree to such disposition of the libel."

GENERAL LAWS, CH. 208, SEC. 24. "After a decree of divorce has become absolute, either party may marry again as if the other were dead, except that the party from whom the divorce was granted shall not marry within two years after the decree has become absolute if the other party is living."

2000 11-57 G. P.

NEW YORK STATE
DEPARTMENT OF HEALTH
CERTIFICATE OF DEATH

REGISTRATION NUMBER 1506

STATISTICAL DISTRICT 4647

REC.

RES.

1. NAME FIRST	MIDDLE	LAST	2. SEX	3A. DATE OF DEATH	3B. HOUR
Frances	(Sister Christine Marie)	Nevins	MALE ☐ FEMALE ☒	MONTH 12 DAY 16 YEAR 80	

4. AGE — LAST BIRTHDAY — 50 YEARS | 5. IF UNDER 1 DAY OR UNDER 1 DAY | 7. U.S. ARMED FORCES? NO ☒ YES ☐ IF YES, SPECIFY WAR OR DATES OF SERVICE | SOCIAL SECURITY NUMBER none

6A. COUNTY OF DEATH Sch'dy | 6B. LOCALITY (CHECK ONE AND SPECIFY) ☐ CITY OF ☐ TOWN OF ☐ VILLAGE OF Sch'dy | 6C. HOSPITAL OR OTHER INSTITUTION (IF NEITHER, GIVE ADDRESS) Ellis Hospital | 6D. IF IN HOSPITAL OR INSTITUTION (CHECK ONE) ☐ DOA ☐ EMERGENCY ROOM ☐ OUTPATIENT ☒ INPATIENT | 6E. IF INPATIENT, ADMISSION DATE 12 16 80

8. STATE OF BIRTH (COUNTRY IF NOT USA) Mass. | 10. CITIZEN OF WHAT COUNTRY? U.S.A. | 11. MARITAL STATUS (CHECK ONE) 1 ☒ NEVER MARRIED 2 ☐ MARRIED OR SEPARATED 3 ☐ WIDOWED 4 ☐ DIVORCED | 12. SURVIVING SPOUSE (IF WIFE GIVE MAIDEN NAME)

13. RACE — WHITE, BLACK, AMERICAN INDIAN, OTHER (SPECIFY) White | 14. OF HISPANIC ORIGIN? IF YES CHECK ONE ☐ YES ☒ NO 1 ☐ MEXICAN 2 ☐ PUERTO RICAN 3 ☐ CUBAN 4 ☐ CENTRAL OR SOUTH AMERICAN 5 ☐ OTHER SPANISH ORIGIN (SPECIFY) | 15. EDUCATION INDICATE HIGHEST GRADE COMPLETED ONLY — ELEMENTARY / HIGH SCHOOL / COLLEGE

16A. USUAL OCCUPATION (DO NOT ENTER RETIRED) Nun | 16B. KIND OF BUSINESS OR INDUSTRY Religious | 16C. NAME AND LOCALITY OF FIRM OR COMPANY Carmelite Monastery Sch'd

17A. STATE N.Y. | 17B. COUNTY Sch'dy | 17C. LOCALITY (CHECK ONE AND SPECIFY) ☐ CITY OF ☐ TOWN OF ☐ VILLAGE OF Sch'dy | 17E. IF CITY OR VILLAGE, IS RESIDENCE WITHIN CITY OR VILLAGE LIMITS? YES ☒ NO ☐ IF NO, SPECIFY TOWN:

17D. STREET AND NUMBER OF RESIDENCE (INCLUDE ZIP CODE) 428 Duane Avenue 12304

18A. NAME OF FATHER		18B. MAIDEN NAME OF MOTHER FIRST	MIDDLE	LAST
Jerome	Nevins	Frances		Waters

19A. NAME OF INFORMANT Sister Mary Michael | 19B. MAILING ADDRESS (INCLUDE ZIP CODE) 428 Duane Ave. Sch'dy, N.Y. 12304

20A. BURIAL, CREMATION, REMOVAL OR OTHER DISPOSITION (SPECIFY) Entombment | 20B. DATE MONTH 12 DAY 19 YEAR 80 | 20B. PLACE OF BURIAL, CREMATION, REMOVAL OR OTHER DISPOSITION Carmelite Monastery | 20C. LOCATION (CITY OR TOWN, STATE) Schenectady, N.Y.

21. NAME AND ADDRESS OF FUNERAL FIRM Gleason, Inc. 730 Union St. Sch'dy, N.Y. 12305

22A. NAME OF FUNERAL DIRECTOR James J. Gleason | 22B. SIGNATURE OF FUNERAL DIRECTOR James J. Gleason | 22C. REGISTRATION NO. 00960

23A. SIGNATURE OF REGISTRAR | 23B. DATE FILED MONTH 12 DAY 18 YEAR 80 | 24. | 24A. BURIAL OR REMOVAL PERMIT (ISSUED) 07333

TO BE COMPLETED BY CERTIFYING PHYSICIAN ONLY — OR — **TO BE COMPLETED BY CORONER OR MEDICAL EXAMINER ONLY**

25. A. TO THE BEST OF MY KNOWLEDGE, DEATH OCCURRED AT THE TIME, DATE AND PLACE AND DUE TO THE CAUSES STATED MONTH 12 DAY 16 YEAR 80 | 25. A. ON THE BASIS OF EXAMINATION AND/OR INVESTIGATION, IN MY OPINION DEATH OCCURRED AT THE TIME, DATE AND PLACE AND DUE TO THE CAUSES STATED ☐ CORONER ☐ CORONER PHYSICIAN ☐ MEDICAL EXAMINER

B. THE PHYSICIAN ATTENDED THE DECEASED FROM 12 8 80 TO: 12 16 80 | C. LAST SEEN ALIVE 12 16 80 | B. PRONOUNCED DEAD ON | C. HOUR AT M. | D. DATE SIGNED MONTH DAY YEAR

D. NAME OF ATTENDING PHYSICIAN, IF OTHER THAN CERTIFIER

26. NAME AND ADDRESS OF CERTIFIER (PHYSICIAN, CORONER, MEDICAL EXAMINER, CORONER'S PHYSICIAN, MEDICAL DIRECTOR) 600 McClellan St Schdy N.Y.

27. DEATH WAS CAUSED BY — ENTER ONLY ONE CAUSE PER LINE FOR (A), (B), AND (C) | APPROXIMATE INTERVAL BETWEEN ONSET AND DEATH

(A) IMMEDIATE CAUSE Asystole and hypotension ASYSTOLE AND HYPOTENSION | 2 weeks

(B) DUE TO, OR AS A CONSEQUENCE OF: Intra cranial hemmorhage INTRACRANIAL HEMMORAGING: PROBABLE ANEURYSM

(C) DUE TO, OR AS A CONSEQUENCE OF: Probable aneurysm

PART II. OTHER SIGNIFICANT CONDITIONS, CONDITIONS CONTRIBUTING TO DEATH BUT NOT RELATED TO CAUSE GIVEN IN PART I (A) None | 28A. AUTOPSY? ☐ YES ☒ NO | 28B. IF YES, WERE FINDINGS CONSIDERED IN DETERMINING THE CAUSE OF DEATH? 1 ☐ YES 2 ☐ NO | 29. WAS CASE REFERRED TO CORONER OR MEDICAL EXAMINER? 1 ☐ YES 2 ☐ NO

30A. SPECIFY IF ACCIDENT, HOMICIDE, SUICIDE, UNDETERMINED, PENDING INVESTIGATION No | 30B. DATE OF INJURY MONTH DAY YEAR | 30C. HOUR OF INJURY | 30D. DESCRIBE HOW INJURY OCCURRED

30E. INJURY AT WORK? YES ☐ NO ☐ | 30F. PLACE OF INJURY HOME, FACTORY, OFFICE BLDG., ETC. | 30G. LOCATION (STREET & NO., CITY OR VILLAGE, TOWN, COUNTY, STATE)

-281-

Frederick R. McManus, D.D., J.D.
Commentary on Roman Catholic Canon
Law Governing Marriage Annulment[102]

In answer to your queries:

1. Under the law of the Latin Church in 1952, a person baptized in the Catholic Church was bound to the Catholic form of marriage, even if she or he was of a mixed marriage, had not been brought up as a Catholic, even was unaware of the Catholic baptism.

   The norm was found in canon 1099, §2, of the 1917 Code of Canon Law, as modified by Pope Pius XII in 1948, effective January 1, 1949. Between 1918 and 1949, an exception had been in effect, namely, an exemption for children of a mixed marriage, even if baptized in the Catholic Church, who from infancy had been members of a non-Catholic church or without religion and who entered marriage with non-Catholics.

   As is evident, this exemption no longer applied in 1952 and thus the marriage of Frances Nevins with an Episcopalian in the Episcopal Church would have been invalid at canon law.

   Had she (or her husband) desired to enter a Catholic marriage, a declaration of nullity would have been a simple administrative matter – a so-called defect of (canonical) form case. In fact, it is most likely that the matter was investigated in 1960 when she sought admission to Carmel. The records of her admission would presumably indicate some resolution of the question.

   For your information, the following is a translation of canon 1099, as found in the 1917 Code of Canon Law – but with the omission of the clause that was abrogated by Pius XII, as mentioned above:

   > §1. The following persons are obliged to observe the form above prescribed [i.e., marriage with the assistance of an authorized priest and at least two witnesses]:
   >
   > n. 1. All who are baptized in the Catholic Church or who have been converted to it from heresy or schism, even though the former or the latter may later have left the Church, whenever they contract marriage among themselves;

n. 2. The same persons above mentioned, if they contract marriage with non-Catholics, either baptized or not baptized, even after obtaining a dispensation from the impediment of mixed religion or disparity of cult;

n. 3. Orientals, if they contract with Latins bound by this form.

§ 2. But, without prejudice to the provisions of §1, n. 1, non-Catholics, whether baptized or not baptized, if they contract among themselves, are nowhere bound to observe the Catholic form of marriage.

2. It is correct that the canon law on this matter has changed since 1952, namely by force of the 1983 Code of Canon Law. Canon 1117 of the new code reads:

With due regard for the prescriptions of canon 1127, §2, the form stated above is to be observed whenever at least one of the contractants was baptized in the Catholic Church or was received into it *and has not left it by a formal act.* (Emphasis added.)

Important as this change is, it has no bearing on marriages entered into in 1952, for example.

Dimitri Plionis, Ph.D. Commentary on
Sr. Christine's use of the Greek Language [103]

September 27, 2008

The passages in question are in New Testament Greek and are from the original Greek version of the document. In general, Frances laments that the English translation does not do justice to the vividness and emotion of the Greek original, which means that she had a very deep understanding of Greek.

On p.14, Frances' sentence is:

No English translation does justice to κοινωνία εις τό ευαγγέλιον or to συγκοινωνούς μου τῆς χάριτος in v. 7.

Translation notes: The meaning of the first fragment above revolves around the meaning of the first word: κοινωνία. There is a wealth of writings about the meaning of this word at the time of Christ (see, for example, *Thayer's Greek-English Lexicon of the New Testament*, p. 352; and Larry Richards' *Zondervan Expository Dictionary of Bible Words*, p. 275-276). A reasonable translation of this word would be something like "fellowship in gospel." The second fragment means something like "my companions in grace." Of course, as Frances remarks, any English translation does not do justice to the original.

Grammatical notes: Frances omits some "aspirational" marks that surely would have been in the Greek original of the New Testament. These marks are no longer in use in the Modern Greek language and Frances seems to be following that usage. However, she seems to be following the original (rather than the modern) use of accents, except that she omitted the accent in the last word. I think that is an oversight: an accent is always required in every polysyllabic (containing more than one syllable) Greek word, and that is true in all versions of Greek. I have corrected this above. There seems to be some kind of a mark under the last letter (α) of the first word above. I don't know if that exists in the original manuscript or is simply a smudge in the fax. There could be a mark under that letter if the case is dative, but I do not have the full sentence and, therefore, I cannot tell from the context whether the case is dative or nominative. However, this type of mark is no longer in use.

On p. 15, Frances has done something different. Rather than giving the phrase in Greek, she has given the Greek phrase using Latin characters! That phrase ("epipotho pantas umas en spalanchnois Christou Jesou" (or is it "Iesou"?)) would have been as follows in Greek:

επιποθῶ πάντας υμάς εν σπλάνχνοις Χριστοῦ Ιησοῦ

(Note: Frances has misspelled the word σπλάνχνοις in the Latin character version! It should be "splanchnois," rather than "spalanchnois".)

The single word in parentheses would be:

επιποθούντων (in Latin characters: "epipothounton")

Translation notes: There are two significant words here: the verb επιποθω̃ and its participle επιποθούντων; and σπλάνχνοις. The verb επιποθω̃ clearly means "long for" or "yearn for" as Frances notes. The essence of the verb is the presence of passion or pain.

The word σπλάνχνοις is the accusative, plural of the noun σπλάνχνον. That noun literally means "inner organs" or "guts."[1] However, in the New Testament it usually takes the meaning of "compassion". Here are two translation notes from *Vine's Expository Dictionary of New Testament Words*.

Compassion, Compassionate [Noun]

splanchnon always used in the plural, is suitably rendered "compassion" in the RV of Col_3:12; 1_John_3:17; "compassions" in Php_2:1, Cp. *splanchnizomai*.

And for the corresponding verb:

Compassion, Compassionate [Verb]

splanchnizomai "to be moved as to one's inwards (splanchna), to be moved with compassion, to yearn with compassion," is frequently recorded of Christ towards the multitude and towards individual sufferers, Matt_9:36; Matt_14:14; Matt_15:32; Matt_18:27; Matt_20:34; Mark_1:41; Mark_6:34; Mark_8:2; Mark_9:22 (of the appeal of a father for a demon-possessed son); Luke_7:13; Luke_10:33; of the father in the parable of the Prodigal Son, Luke_15:20. (Moulton and Milligan consider the verb to have been coined in the Jewish dispersion).

So, the translation of this phrase is something like:

"I long for you all in the compassion of Jesus Christ." (Again, something lost in translation.)

Grammatical note: In rendering the phrase in Greek, I have retained Frances' usage of omitting the aspirational marks and her usage of accents.

All the best,

Dimitri Plionis, Ph.D.

---

[1] This caused me to reminisce about my mother, who often used this word to tell me how she felt I was a part of her. Thank you for this.

◆ SELECTED BIBLIOGRAPHY ◆

Selected Bibliography

1. Bellito, C. Izbicki, T. and Christianson, G.: *Intro-ducing Nicholas of Cusa, A Guide to a Renaissance Man* (NY: Paulist, 2004).

2. Burrows, Ruth. *Carmel, Interpreting a Great Tradi-tion* (London: Sheed and Ward, 2000).

3. ---. *Fire Upon the Earth, Interior Castle Explored, St. Teresa's Teaching on the Life of Deep Union with God* (New Jersey: Dimension Books, 1981).

4. Casey, Michael. *Sacred Reading, The Ancient Art of Lectio Divina* (Missouri: Liguori, 1996).

5. ---. *Strangers to the City: Reflections on the Beliefs and Values of the Rule of St. Benedict* (Brewster, Ma: Paraclete, 2005).

6. Croix, Paul De La. *Some Schools of Catholic Spiri-tuality. Carmelite Spirituality*, ed. by Jean Gauthier, trans. by Katheryn Sullivan (Paris: Descles, 1959).

7. Cunningham, Lawrence. *Thomas Merton and the Monastic Vision* (Grand Rapids: Eerdsman, 1999).

8. Gorres, Ida. *The Hidden Face. A Study of St. Therese of Lisieux* (New York: Pantheon, 1959).

9. Johnson, Elizabeth. *Friends of God and Prophets. A Feminist Theological Reading of the Communion of Saints* (New York: Continuum, 2005).

10. Martinez, Luis. *The Sanctifier* (New Jersey: St. Anthony, 1959). See also: Trevino, Joseph. *The Spiritual Life of Archbishop Martinez* (St. Louis: Herder, 1966).

11. McGinn, Bernard. *The Foundations of Mysticism* (New York: Crossroad, 1992).

12.   Six, Jean-Francois. *Light of the Night, The Last Eighteen Months in the Life of Therese of Lisieux* (Notre Dame, Indiana: Notre Dame University, 1998).

13.   Von Balthasar, Hans Urs. *Two Sisters in the Spirit, Therese of Lisieux and Elizabeth of the Trinity* (San Francisco: Ignatius, 1992).

14.   Williams, Rowan. *Teresa of Avila.* Outstanding Christian Thinkers Series, ed. by Brian Davis (Harrisburg: Morehouse, 1996).

15.   ---. *Wound of Knowledge, Christian Spirituality from the New Testament to St. John of the Cross* (Cambridge: Cowley, 1991).

About the Author:

Joan Ward Mullaney, Ph.D. served as Professor and Dean, Catholic University of America. She was awarded Catholic University's highest honor, the President's Medal, by the Board of Trustees. She also was awarded the Benemerenti Medal by Pope John Paul II. She lives in Pittsfield, Massachusetts. Dr. Mullaney welcomes those who read this book to comment on the life of Frances Nevins. Send comments to book distributor, Monastery Greetings (see front cover).

Schenectady Carmel Chapel
428 Duane Avenue, Schenectady, NY

FRANCES NEVINS - INDEX

- A -

- B -